Progress in

EXPERIMENTAL PERSONALITY RESEARCH

VOLUME 11

NORMAL PERSONALITY PROCESSES

CONTRIBUTORS TO THIS VOLUME

SYDNEY HANS

JEROME KAGAN

HANS KREITLER

SHULAMITH KREITLER

JAMES T. LAMIELL

DIANE LOPEZ

RICHARD LYNN

ALICE MARKOWITZ

RICHARD A. SHWEDER

HEIDI SIGAL

PROGRESS IN
Experimental
Personality Research

Edited by
Brendan A. Maher and Winifred B. Maher

DEPARTMENT OF PSYCHOLOGY
AND SOCIAL RELATIONS
HARVARD UNIVERSITY
CAMBRIDGE, MASSACHUSETTS

VOLUME 11

NORMAL PERSONALITY PROCESSES

1982

ACADEMIC PRESS

A Subsidiary of Harcourt Brace Jovanovich, Publishers

New York   London

Paris   San Diego   San Francisco   São Paulo   Sydney   Tokyo   Toronto

ACADEMIC PRESS, INC.
111 Fifth Avenue, New York, New York 10003

United Kingdom Edition published by
ACADEMIC PRESS, INC. (LONDON) LTD.
24/28 Oval Road, London NW1 7DX

LIBRARY OF CONGRESS CATALOG CARD NUMBER: 64–8034

ISBN 0–12–541411–0

PRINTED IN THE UNITED STATES OF AMERICA

82 83 84 85   9 8 7 6 5 4 3 2 1

CONTENTS

The Case for an Idiothetic Psychology of Personality: A Conceptual and Empirical Foundation

JAMES T. LAMIELL

Fact and Artifact in Trait Perception: The Systematic Distortion Hypothesis

RICHARD A. SHWEDER

The Theory of Cognitive Orientation: Widening the Scope of Behavior Prediction

HANS KREITLER AND SHULAMITH KREITLER

Validity of Children's Self-Reports of Psychological Qualities

JEROME KAGAN, SYDNEY HANS, ALICE MARKOWITZ, DIANE LOPEZ, AND HEIDI SIGAL

National Differences in Anxiety and Extroversion

RICHARD LYNN

CONTENTS

CONTRIBUTORS

Numbers in parentheses indicate the pages on which the authors' contributions begin.

SYDNEY HANS,* *Department of Psychology and Social Relations, Harvard University, Cambridge, Massachusetts 02138* (171)

JEROME KAGAN, *Department of Psychology and Social Relations, Harvard University, Cambridge, Massachusetts 02138* (171)

HANS KREITLER, *Department of Psychology, Tel Aviv University, Ramat Aviv, Tel Aviv, Israel* (101)

SHULAMITH KREITLER, *Department of Psychology, Tel Aviv University, Ramat Aviv, Tel Aviv, Israel* (101)

JAMES T. LAMIELL, *Department of Psychology, University of Illinois at Urbana-Champaign, Champaign, Illinois 61820* (1)

DIANE LOPEZ, *Department of Psychology and Social Relations, Harvard University, Cambridge, Massachusetts 02138* (171)

RICHARD LYNN, *Department of Psychology, New University of Ulster, Coleraine, Northern Ireland* (213)

ALICE MARKOWITZ, *Department of Psychology and Social Relations, Harvard University, Cambridge, Massachusetts 02138* (171)

RICHARD A. SHWEDER, *Committee on Human Development, University of Chicago, Chicago, Illinois 60637* (65)

HEIDI SIGAL, *Foundation for Child Development, New York, New York 10017* (171)

*Present address: Department of Psychiatry, University of Chicago, Chicago, Illinois 60637.

PREFACE

This, the eleventh volume of the publication, begins a pattern whereby we will devote each alternate volume to personality processes or to psychopathology. The present volume focuses upon issues of relevance to the experimental study of normal personality, with special emphasis upon problems of measurement and method.

For some years now the study of personality has been shadowed by the problem of the longitudinal and transsituational consistency of personality. Positions taken in the controversy have included, among others, the view that (a) situational or contextual variables are the prime determinants of behavior, with personal dispositions accounting for unimportant proportions of the variance; (b) transsituational consistency can be found if we establish the individual cognitive basis upon which situations may be regarded as sufficiently similar to warrant the expectation of the generalization of behavior across them; (c) some people are personally consistent and others are not; (d) current methods of personality measurement are inadequate to the task of demonstrating the consistency that may really be there; and (e) that more or less all of the foregoing are correct and the problems to be solved require the proper description of the parameters of disposition–situation interactions in personal behavior.

Lamiell's article opens this volume with an innovative proposal for a new approach to the measurement of personality, together with a report of promising applications of this approach to empirical problems. Shweder's contribution which follows provides an analysis of the central role that he believes is played by the "illusory correlation" effect in human assessments of the traits of other people as well as of self. Both of these articles represent systematic attempts to move forward the experimental study of personality by careful analysis of the assumptions that underlie present measurement technology and the weaknesses inherent in these assumptions.

The Kreitlers report in detail a new framework for the study of personality, based upon the analysis of cognitive processes; they demonstrate interesting relationships between their measures and behavioral data. Their article may be expected to stimulate research efforts directed at testing the range of the explanatory power of their framework. Kagan and his associates address the problem of measurement validity in the assessment of behavior and personality in children. As frequently proves to be the case, improved reliability may be attained to the extent that the researcher abandons the one-measure, one-time, and one-observer technique in favor of multiple data sources over several situations.

Finally, Lynn reports the current state of evidence bearing on his provocative model of national differences. No matter what interpretations of the data may appeal to the individual reader, the wealth of observation demands explanation. Lynn's work will undoubtedly stimulate many psychologists to develop alternatives to his hypotheses. The onus of doing so will, of course, be on the critic.

BRENDAN A. MAHER
WINIFRED B. MAHER

CONTENTS OF PREVIOUS VOLUMES

THE CASE FOR AN IDIOTHETIC PSYCHOLOGY OF PERSONALITY: A CONCEPTUAL AND EMPIRICAL FOUNDATION

James T. Lamiell

DEPARTMENT OF PSYCHOLOGY
UNIVERSITY OF ILLINOIS AT URBANA-CHAMPAIGN
CHAMPAIGN, ILLINOIS

I. Introduction and Statement of Purpose

Anyone familiar with the developments in personality psychology during the past decade is well aware that the period has been an extremely difficult one for the discipline. Confronted with Mischel's (1968) renowned challenge to the critical assumption inherent within the concept of personality itself, that is, the assumption of the "consistency of particular predispositions within any individual" (Mischel, 1968, p. 9), the major problem in personality psychology became one of repairing or reconstructing its very foundation. Thus did Mischel (1969) point to the necessity of somehow reconciling "our shared perception of continuity (in the behavior or psychological functioning of individuals) with the equally impressive evidence that on virtually all of our dispositional measures of personality substantial changes occur in the characteristics of the individual longitudinally over time and, even more dramatically, across seemingly similar

1

settings cross-sectionally'' (p. 1012, parentheses added). In a similar vein, Bem and Allen (1974) emphasized the importance of resolving the ''sharp discrepancy between our intuitions, which tell us that individuals do in fact display pervasive cross-situational consistencies in their behavior, and the vast empirical literature, which tells us that they do not'' (pp. 507–508).

The ''classic debate'' (Epstein, 1980, p. 790) that materialized in personality psychology in the wake of Mischel's (1968) seminal work has generated a literature so voluminous that it could not possibly be throughly reviewed here (see, e.g., Endler & Magnusson, 1976a; Magnusson & Endler, 1977a; London, 1978a; Pervin, 1978). Suffice it to note instead that three major themes appear to have evolved within that literature. One is the view that a variety of technical refinements in the procedures used to measure individual differences would lead to better evidence of consistency in personality, and thus would contribute greatly to a solution of the problem represented by Mischel's (1968) findings (see especially Epstein, 1979, 1980; see also Block, 1968, 1971, 1977, 1978; Hirschberg, 1978; Hogan, DeSoto, & Solano, 1977; McGowan & Gormly, 1976). The second is the view that Mischel's (1968) findings might be genuinely indicative of systematic temporal and transsituational inconsistencies in the behavior/psychological functioning of individuals, rather than of ill-conceived or poorly constructed measures of individual differences, and, therefore, that studies of the interactive effects of person and temporal/situational factors on behavior should be of primary concern to personologists (see, e.g., Argyle & Little, 1972; Bowers, 1973; Cronbach, 1975; Ekehammar, 1974; Endler & Magnusson, 1976b; Magnusson & Endler, 1977b; Mischel, 1973, 1977).

The third major theme that has emerged during the past decade seems to be shared in large part by adherents to each of the two basic positions just discussed. This theme is that the scientific study of personality must become increasingly *cognitive* in its orientation, that is, increasingly attentive to the *psychological meanings* that persons impose on their actions and on their social ecologies (cf. Golding, 1977, 1978). Mischel (1979) has articulated this development as follows:

> In the previous decade many of us realized the incompleteness of a personality psychology that failed to include and consider seriously the role of specific situations in the analysis of behavior. In the decade now ending, many of us have come to recognize increasingly that an adequate analysis of behavior cannot proceed without serious attention to the cognitive processes of both the actors and the observers, the subjects and the scientists, of our field. (p. 752)

Without questioning the *theoretical* significance of personality psychology's rediscovery (cf. Kelly, 1955; Rychlak, 1968) of the importance of the cognitive aspects of human psychological functioning (see Fiske, 1978a, 1978b, 1979), the present author has recently voiced opposition to both of the first two major themes discussed above, which are essentially *methodological* in nature. More specifically, it has been argued (Lamiell, 1981) that further progress in the scientific study of personality is not likely to be facilitated either by increasing psychometric sophistication in the measurement of individual differences, by focusing on the interaction terms in multifaceted research designs, or more generally, by refining or extending any of the basic research strategies that have traditionally dominated empirical inquiry in the field. As an alternative to those strategies, it has been suggested that personologists might profitably adopt an "idiothetic" framework, that is, one in which problems of personality measurement would be approached idiographically, and in which nomothetic principles would be sought in answers to questions concerning the process of personality development.

The major objectives of the present contribution are (a) to articulate more fully the case for adopting the idiothetic framework as a basis for the scientific study of personality, and (b) to present the empirical evidence that has thus far been accumulated in support of the utility of that framework. It is hoped that, at its conclusion, this article will have helped to clarify not only the formal compatibility between the idiothetic framework and the traditional metatheoretical concerns of personality psychology, but also how the adoption of that framework might well facilitate the current movement of the field toward what Mischel (1979) describes as the *interface of cognition and personality*. More than anything else, this article constitutes an attempt to explicate the problems involved in aligning the methodology of personality *research* with the traditional and contemporary concerns of personality *theory*.

II. The Need for an Alternative Research Strategy in Personality Psychology

A. A FORMULATION OF OBJECTIVES

In accordance with the purposes of this article, it is necessary to begin the discussion with some consideration of the overriding metatheoretical objectives of the scientific study of personality, for it is only vis-à-vis some articulation of those objectives that the adequacy or inadequacy of the various research strategies which currently dominate the discipline can be meaningfully evaluated.

Attempting to specify a set of objectives for the scientific study of personality on which most contemporary personologists could agree is, of course, a hazardous undertaking. Within the introductory pages of virtually any personality text, one can find some statement to the effect that contemporary personologists continue to *dis*agree on a multitude of important issues, a point to which Fiske (1973, 1974, 1978a, 1978b, 1979) has repeatedly drawn attention.

On the other hand, the mere existence of personality journals and textbooks, and thus an identifiable subdiscipline within psychology, suggests that there must be some central concerns, however implicit or ill-specified, that all (or at least the vast majority of) personologists would agree they share, and which might therefore serve to define the overriding metatheoretical objectives of the discipline. Elsewhere (Lamiell, 1981) I have cited Levy (1970) as providing a lucid and reasonably concise identification of those objectives:

> Colloquially, it might be said that in personality we are interested in learning the best way to describe what kind of a person a man [sic] is, how he got that way, what keeps him that way, what might make him change, and how we might use all this to explain why he behaves as he does and predict how he will behave in the future. (p. 29)

> In stipulating the domain of personality and specifying its matrix of inquiry, we have by implication also stated the goals of the psychology of personality. We ask that the science of psychology provide us with [among other things] knowledge that will be as reliable and comprehensive as possible with respect to the phenomena of personality. This knowledge, compounded by observation and theory, should make individual human behavior intelligible, and it may be useful in the prediction and control of this behavior. The development of this knowledge is the sole purpose of the psychology of personality. (pp. 34–35)

For the purposes of the discussion that follows, there are three specific features of these passages that warrant magnification. The first is that the most basic (though clearly not the only) problem in the scientific study of personality is the development of a viable framework for personality *description,* that is, a set of procedures that could be used to derive an empirically based account of what "kind of a person" any given individual is at a given period in his/her life.

The second important aspect of Levy's (1970) remarks is that, given an adequate means of describing personality, the questions of major theoretical import center around the process of personality *development,* that is, how personalities emerge, how they are maintained, and how they change over time. The assumption is that an adequate means of describing an individual's personality at any given point in time, coupled with an understanding of the way in which personalities develop, would contribute importantly to attempts to explain and predict human behavior and psychological functioning.

The third important feature of the previous quotations is only implicit in the singular nouns and pronouns used by Levy (1970) in the first passage, but is made explicit in the second passage, where it is directly asserted that the knowledge produced by the scientific study of personality should make *individual* human behavior intelligible. By no means should this be construed as a denial by Levy of the efficacy of searching for general or nomothetic principles of personality. Rather, it would seem more appropriate to interpret the above as an assertion that general or nomothetic principles of personality should be validated, and should thus contribute to the understanding, explanation, and prediction of behavior, *at the level* of the individual. Stated otherwise, general or nomothetic principles of personality would be those which have been shown—within the constraints necessarily imposed by induction in any domain of scientific inquiry—to be applicable to *any given individual*.

To summarize, an attempt has been made here to draw attention to three critical facets of the overriding, metatheoretical objectives of the scientific study of personality: (1) the discipline must seek to develop a viable framework for empirical personality description; (2) given such a framework, programmatic personality research should ultimately be directed toward an elucidation of the basic processes presumed to govern personality development; and (3) the knowledge produced by the science of personality should seek to establish general principles that would contribute to the understanding, explanation, and prediction of human behavior and psychological functioning at the level of the individual.

Assuming that the recent identity crisis in personality psychology has neither completely obscured nor radically altered these overriding objectives (cf. Phares & Lamiell, 1977; Sechrest, 1976), it will be argued that personality psychology is in need of some viable alternative to all of the basic research strategies that currently dominate empirical inquiry in the field. The basis for this argument is that none of the prevailing strategies adequately confronts what is clearly the most fundamental problem of all in the scientific study of personality: that of developing a viable framework for empirical personality *description*. Recent discussions of the persistence of this problem by investigators with markedly different orientations can be found in Harris (1980) and in Mehrabian and O'Reilly (1980). Failing in this regard, it is difficult to see how the prevailing research strategies could possibly prove adequate vis-à-vis the remaining metatheoretical concerns already discussed, however useful those strategies might be for other purposes. With this in mind, let us proceed to a more detailed consideration of the problem.

B. THE AGGREGATION PROBLEM

To most people—personologists and lay persons alike—the task of personality description is essentially one of identifying, within any given individual, those qualities, attributes, or characteristics that he/she manifests at certain levels with some degree of regularity or consistency over time and across situations. The first major difficulty that one encounters in attempting to glean from the extant literature in personality psychology a generally viable approach to this task results from what might be termed *the aggregation problem,* that is, the long-standing and widespread practice among personality investigators of treating as a *statistical* issue what is actually an issue of *measurement*. In order to arrive at a clear conception of the nature of this problem, it is helpful to begin with a brief discussion of the basic framework from which the vast bulk of the extant empirical literature in personality psychology has emerged.

Empirical personality research typically begins with an attempt by the investigator to express formally information about one or more (usually many) persons with respect to one or more underlying attributes of a set (or sets) of empirical observations. This is, of course, the essence of personality *assessment*, and the process can be formally represented in terms of the following general model:

$$S_{\text{pao}} = \overset{m}{\underset{i=1}{f}} (V_{\text{pio}}) (R_{\text{iao}}) \tag{1}$$

where S_{pao} refers to the "raw" score assigned to person p to represent quantitatively his/her manifestation of some underlying attribute a of a set of m empirical observations on a given measurement occasion o, V_{pio} is one of m variables in terms of which the empirical observations about person p on measurement occasion o are expressed or recorded, and R_{iao} is one of m "relevance values" indicating the degree to which the recording made on a given V_i on measurement occasion o is presumed to reflect or indicate the underlying attribute a. In words, Eq. (1) simply states that the "raw" score assigned to person p on measurement occasion o to represent his/her manifestation of attribute a is some function (traditionally additive, cf. Nunnally, 1967) of m empirical statements about person p, each of which is weighted by its presumed relevance to attribute a.

The specific nature of the V_i component of Eq. (1) depends, of course, on the particular assessment device in use. For example, it might be comprised of coded responses to projective test stimuli, checkmarks on the items of a self-report inventory, memory-based ratings on the m different items provided by persons other than person p, or immediately recorded direct observations of behavior. Moreover, observations on any given V_i might be recorded categorically (e.g., true–false, occurred–did not occur) or continuously (e.g., on scales of frequency, intensity, duration; scales ranging from "strongly agree" to "strongly disagree"). It should also be noted that V_i can be defined at various levels of abstraction, depending upon the investigator's purposes and/or theoretical predilections (cf. Fiske, 1978b; Golding, 1978).

As Eq. (1) indicates, formal personality assessment also requires some implicit or explicit definition of the relevance of the information conveyed by recordings on the V_is to the underlying attribute (or attributes in a multidimensional scheme) being measured (Bem & Allen, 1974; Bem & Funder, 1978; Funder, 1980). These "relevance values" might be determined intuitively, deduced rationally from a theory, or specified on the basis of empirical considerations (Hase & Goldberg, 1967). Examples of the latter would include the loadings derived from a factor analysis of the intercorrelations among the V_is (e.g., Hase & Goldberg, 1967), coefficients derived from multiple regression analyses involving the V_i and specified criterion variables (e.g., Mehrabian & O'Reilly, 1980), or the scale values of the V_i derived from a multidimensional scaling procedure (e.g.,

Shweder, 1975). In essence, the R component of Eq. (1) represents the process of *abstraction* that is normally an integral part of personality assessment (cf. Goldfried & Kent, 1972). That is, the "relevance values" reflect someone's (usually, but not necessarily, the investigator's) views concerning the degree to which recordings made for the respective V_is "contain" or "reveal" the underlying attribute being measured.

Having generated an array of S_{pao} values in accordance with the procedures represented by Eq. (1), the next concern of the personality investigator is usually that of demonstrating that those scores are scientifically defensible vis-à-vis the task of personality description, that is, the task of identifying those attributes which individuals manifest at certain levels with some degree of consistency over time and across situations. By far the most widely used strategy for addressing this concern has been to correlate the scores assigned to a number of persons on a particular attribute on one measurement occasion (or in one situation) with the scores assigned to those same persons on the same attribute on some subsequent measurement occasion (or in some other situation). The reliability and validity coefficients generated by this procedure have been employed as the empirical criteria for determining whether or not the S_{pao} values in question convey interpretable information concerning the personalities of the individuals assessed. The rationale underlying this approach is that those attributes for which highly reliable and valid individual differences measures can be devised are the ones with respect to which individuals do in fact demonstrate appreciable temporal and transsituational consistency, and thus, by definition, the ones with respect to which scientifically defensible personality descriptions can be formulated.

The extent to which this basic rationale has dominated the thinking of personality investigators over the years would seem to be amply reflected in the substance and enormous impact of Mischel's (1968) previously cited challenge to the assumption of the "consistency of particular predispositions *within the individual*" (emphasis added). Evidence of the long-standing adherence to that rationale abounds throughout the literature of the discipline (see, e.g., Beck, 1953; Bem & Allen, 1974; Campbell & Fiske, 1959; Endler & Magnusson, 1976b; Epstein, 1979, 1980; Eysenck, 1954; Falk, 1956; Hartshorne & May, 1928; Hase & Goldberg, 1967; Hirshberg, 1978; Hogan *et al.*, 1977; Holt, 1962; Kenrick & Stringfield, 1980; McGowan & Gormly, 1976; Mehrabian & O'Reilly, 1980; Nunnally, 1967; Shweder, 1975; Zanna, Olson, & Fazio, 1980).

Unfortunately, this rationale rests on the faulty premise that the reliability and validity coefficients obtained in studies of individual differences provide adequate empirical grounds for inferring the degree of consistency with which the *individuals* in a sample have manifested a particular attribute or characteristic over time or across situations. The premise is faulty simply because such coefficients are *group statistics*, computed on the basis of data summed *across persons*. It is the aggregate nature of those coefficients which virtually precludes their appropriateness as grounds on which to infer anything about (in)consistency in the levels at which any *one* individual has manifested a particular attribute or characteristic. Indeed, a reliability or validity coefficient cannot be unequivocally interpreted in this manner unless it is perfect (i.e., unity), because it is *only* then that the degree of consistency (in relative position with respect to some attribute) manifested by the individuals *as a group* unambiguously reflects the degree of consistency (in relative position) manifested by *each* individual *in* the group.

Before proceeding any further, it should be noted that the point being developed here is equally applicable to the interpretation of the omega-square ratios (cf. Bowers, 1973; Endler, 1975) and generalizability coefficients (Golding, 1975) used in the so-called "variance components" approach to the study of (in)consistencies in personality (cf. Magnusson & Endler, 1977b). They, too, are aggregate statistics, computed on the basis of data summed across persons.

Obviously, the reliability and validity coefficients (and omega-square ratios and generalizability coefficients) derived from individual differences research are rarely, if ever, perfect, and there is little reason to believe that their deviations from unity can be attributed entirely to measurement error. However, the prevailing view in empirical personality psychology has long been that *whatever* their size, such coefficients will support adequately some generalizations about (in)consistency in the levels at which particular attributes have been manifested by the individuals one has studied. Thus, "high" coefficients have been taken to mean that the individuals assessed were relatively consistent in their manifestations of an attribute, while "low" coefficients have been taken to mean that the individuals assessed were relatively inconsistent in their manifestations of the attribute. The inappropriateness of such interpretations can easily be seen by considering the data plotted in Fig. 1.

These data have been taken from a study to be discussed in greater detail below. For our present purposes, it is sufficient to note that in each panel of Fig. 1, z scores indicating the relative positions of 19 individuals on a measure of a particular attribute have been plotted for two measurement occasions. Thus, each line in the figure represents a single individual, and the slope of a line reflects the degree to which an individual's relative position in the group shifted from the first measurement occasion to the second (left panel), and from the second measurement occasion to the third (right panel).

As indicated at the top of Fig. 1, the Pearson product–moment correlation coefficient (i.e., the average of the cross-products of z scores) for the Occasion 1–Occasion 2 data is .60. As traditionally interpreted, this "reliability coefficient" would be taken as grounds for a generalization that the individuals sampled were fairly consistent over time in their manifestations of the attribute in question. Yet, as an inspection of the left panel of the figure reveals, the 19 individuals in the sample were clearly not *equally* (in)consistent over the two

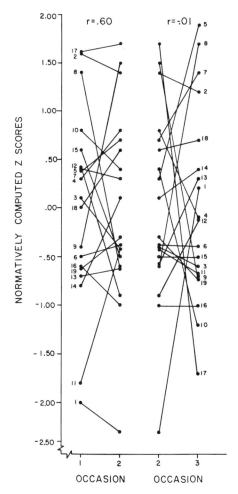

FIG. 1. A "microscopic picture" of data underlying two reliability coefficients.

measurement occasions in their relative positions on the attribute. Some individuals were, to be sure, quite consistent in this regard (e.g., persons 2, 5, 6, 13, and 17). Other individuals, however, shifted substantially in their relative positions in the group from the first to the second measurement occasion (e.g., persons 8, 9, 12, 14, and 15).

The observation that the individuals in the sample were not equally (in)consistent in their manifestations of the attribute in question clearly illustrates a very basic but critically important point: There is *no* single quantitative expression of (in)consistency computed for the *group* (e.g., a reliability coefficient of .60) that can accurately reflect what is going on with respect to the question of (in)consistency at the level of the *individual*.

The problem is identical when one considers the data in the right-hand panel of Fig. 1. There, the reliability coefficient was found to be $-.01$, and, as traditionally interpreted, would be taken as grounds for the generalization that the individuals sampled were extremely inconsistent from the second to the third measurement occasions in their manifestations of the attribute. For *some* of the individuals in the group, this conclusion might well be appropriate. Specifically, it can be seen in Fig. 1 that persons 1, 5, 8, 9, 10, and 17 shifted substantially in their relative positions in the group from the second to the third measurement occasions. However, it can also be seen that persons 2, 3, 6, 14, 15, 16, and 18 shifted very little or not at all in their relative positions. That is, those seven individuals were extremely *consistent* from Occasion 2 to Occasion 3 in their relative positions in the group, the $-.01$ reliability coefficient notwithstanding.

Again, the fact that the individuals in the sample were *not equally* (in)consistent in their manifestations of the attribute in question *means* that there is no index of (in)consistency computed for the group that can be assumed to reflect accurately the (in)consistency of any given individual in the group.

It may be appropriate to interject here that it is by no means certain that the (in)consistency of an individual's *relative position in a group* is an issue of critical relevance to the concept of personality (cf. Lay, 1977; Magnusson & Endler, 1977b). That it might not be would seem to be implied by those authors who have sought to emphasize the relevance of the findings generated by individual differences research to the question of (in)consistency in *behavior* (cf. previously cited quotation of Bem & Allen, 1974; see also Epstein, 1979, 1980), inasmuch as (in)consistency in behavior and (in)consistency in relative position in a group are not necessarily empirically equivalent phenomena.

However, to adopt the individual differences research strategy as a framework within which to address the consistency/inconsistency issue is, *methodologically* speaking, to adopt the (in)consistency-in-relative-position view by default. Thus, it is only to that aspect of the question that the findings generated by such research could possibly be said to speak in any sense. Whether or not (in)consistency in relative position in a group is precisely the *theoretical* question that an investigator might *wish* to address (or thinks he/she is addressing) does not, of course, alter this fact at all.

The importance of the distinction between what some authors have called "absolute" and "relative" consistency (cf. Lay, 1977; Magnusson & Endler, 1977b) will become more apparent in our later discussion of the measurement model problem in personality research (cf. Section II,C). Returning to the matter at hand, it does seem clear from the extant literature in personality psychology that (in)consistency of one sort or another *at the level of the individual* is generally agreed to be a phenomenon of fundamental theoretical importance.

Given a reliability or validity coefficient that deviates for any systematic reason from unity, *it is simply not possible to tell* how consistent or inconsistent *any* one individual has been in the levels—"absolute" *or* relative—at which he/she has manifested a particular attribute. With respect to the issue of (in)consistency, all that can be reasonably safely inferred on the basis of such a coefficient is that the individuals in one's sample were *not equally* (in)consistent in their manifestations of the attribute in question, in which case there is obviously *no generalization about temporal or transsituational (in)consistency at the level of the individual that could possibly be valid.*

Since the degree of consistency with which an *individual* manifests particular attributes is precisely what an investigator must know in order to determine the relevance of those attributes to a description of the subject's personality, it is perhaps apparent at this point why the empirical findings generated by the assessment and study of individual differences (whether alone or in interaction with situational variables) have not yielded and in all likelihood will never yield a viable (and methodologically defensible) framework for empirical personality description.

It is interesting to note that the limitations of the individual differences research strategy vis-à-vis the fundamental problem of personality description have been discussed in a variety of ways by many previous authors (see, e.g., Allport, 1937, 1962, 1966; Baldwin, 1942, 1946; Harris, 1980; Kelly, 1955; Norman, 1967; Rosenzweig, 1958; Stephenson, 1953; Tyler, 1959, 1978). Unfortunately, and for reasons that are not entirely clear to the present author, such caveats have been largely ignored (cf. Sanford, 1963). With very few exceptions (to be discussed presently), empirical personality research continues to be dominated by the erroneous notion that aggregate indices of the (in)stability of *differences between* individuals in their manifestations of various attributes will (a) adequately support generalizations concerning (in)consistency in the manifestation *by individuals* of those attributes, and (b) is, therefore, directly relevant to the fundamental problem of identifying those attributes in terms of which scientifically defensible personality descriptions can be formulated.

Perhaps mindful to some degree of the inappropriateness of this notion, a relative handful of investigators have at times employed alternatives to the traditional individual differences strategy as a means of conducting empirical studies in personality. In adopting those alternative strategies, however, investigators have still failed to address satisfactorily the fundamental problem of empirical personality description.

Consider, for example, the work of Baldwin (1942, 1946), who reported correlations between attributes, computed for single individuals over time. Such interattribute correlations can reveal the pattern of *co*variation between pairs of attribute measures within an individual (Carlson, 1971). Such correlations do not, however, properly address the question of (in)consistency in the levels at which any one attribute has been manifested by the individual, which, again, is the question that lies at the very heart of the problem of personality description.

A high interattribute correlation is, by definition, evidence of variability (not consistency) within an individual on two attributes over measurement occasions. Moreover, a low interattribute correlation could mean that an individual was highly variable on two attributes in ways which did not happen to coincide, *or* that the individual was highly *consistent* on one or both attributes. In the limiting case, perfect consistency in the manifestation of a given attribute would result in a zero interattribute correlation between that attribute and every other attribute. In sum, interattribute correlations such as those reported by Baldwin are no more adequate than conventional reliabilities and validities for the purpose of detecting (in)consistencies in the levels at which particular attributes are manifested by an individual over time (or across situations).

A somewhat different interpretive problem arises from the use of "O correlations" (Cattell, 1966) based on attribute profiles obtained for single individuals on different measurement occasions, an example of which approach can be found in Harris (1980). Such correlations *can* be used to address the question of (in)consistency at the level of the individual with respect to a *set* of attributes or characteristics. This is rather different, however, from the question of (in)consistency at the level of the individual with respect to *any particular* attribute or characteristic.

It was explained previously that a conventional reliability or validity coefficient that deviates for any systematic reason from unity is prima facie evidence that the individuals assessed were not equally (in)consistent in their manifestations of the attribute in question. For the very same logical reason, an O correlation that deviates for any systematic reason from unity is prima facie evidence that the individual being investigated was not equally (in)consistent with respect to all of the attributes in question. To see this, one need only return to Fig. 1 and imagine that the data in each of its panels represent measures taken for a single person on each of 19 attributes on two occasions. Clearly, the correlation of .60 could not be taken as an indication that the individual was moderately consistent on *all* of the attributes, nor could the correlation of −.01 be taken as evidence that the individual was extremely inconsistent on *all* of the attributes.

To reiterate, all that can be reasonably safely inferred from an O correlation that deviates for any systematic reason from unity is that the individual was not equally (in)consistent with respect to all of the attributes in question. Now, if it is the degree of consistency with which an individual manifests a particular attribute that determines the relevance of that attribute to a description of the individual's personality, then it would follow from what has just been said that an O correlation that deviates for any systematic reason from unity constitutes prima facie evidence that not all of the attributes in the profile are equally relevant to a description of that individual's personality, at least at that period in his/her life. Unfortunately, the correlation itself provides no clues as to which attributes are relevant and which are not. Thus, as useful as O correlations can be for certain purposes, they do not provide an adequate foundation for empirical personality description.

At the conclusion of Section II,A, it was suggested that the various correlational/variance partitioning strategies that have long dominated empirical personality research have failed to address satisfactorily the most fundamental problem in the discipline: that of developing a viable framework for personality description. That the persistence of this problem has impeded, and continues to impede, significant theoretical advances in the scientific study of personality has been noted by other authors as well (Harris, 1980; Mehrabian & O'Reilly, 1980; see also Sechrest, 1976). Moreover, and perhaps reflecting frustration with the failure to resolve this problem empirically despite decades of psychometrically sophisticated research (Tyler, 1978), London (1978b) has gone so far as to suggest that the question of which attributes shall be deemed relevant to the description and study of personalities might have to be decided by a panel of acknowledged experts in the field.

However, in light of the previous discussion, the reason that the extant empirical literature in personality psychology has failed to yield a generally viable framework for personality description has perhaps become apparent: Personality investigators have for years persisted in a massive effort to resolve with *statistics* (e.g., conventional reliability and validity coefficients, omega-square ratios, generalizability coefficients, interattribute correlations, and O correlations) what is fundamentally a problem in *measurement* (for general discussions of the importance of distinguishing questions of measurement from questions of statistics or hypothesis testing, see Birnbaum, 1974a; Gaito, 1980). More specifically, it is a problem of assigning numerical values to individuals in such a way as to represent, for *each* of those individuals, the levels at which he/she manifests *particular* qualities, attributes, or characteristics on each of a number of measurement occasions. Having created these numerical values, an investigator could reasonably proceed to array them in attributes-by-measurement occasions profiles *for single individuals*. The investigator would then be in a position to identify those attributes with respect to which any given individual is consistent, against the background, or within the context, of those attributes with respect to which that same individual is inconsistent. The former would presumably be the ones used to describe that individual's personality at that period in his/her life. It is to a more detailed consideration of this perspective, and its implications, that we now turn.

C. The Measurement Model Problem

1. The Nature of the Problem

Recognizing the problem of empirical personality description as one of measurement rather than one of statistics, the question becomes: How is one to go about the task of representing empirically the levels at which an individual manifests each of a number of attributes on each of a number of measurement occasions? As a way of introducing our consideration of this question, it is instructive to consider Fig. 2.

In Fig. 2, the points along the abscissa represent different occasions on (or situations in) which measures of an individual have been taken. Points on the ordinate represent various levels of the manifestation of any given attribute. Finally, lines A, B, C, and D in the figure connect points representing the levels (from "low" to "high") at which a single individual has manifested each of four attributes on each of the different measurement occasions.

In effect, Fig. 2 is a graphic portrayal of the sort of profile described previously in discussing how a personologist would approach the task of empirical personality description. As can be seen in the figure, the individual in question appears to have been quite consistent across measurement occasions in the levels at which he/she has manifested Attribute A, and rather variable or inconsistent in the manifestations of Attributes B, C, and D.

This general approach to the problem of empirical personality description might well seem straightforward enough. However, the important methodological question is this: How does one determine precisely the y-axis coordinates of points such as those plotted in Fig. 2? That is, what, specifically, does the "low," "high," or "moderate" manifestation by an individual of a particular attribute on a particular measurement occasion mean? In short, what is to be the underlying rationale or measurement model by which profiles of the sort represented by Fig. 2 are to be constructed? These are the questions which give rise to what has here been called *the measurement model problem* in personality research.

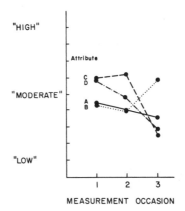

FIG. 2.   Attributes-by-measurement occasions profile for an individual. (Adapted from Lamiell, 1981.)

It is important to understand at the outset that answers to these questions are *not* simply "given" in the S_{pao} values generated via the assessment procedure represented by Eq. (1) above. It has long been recognized that the "raw" S_{pao} value assigned to a given individual for a particular attribute on a specific measurement occasion cannot be meaningfully interpreted in and of itself. In this sense, it can be said that there is no such thing as "absolute" measurement. Instead, the meaningful interpretation of any single S_{pao} value requires that it be *contrasted* in some way with other values, that is, *placed in some context*. It is at this point where the notion of a measurement model becomes relevant. Stated otherwise, it is the measurement model that a personality investigator employs (implicitly or explicitly) that defines the rationale whereby the y-axis coordinates of points such as those plotted in Fig. 2 are determined.

Cattell (1944) pointed out that in approaching this (or any other) problem in psychological measurement, an investigator may choose from three basic models: normative, ipsative, and interactive. The first two of these models are undoubtedly the ones most familiar to personality investigators, inasmuch as one or the other (and at times a mixture of both) is adopted implicitly when "raw" assessments are analyzed in terms of any of the various statistical indices of (in)consistency in personality previously discussed. Interestingly, however, programmatic applications of what Cattell (1944, p. 299) specifically referred to as the "queen" of psychological measurement—that is, interactive measurement— are virtually nonexistent in the literature of empirical personality psychology. This point is particularly noteworthy in view of the fact that, upon careful analysis, it can be seen that reliance on either the normative or ipsative measurement model, or some combination of these, can impose certain conceptually costly constraints on the task of empirical personality description; constraints that can be eliminated only by the adoption of an interactive measurement model.

In consideration of this matter, I have proposed (Lamiell, 1981) a measurement model which, though labeled "idiographic" (cf. Allport, 1962), would seem to conform in its essential features to what Cattell (1944) had in mind when he used the term "interactive" measurement. In any event, that model was specifically proposed as one in terms of which the fundamental problem of empirical personality description might most usefully be approached. In attempting to develop this point more fully here, it is helpful to consider explicitly the formal differences between that model and the more traditional normative and ipsative ones.

2. Formal Characteristics of the Alternative Measurement Models

As Kleinmuntz (1967) has pointed out, the essence of the normative measurement model is that "all meaning for a given score a person derives from comparing his score with those of other persons" (p. 47). More specifically, the meaning of the "raw" score (S_{pao} value) assigned to person p for attribute a on measurement occasion o is defined by contrasting that score with (i.e., placing it within the context of) the scores assigned to other persons for attribute a on measurement occasion o (or, at least, on measurement occasions deemed equivalent to o). Using the notation adopted above for Eq. (1), the most common application of this model can be formally represented as follows:

$$Z_{pao} = (S_{pao} - \overline{S}_{.ao})/SD_{.ao} \tag{2}$$

where Z_{pao} represents the meaningfully interpreted level at which person p would be said to have manifested attribute a on measurement occasion o, S_{pao} is defined as previously, $\overline{S}_{.ao}$ represents the mean, computed across persons, of the "raw" scores assigned to those persons for attribute a, measurement occasion o, and $SD_{.ao}$ represents the standard deviation of those same "raw" scores.

Equation (2) represents the measurement model adopted by default when an individual differences investigator computes conventional (Pearson product–moment) reliability and validity coefficients. For reasons already explained, those correlations are rarely, if ever, informative vis-à-vis the fundamental problem of empirical personality description. However, by applying the model represented by Eq. (2) in the appropriate way to an appropriate set of "raw" attribute scores (S_{pao} values), an attributes-by-occasions profile of interpretable data *for a single individual* could conceivably be constructed, and in turn used as the basis for empirically describing the personality of that individual. In other words, the fact that conventional reliability and validity coefficients normally cannot themselves be properly used as the basis for determining which attributes are relevant to a description of the personality of any given individual does not, in and of itself, preclude the possibility that the measurement model which underlies the computation of those indices could be usefully employed for such purposes.

However, within an attributes-by-measurement occasions profile constructed for a single individual on the basis of the normative measurement model, the levels at which the individual would be said to have manifested particular attributes on the various measurement occasions would not depend uniquely on the set of empirical observations originally obtained, and then summarized, *for that individual* in accordance with Eq. (1). Rather, those specified levels would also reflect, in part, the empirical observations obtained and summarized [via Eq. (1)] for each of the other persons with whom the individual in question happens to have been compared.

One very important implication of this fact is that the degree of consistency with which an individual would later be said to have manifested a particular attribute across measurement occasions would not, in profiles constructed on the basis of a normative measurement model, be uniquely dependent on his/her *own* (in)consistency with respect to the *set of empirical referents* for that attribute [i.e., the information contained in the right-hand side of Eq. (1)].[1] Indeed it would be possible for an individual to be *perfectly* consistent, across measurement occasions, with respect to the set of empirical referents for an attribute, and yet for his/her normatively defined status on that attribute to change. This could occur merely as a result of inconsistencies on the part of others with whom that individual has been compared. Similarly, it would be possible for an individual to change dramatically, across measurement occasions, with respect to the set of empirical referents for a given attribute, and yet for his/her normatively defined status on that attribute to remain constant. This could occur if the other persons with whom that individual has been compared happen to change in the same way.

As one way of ensuring that the observed (in)consistencies of an individual are entirely dependent upon his/her own (in)consistencies, and not at all on the (in)consistencies of other persons, an investigator could conceivably adopt a measurement model whereby the level at which an individual is said to have manifested a given attribute on a given measurement occasion would be defined with reference to the levels at which that same individual has manifested that same attribute on other measurement occasions. This is the basic rationale which underlies one of the two possible forms of ipsative measurement, and it can be formally represented in terms of the following equation:

$$Z_{pao} = (S_{pao} - \bar{S}_{pa.})/SD_{pa.} \tag{3}$$

where Z_{pao} represents the meaningfully interpreted level at which person p would be said to have manifested attribute a on measurement occasion o, S_{pao} is defined as previously, $\bar{S}_{pa.}$ represents the mean, computed across occasions, of the "raw" scores assigned to person p for attribute a, and $SD_{pa.}$ represents the standard deviation of those same "raw" scores.

Equation (3) represents the measurement model adopted by default when an investigator computes interattribute correlations of the sort discussed previously in connection with the work of Baldwin (1942, 1946). Again, while such correlations are not themselves well suited to the problem of empirical personality description, an attributes-by-occasions profile of interpretable data for a single individual could conceivably be constructed by applying Eq. (3) in the appropriate way to an appropriate set of data.

---

[1] The notion of (in)consistency with respect to a *set* of empirical referents for a given attribute must be carefully distinguished from the notion of (in)consistency with respect to any *one* empirical referent for an attribute. It has long been recognized that an individual can be inconsistent with respect to some particular behavior, for example, yet consistent in the overall degrees to which his/her *patterns* of behavior reflect particular attributes. It is for this reason that most personality assessment procedures involve observations on many empirical referents for a single attribute, rather than just one. The use of the phrase "(in)consistency with respect to a *set* of empirical referents for a given attribute" is intended to serve this important distinction.

Unlike profiles constructed in accordance with the normative measurement model, those constructed in accordance with the ipsative model represented by Eq. (3) would be such that the degree of consistency with which an individual would be said to have manifested any one attribute would be uniquely dependent on his/her *own* (in)consistency with respect to the set of empirical referents for that attribute. However, in adopting such a measurement model, an investigator risks losing information about differences between the *levels* at which an individual manifests *different attributes*.

Suppose, for example, that an investigator has obtained measures for a single individual on two attributes on each of three measurement occasions. Suppose further that the "raw" scores (S_{pao} values) on the scales used to measure each of the two attributes can range in value from 0 (lowest possible score) to 10 (highest possible score). Under the logic of the measurement rationale represented by Eq. (3), an individual assigned "raw" scores of 8, 9, and 8 on the first attribute (consistently "high" scores) would obtain ipsatively defined z scores of $-.58$, 1.15, and $-.58$, respectively (rounded to two decimals). If the same individual obtained "raw" scores of 1, 2, and 1 on the second attribute (consistently "low" scores), his/her ipsatively defined z scores on that attribute would again be $-.58$, 1.15, and $-.58$.

It is in the specific sense just illustrated that reliance by an investigator on the measurement model represented by Eq. (3) could result in the loss of information about an individual with respect to the different levels at which he/she manifests various attributes over measurement occasions. One way of resolving this problem would be to resort to the second of the two possible forms of ipsative measurement, whereby the level at which an individual is said to have manifested a given attribute on a given measurement occasion would be defined with reference to the levels at which he/she manifested other attributes on the same (or some comparable) measurement occasion. This form of ipsative measurement can be formally represented as follows:

$$Z_{pao} = (S_{pao} - \overline{S}_{p.o})/SD_{p.o} \tag{4}$$

where Z_{pao} represents the meaningfully interpreted level at which person p would be said to have manifested attribute a on measurement occasion o, S_{pao} is defined as previously, $\overline{S}_{p.o}$ represents the mean, computed across attributes, of the "raw" scores assigned to person p on measurement occasion o, and $SD_{p.o}$ represents the standard deviation of those same "raw" scores.

In order to sensibly apply the measurement model represented by Eq. (4), it is obviously necessary for the different attribute measures to be defined in comparable units. For example, it would make little sense to compute the mean and standard deviation of an individual's "raw" scores on the attributes of height, as measured in inches, and weight, as measured in pounds.

One way of resolving this problem is to redefine "raw" attribute scores in accordance with the normative measurement model *prior* to the application of Eq. (4). In essence, this is the strategy adopted by Harris (1980) in his recently reported work on the problem of "nomovalidation and idiovalidation." As a way of formally representing this strategy, Eq. (4) can be rewritten as:

$$Z'_{pao} = (Z_{pao} - \bar{Z}_{p.o})/SD_{z,p.o} \tag{4a}$$

where Z'_{pao} new represents the meaningfully interpreted level at which person p would be said to have manifested attribute a on measurement occasion o, Z_{pao} represents the normatively defined level at which person p would be said to have manifested attribute a on measurement occasion o, $\bar{Z}_{p.o}$ represents the mean, computed across attributes, of the normatively defined Z scores for person p on measurement occasion o, and $SD_{z, p.o}$ represents the standard deviation of those same normatively defined z scores.

Equation (4a) is an approximate representation of the measurement model on which the O correlations reported by Harris were based [the representation is not, strictly speaking, precise, because the right-hand side of Eq. (4a) was actually defined by Harris in terms of T scores, which are normalized z scores]. Once again, such correlations do not resolve adequately the problem of empirical personality description, whether or not the z scores have been normalized. Nevertheless, data of the sort generated by Eq. (4a) could conceivably be used as the basis for constructing attributes-by-occasions profiles for single individuals. In order to distinguish the profiles constructed in accordance with Eqs. (3) and (4a), the former will hereafter be referred to as "ipsative," and the latter as "normative–ipsative."

Unlike profiles constructed according to the ipsative measurement model, those constructed in accordance with the normative–ipsative model would retain information concerning the different levels at which particular attributes have been manifested by an individual across measurement occasions. However, such profiles would also be subject, in part, to the same constraints identified earlier in discussing "pure normative" profiles. In addition to and quite independent of this fact, it should be apparent that, under the logic of the rationale represented by Eq. (4a), the levels at which, and thus the degree of consistency with which an individual would be seen to manifest any one attribute would be influenced in part by the levels at [and (in)consistency with] which he/she manifests the other attributes. In other words, just as information concerning an individual's manifestation of a particular attribute would not be specific *to that person* under the terms of the normative measurement model, the information would not be specific *to that attribute* under the terms of the normative–ipsative measurement model.

The single most important methodological feature distinguishing the interactive measurement model proposed by the present author (Lamiell, 1981; see also Allport, 1962; Cattell, 1944) from all of the other models discussed thus far is

that, under the terms of the interactive model, the meaning of the "raw" S_{pao}
value assigned to a given individual for a particular attribute on a specific measurement occasion does not hinge in any way on other S_{pao} values obtained by
the investigator in some larger data set. Stated otherwise the meaning of the S_{pao}
value assigned to person p for attribute a on measurement occasion o is not
derived by contrasting it directly with the "raw" scores assigned to (a) other
persons for the same attribute on the same measurement occasion (the normative
rationale), (b) the same person for the same attribute on other measurement
occasions (the ipsative rationale), or (c) the same person for other attributes on
the same measurement occasion (the normative–ipsative rationale). Instead, in
interactive measurement, the "raw" score assigned to person p for attribute a for
measurement occasion o is interpreted with reference to the extreme alternative
scores that could *possibly* have been assigned to that person for that attribute on
that measurement occasion, given the constraints necessarily imposed—
regardless of one's measurement rationale—*by the assessment procedure itself*,
that is, given the V_{pio} s, R_{iao} s, and integration function of Eq. (1). This rationale
can be formally represented as follows:

$$I_{\text{pao}} = (S_{\text{pao}} - S'_{\text{pao min}})/(S'_{\text{pao max}} - S'_{\text{pao min}}) \qquad (5)$$

where I_{pao} represents the meaningfully interpreted level at which person p would
be said to have manifested attribute a on measurement occasion o, S_{pao} is defined
as previously, and $S'_{\text{pao max}}$ and $S'_{\text{pao min}}$ refer, respectively, to the maximum
and minimum obtainable "raw" scores on attribute a, given the V_{pio}, R_{iao},
and integration function of Eq. (1).

Under the terms of the measurement model represented by Eq. (5), the y-axis
coordinate of any one "raw" S_{pao} value in a profile such as that represented by
Fig. 2 would be uniquely and entirely dependent upon information obtained for a
particular individual on a *particular* measurement occasion with respect to the
set of empirical referents for a *particular* attribute. If these are the conditions that
an investigator wishes to create in approaching the task of empirical personality
description, then it can be seen that the interactive measurement model would
indeed provide a means of eliminating the constraints imposed on that task by the
adoption of one or another of the previously discussed models.

3. Comment

In principle, any of the alternative measurement models discussed above could
be used by an investigator for the purposes of constructing attributes-by-
measurement occasions profiles for single individuals. In this sense, any one of
those models could be methodologically defended as an approach to the fundamental problem of empirical personality description.

However, and as a simple inspection of Eqs. (2), (3), (4), (4a), and (5)
reveals, these alternative measurement models are clearly *not formally equiva-*

lent to one another. That is, the nature of the *contrast* by virtue of which a single "raw" S_{pao} value is given meaning changes from one measurement model to the next. As a result, it cannot be uncritically assumed that the attributes-by-measurement occasions profiles that could conceivably be constructed for a single individual by applying the various models, in turn, to a common set of "raw" S_{pao} values would be equivalent to, and thus intersubstitutable for, each other. Quite to the contrary, and as we shall see, the "picture" of an individual that a personality investigator creates out of "raw" assessments can depend very much on the particular "camera" he/she uses.

What all of this implies, of course, is that while any of the alternative measurement models *could* be adopted by an investigator vis-à-vis the problem of empirical personality description, the particular model that one *does* adopt cannot be regarded as an atheoretical decision (Cattell, 1965). Thus, that decision should be firmly grounded in some explicit consideration of precisely the sorts of phenomena one wishes to address. It is in this context, for example, that the previously discussed distinction between "absolute" and "relative" consistency becomes critical.

The interactive measurement model represented by Eq. (5) is the model on which the "idiothetic" (Lamiell, 1981) psychology of personality is based. On a variety of methodological and metatheoretical grounds (including but not limited to a consideration of the aggregation problem discussed in Section II,B), I have argued the potential advantages of adopting the "idiothetic" approach as a general orientation for the scientific study of personality. While these arguments will be elaborated at the conclusion of this article, this next section will be used to develop the point that the case for adopting the "idiothetic" framework, and the interactive measurement model on which it is based, need not necessarily rest on methodological and theoretical considerations alone.

To this end, it is instructive to begin by returning to a consideration of one of the three major themes identified earlier as having emerged from the personality literature of the 1970s. Specifically, reference is being made here to the growing consensus that further progress in the scientific study of personality is going to require increasing "attention to the cognitive processes of both the actors and the observers, the subjects and scientists of our field" (Mischel, 1979, p. 752).

If this notion of attending to the cognitive processes of the subjects (as well as the scientists) of our field is to be taken seriously, then it would seem to follow that one major objective of personality investigators in the 1980s is going to be to achieve a fuller understanding of the nature of the cognitions which underlie the formulation of subjective personality impressions. Obviously, substantial efforts in this general direction have already been made (cf. Wegner & Vallacher, 1977), a fact which is amply reflected in research on such topics as (a) the structure of implicit personality theories (e.g., Jackson & Messick, 1963; Kim & Rosenberg, 1980; Passini & Norman, 1966; Rosenberg, Nelson, &

Vivekananthan, 1968; Rosenberg & Sedlak, 1972; Schneider, 1973; N. Wiggins, 1973), (b) information integration in the formation of subjective/clinical personality impressions (e.g., Anderson, 1965; Anderson & Shanteau, 1977; Birnbaum, 1974b; Dawes, 1974; Goldberg, 1968; J. S. Wiggins, 1973), and (c) the so-called "illusory correlation" phenomenon in social perception (e.g., Berman & Kenny, 1976; D'Andrade, 1965; Lay & Jackson, 1969; Mulaik, 1964; Shweder, 1975, 1977; Shweder & D'Andrade, 1979, 1980).

As interesting and informative as research on these topics has been in certain respects, virtually all of that research is based on the assumptions (often only implicit by virtue of the methodologies employed) that (a) subjective personality impressions are grounded ultimately in the individual differences conception of personality that has, throughout the twentieth century, so thoroughly dominated the thinking of personality investigators themselves, and thus that (b) such subjective impressions can be adequately studied, represented, and understood within the individual differences framework. To the best of the present author's knowledge, the possibility has not heretofore been seriously and systematically considered that the subjective perspective on personality-relevant phenomena [e.g., various aspects of the (in)consistency question] might *not* be grounded in the traditional individual differences conception of personality at all, and thus might not be adequately studied, represented, or understood within the constraints imposed by that orientation (cf. Lamiell, 1980).

In the following section, empirical findings will be considered which suggest that while the actors and observers in personality research might well be functioning as implicit *personality* theorists, they might not be functioning as implicit *individual differences* theorists (or, one might say, as implicit differential psychologists). More specifically, the evidence presented indicates that the subjective perspective on personality-relevant phenomena conforms neither to (a) the aggregate viewpoint typically taken by the individual differences investigator, nor, when the issues are framed at the level of the individual, to (b) the *normative* viewpoint on which the individual differences orientation is by definition predicted.

Regarding point (b), the evidence suggests that, in formulating subjective impressions of their own and others' personalities, a process which can be thought of as the subjective analog of the measurement model problem discussed previously, lay persons rely on a cognitive rationale that is essentially interactive rather than normative or ipsative in nature. If this is true, and given that the "idiothetic" approach to the scientific study of personality is also predicted on a rationale that is interactive rather than normative or ipsative in nature, it is not difficult to see how the adoption of that approach could prove useful over and above the methodological/metatheoretical issues discussed in this article and by Lamiell (1981). Beyond those considerations, the "idiothetic" framework might well provide the most viable means of reconciling the traditional concerns of personality theory with the more "contemporary" (at least in the mainstream) objective of illuminating the *interface of cognition and personality* (Mischel, 1979). With this possibility in mind, let us turn to a consideration of the evidence.

III. Toward the Interface of Cognition and Personality via Interactive Measurement

A. STUDY I: SUBJECTIVE PERCEPTIONS OF INTERNAL (IN)CONSISTENCIES IN BEHAVIOR PATTERNS

The thinking that has given rise to the "idiothetic" approach to the study of personality actually began to emerge out of a study conducted by the present author and two graduate student colleagues on the so-called "illusory correlation" phenomenon. Since a detailed presentation of that study is available elsewhere (Lamiell, Foss, & Cavenee, 1980), and in consideration of present space limitations, only a general overview of the work is presented here.

As articulated most recently by Shweder (1975, 1977a, 1977b, 1977c, 1980) and by Shweder & D'Andrade (1979, 1980), the illusory correlation hypothesis states that, under difficult memory conditions

> respondents on interpersonal checklists, personality inventories and questionnaire interviews unwittingly substitute a theory of conceptual likenesses for a description of behavioral co-occurrences. Considerations about similarity are confounded with judgments about probability to such an extent that items alike in concept are inferred to be behaviorally characteristic of the same person even when, as is typically the case, conceptual relationships among items do not correspond with the actual behavioral relationships among the items. (Shweder, 1975, pp. 481–482)

As an empirical index of the degree to which pairs of items are inferred to be "behaviorally characteristic of the same person," Shweder has employed, throughout the above-cited research, correlations between the ratings made by a given rater on pairs of items, computed across rating protocols (i.e., across ratees). Where m equals the number of items rated in each protocol, this procedure results in $m(m-1)/2$ interitem correlations. These correlations have in turn been correlated with independently obtained judgments of the conceptual (dis)similarities among the items. The resulting correlation [i.e., that between the $m(m-1)/2$ interitem correlations and the $m(m-1)/2$ conceptual (dis)similarities] has been used as an index of the degree of correspondence between conceptual schemes and behavior reports.

Lamiell *et al.* (1980) pointed out that, as an aggregate index computed by summing data across ratees, the correlational measure of interitem "attributional (dis)similarity" [i.e., (dis)similarity between ratings for item pairs] is logically inappropriate for purposes of testing the assertion—clearly implied by the illusory correlation hypothesis—that substantial correspondence between conceptual schemes and behavior reports exists *at the level of the individual ratee* (who, in instances of self-report, is the same person as the rater). Thus, Lamiell *et al.* argued that in order to test the illusory correlation hypothesis properly an index of interitem attributional (dis)similarity computed *within* single protocols is logically required. Those authors went on to suggest that the computation, for all possible pairs of items, of the absolute differences between item ratings within a single protocol would provide the theoretically required index. Correlations between those $m(m-1)/2$ absolute differences and the $m(m-1)/2$ conceptual (dis)similarities would then provide an index of the linear correspondence between conceptual schemes and behavior reports that could be computed and interpreted at the level of the individual ratee.

Lamiell *et al.* then reported the results of two parallel analyses of a single data set, based first on (a) the correlational, and then on (b) the absolute differences measure of interitem attributional (dis)similarity. For (a), the results obtained were virtually identical to those reported in previous tests of the illusory correlation hypothesis, apparently providing further empirical support for that hypothesis. However, when the same data were reanalyzed according to (b) above, findings quite incompatible with the illusory correlation hypothesis were obtained.

The latter analyses revealed that, when averaged across ratees, the degree of correspondence between one's conceptual scheme and one's descriptions of self or others is considerably lower than previously reported results had made it appear. Of much greater importance, it was found that within single raters and within self-reports, the degree of correspondence between conceptual schemes and behavior reports (a) *varied* substantially across ratees, and (b) was systematically related to subjective judgments of the *internal consistency* or *coherence* in the reported behavior patterns. As a direct result of the aggregate methods that had been employed in previous studies of the illusory correlation phenomenon, this relationship—which is of immediate relevance to prevailing theoretical interpretations of the illusory correlation phenomenon—had not been and could not have been detected (cf. Lamiell, 1980).

In discussing the implications of their work, Lamiell *et al.* noted that while their findings contraindicated Shweder's theoretical interpretation of the illusory correlation phenomenon, those same findings did little to support the utility of the traditional individual differences conception of personality, which had also been questioned by Shweder (1975). The reason for this is that the technique of computing absolute differences between item ratings within single protocols is *itself* incompatible with the normative measurement model on which the individual differences conception is predicated, and, instead, conforms more closely to a rationale that is essentially interactive in nature.

Under the terms of the normative measurement model, the rated level of any given item of behavior in the protocol of a single ratee is regarded as interpretable only in comparison with the rated levels of that same item in the protocols of other ratees. Thus, in order to investigate the relationship between conceptual schemes and behavior reports at the level of the individual ratee, and at the same time remain within the constraints of the individual differences framework, Lamiell *et al.* would have had to standardize item ratings across ratees *prior* to the calculation of iteritem absolute differences.

Mindful of this fact, Lamiell *et al.* proceeded to conduct the analyses just described. With respect to their means and variabilities, the resulting correspondence values between the conceptual schemes and behavior reports were virtually identical to those obtained when absolute differences between unstandardized item ratings had been used. However, the previously obtained relationships between the correspondence values and the subjective judgments of internal consistency or coherence were, in these analyses, substantially obscured. That is, ratee-by-ratee analyses of the correspondence between conceptual schemes and behavior reports, when conducted in methodological accordance with the normative assumption of the individual differences framework, left subjective impressions of internal consistency or coherence in reported behavior patterns largely unaccounted for.

Quite apart from the implications of the Lamiell *et al.* findings vis-à-vis the illusory correlation hypothesis (cf. Lamiell, 1980; Shweder, 1980), those findings raised at least two intriguing possibilities concerning the nature of the lay perspective on personality-relevant phenomena. First, the findings suggested that, with respect to at least one issue of long-standing theoretical concern to personologists—that of internal consistency of coherence in behavior patterns (cf. Lay, 1977; Magnusson & Endler, 1977b)—lay persons' cognitions cannot be adequately reflected in the aggregate data that individual differences investigators have routinely brought to bear on the phenomenon. Instead, lay persons appear to be quite capable of dealing with the phenomenon *at the level of the individual*. This point is both intriguing and important because the individual level of analysis is much better suited to the *theoretical* concerns of personologists than is the aggregate level of analysis at which personologists themselves have traditionally worked.

Beyond this, however, the Lamiell *et al.* findings suggested that even when the question of internal consistency or coherence is framed at the level of the individual, the lay perspective cannot be adequately represented, studied, or understood within the constraints imposed by the normative measurement model employed by individual differences investigators. To the contrary, the findings suggested that the cognitions which underlie subjective perceptions of internal consistency or coherence conform more closely to an interactive rationale.

To summarize, as concerns the broad problem of understanding the cognitive processes of the actors and observers in personality research, the Lamiell *et al.* findings suggest that the individual differences framework may be inadequate, not only by virtue of its usual (aggregate) level of analysis, but also by virtue of the normative measurement model on which it is based.

Given these possibilities, both emanating from a study pertinent to the subjective perception of internal consistency/coherence in behavior patterns, it was but a small step to entertain the possibility that the subjective perspective on other matters of long-standing theoretical concern to personologists would likewise differ fundamentally and importantly from the traditional individual differences view. Accordingly, a second study was carried out by the present author in collaboration with Steven J. Trierweiler, this time to investigate whether or not the subjective perspective on the question of temporal (in)consistencies in the manifestation of particular attributes could be adequately represented in terms of the aggregate data typically relied on by individual differences investigators themselves.

B. STUDY II: SUBJECTIVE PERCEPTIONS OF TEMPORAL (IN)CONSISTENCIES IN THE MANIFESTATION OF PARTICULAR ATTRIBUTES

1. Method

Participants in the study included 19 student volunteers (11 females, 8 males) enrolled in an undergraduate psychology course at the University of Illinois. The participants were informed that the purpose of the study was to investigate the way in which people make personality-relevant judgments about themselves.

During the first week of course meetings, each participant judged the similarity between all possible pairs of the 18 activities listed in Table I. These activities had been selected on the basis of a previous survey aimed at identifying activities representative of those in which college students might possibly engage. The order in which the 153 activity pairs [18 (17)/2] were presented was determined on a random basis, and then held constant across persons.

The similarity judgments were recorded on an 11-point scale, labeled at the endpoints by the phrases ''There is no similarity between these two activities'' (0), and ''These two activities are virtually identical'' (10). These similarity judgments were later submitted to multidimensional scaling analyses, so as to derive a geometric representation of the underlying attributes in terms of which each participant construed the 18 activities. For reasons to be discussed, a four-dimensional solution was selected as ''best.'' The coordinates of the activities on these four dimensions were then used to define operationally the four underlying attributes in terms of which temporal (in)consistencies were subsequently examined (cf. Table I).

TABLE I
PROJECTIONS OF 18 ACTIVITIES ON FOUR DIMENSIONS OF AN INDSCAL SOLUTION

Activity	Dimension[a]			
	A	B	C	D
1. Studying or reading intellectual material	.17	−.28	.42	−.18
2. Participating in artistic or creative activities	.34	.00	.03	−.14
3. Casual dating	−.03	−.06	−.39	−.03
4. Engaging in premarital sex	.14	.48	−.10	−.17
5. Participating in athletic activities	.34	.12	−.06	.47
6. Reading/viewing pornographic materials	−.20	.31	.24	−.30
7. Watching television	−.39	−.21	.08	.02
8. Listening to music	−.13	−.08	−.17	−.25
9. Working at a part-time job	.00	−.15	.47	.41
10. Playing cards	−.38	−.25	−.16	.16
11. Partying	−.22	.17	−.28	.03
12. Attending live entertainment or movies	−.12	−.07	.13	−.23
13. Participating in outdoor activities (camping, hiking, etc.)	.32	.03	−.24	.35
14. Participating in events of a religious nature	.32	−.32	.02	−.13
15. Cutting classes	−.15	.15	.06	.32
16. Getting high on alcohol and/or marijuana	−.16	.18	−.20	−.02
17. Using drugs other than alcohol or marijuana	−.06	.34	.06	−.13
18. Attending lectures/seminars (outside of coursework)	.22	−.37	.34	−.18

[a] Intuitive interpretation of dimensions: A, Filling spare time, diversionary, or "idle" (−) vs Physically and/or mentally involved, or "earnest" (+); B, Hedonistic, or oriented toward physical pleasure (+) vs Nonhedonistic, or not oriented toward physical pleasure (−); C, Socially oriented (−) vs Nonsocially oriented (+); D, Low in motor activity (−) vs High in motor activity (+).

At the end of the first week of course meetings, each participant was given three activity report forms, each of which consisted of a list of the 18 activities, and a 10-point frequency-of-occurrence rating scale for each activity, labeled at the endpoints with the terms "never" and "very frequently." Each participant was asked to complete the activity report forms at 2-day intervals over the next 6 days, describing each time his/her activity pattern over the previous 2 days. The three protocols thus generated by each participant were later used as the "stimulus materials" for the participants' self-ratings on the four underlying attributes, defined by the multidimensional scaling analyses just discussed.

In the third week of course meetings, each participant was presented with the three activity protocols he/she had previously generated, ask to consider carefully the information in each, and to arrive at an overall rating of each protocol on each of the four criterion attributes. All self-ratings were made on 11-point scales, labeled at the endpoints by descriptors of the dimension poles, and at the midpoints by phrases indicating neither one extreme nor the other. For example, Attribute A was labeled by the investigators (on a strictly intuitive basis) as "Filling spare time, diversionary, or 'idle' vs Physically and/or mentally involved, or 'earnest.' " The midpoint for the rating scale corresponding to this attribute was labeled "Neither particularly 'idle' nor particularly 'involved.' "

The rating scales for the other three criterion attributes were similarly constructed. The endpoints of these rating scales were labeled, respectively, "Hedonistic or oriented toward physical pleasure vs Nonhedonistic, or not oriented toward physical pleasure" (Attribute B); "Socially oriented vs Nonsocially oriented" (Attribute C), and "Low in motor activity vs High in motor activity" (Attribute D).

Thus, each participant provided a total of 12 self-ratings: one for each of the four criterion attributes on each of three self-reported activity protocols. The standard deviation, computed across protocols, of an individual's three self-ratings on a given criterion attribute was used in subsequent analyses as a measure of subjective temporal (in)consistency in the manifestation of that attribute.

Finally, each respondent was again asked to consider his/her three self-report protocols, and to make a single, overall judgment of his/her psychological (in)consistency over time. For purposes of this judgment, no reference was made to any particular attribute. Rather, the judgments were made on an 11-point scale, labeled at the endpoints by the phrases "Psychologically speaking, (this person) was extremely consistent over time" (0), and "Psychologically speaking, (this person) was extremely inconsistent over time" (10). The midpoint of this scale was labeled "Psychologically speaking, (this person) was neither extremely consistent nor extremely inconsistent over time."

2. Results

As a first step in the data analysis, it was necessary to assign "raw" scores (S_{pao} values) to each activity protocol so as to represent empirically subjective impressions of the activity protocols with respect to each criterion attribute on each measurement occasion. This was done in accordance with a procedure which assumes that the cognitive "computation" of subjective S_{pao} values can be formally represented as an intuitive or implicit application of Eq. (1), that is, as a subjective analog of formal personality assessment.

The subjective V_{pio} component of Eq. (1) was defined operationally in terms of the frequency values for each of the 18 activities in each protocol. These values were numerically coded on a zero-to-nine scale, with zero indicating "never" engaged in a given activity, and nine indicating "very frequently" engaged in a given activity.

The subjective R_{iao} values of Eq. (1) were operationally defined in the present study by the coordinates of the 18 activities in the four-dimensional configuration retained after the multidimensional scaling analyses of the pair-wise similarity judgments of the activities. In conducting these analyses, the INDSCAL procedure developed by Carroll and Chang (1970) was used.

The mean indices of fit computed for the one-, two-, three-, and four-dimensional solutions of INDSCAL were .52, .62, .67, and .73, respectively. Additional dimensions did not noticeably increase fit, nor were solutions comprised of more than four dimensions easily interpretable. Of the above-mentioned solutions, the four-dimensional configuration was most easily interpreted, and was therefore retained for use in subsequent analyses.

The projections of the 18 activities on each of the four dimensions of this configuration are shown in Table I, and the investigators' intuitive interpretations of the dimensions are provided at the bottom. It should be pointed out that the variance of the index of fit for the four-dimensional solution, computed across respondents, was extremely small (.001). For this reason, the values shown in Table I were assumed, in the present study, to reflect adequately each respondent's conceptualization of the 18 activities.

With the subjective V_{pio} and R_{iao} components of Eq. (1) thus defined, simple matrix multiplication yielded estimates of the subjective S_{pao} values of Eq. (1). Specifically, the occasions-by-activities matrix of subjective V_{pio}s defined for each respondent by his/her set of three activity report protocols (scored in the manner specified above) was postmultiplied by the activities-by-attributes matrix of subjective R_{iao} values shown in Table I, yielding the desired occasions-by-attributes matrix of subjective S_{pao} values for each respondent. Consistent with tradition in formal personality assessment, this procedure obviously assumes that the subjective integration function ($f_{i=1}^m$) of Eq. (1) is additive. The complete persons-by-occasions-by-attributes matrix of subjective S_{pao} values estimated by these procedures is provided in Table II.

Given data of the sort shown in Table II, the individual differences investigator would presumably address the question of temporal (in)consistency in the manifestation of each attribute by conducting a person-by-occasions analysis of variance (ANOVA) on the S_{pao} values used to represent the status of persons with respect to that attribute. Since four attributes were assumed to be represented in the data of the present study, four such ANOVAs were conducted (one for each column of data in Table II). The results of these ANOVAs are summarized in Table III.

As can be seen in Table III, the percentage of variance due to the persons' components of the present data ranged from a low of 43% for Attribute C to a high of 76% for Attribute A. All ANOVAs yielded statistically significant "persons effects." By comparison, it can be seen that the percentage of variance due to the occasions components of the present data ranged from a low of 1% for Attribute A to a high of 12% for Attribute C. A statistically significant effect was obtained only for Attribute C.

Under the currently accepted conventions for interpreting such data, the

JAMES T. LAMIELL

TABLE II

RESPONDENTS-BY-OCCASIONS-BY-ATTRIBUTES MATRIX OF SUBJECTIVE S_{pao} VALUES

Respondent	Occasion	Attribute			
		A	B	C	D
1	1	2.28	−.49	−3.82	−.47
	2	−.76	−1.22	−7.32	−2.36
	3	1.53	−2.29	−1.09	.00
2	1	3.68	−5.12	4.39	−3.59
	2	5.32	−4.57	3.88	1.79
	3	3.70	−1.81	1.55	.90
3	1	−1.47	−3.37	.90	−2.27
	2	−1.44	−3.00	−1.33	−2.52
	3	.45	−4.40	−3.27	−3.64
4	1	−1.89	−1.69	1.43	−2.11
	2	−1.39	−1.51	2.27	−1.10
	3	−4.05	−1.56	−1.97	−3.77
5	1	3.22	−3.37	1.46	−1.05
	2	1.33	−2.66	.77	−3.13
	3	5.17	−5.09	3.55	−2.72
6	1	−.42	.44	−.53	−2.56
	2	−1.85	2.10	−1.54	−1.04
	3	−4.07	2.14	−2.76	−1.21
7	1	2.32	−7.39	1.56	−.37
	2	2.21	−8.14	1.83	−.43
	3	2.98	−7.92	2.16	−.38
8	1	.48	−2.72	3.82	−.34
	2	−.90	1.92	−1.86	−1.28
	3	.60	−2.60	3.13	2.19
9	1	1.20	−1.73	−.25	.96
	2	1.39	−2.50	4.18	−1.70
	3	−.54	−1.98	−3.67	.83
10	1	2.98	−3.90	2.36	−1.93
	2	2.98	−2.43	1.03	−3.30
	3	.65	1.83	−4.94	−3.78
11	1	−5.06	−1.07	−3.55	−2.41
	2	−3.51	−.53	−1.49	−1.22
	3	−6.16	−.87	−3.67	.27
12	1	−1.16	−1.63	1.58	.45
	2	.54	−2.76	−2.90	3.12
	3	−2.95	−.83	−2.06	2.70

(*continued*)

TABLE II—*Continued*

| Respondent | Occasion | Attribute | | | |
		A	B	C	D
	1	−.43	−3.29	−1.04	1.04
13	2	−3.15	−2.46	−1.96	1.12
	3	−1.01	−2.48	−.85	1.44
	1	2.78	−.29	−1.23	2.02
14	2	1.34	−1.29	−.01	.99
	3	−1.42	−1.13	−.53	−2.18
	1	.85	−2.79	1.93	.44
15	2	−.72	−1.14	−1.63	−1.97
	3	−.87	−1.12	−3.04	−1.25
	1	−.56	−3.92	−.79	−2.06
16	2	−2.22	.89	−3.23	.94
	3	4.30	−.05	−4.57	1.53
	1	−1.92	−2.09	4.19	2.59
17	2	−3.13	−3.25	4.70	−.42
	3	−4.50	2.91	−6.50	−7.07
	1	2.13	−2.66	.61	−.26
18	2	1.93	−3.31	1.48	−2.87
	3	1.49	−4.82	.29	−4.05
	1	−.81	−2.93	−.77	−3.63
19	2	−.63	−3.06	−1.10	−3.49
	3	1.26	−1.85	−3.67	−2.45

omega-square ratios in Table III would be taken as grounds for a generalization that the 19 individuals investigated were moderately to substantially consistent over time in their self-reported manifestations of the four attributes assessed. Conceptually, what such generalizations would imply is that, excepting minor variations attributable to measurement error (or, perhaps, to other random factors), the level of consistency with which any given attribute was manifested by the *group* of individuals (which an omega-square ratio actually reflects) could serve as an adequate empirical indicator of the level of consistency with which that attribute was manifested by any given individual *in* the group.

For reasons already discussed in detail, such interpretations are rarely, if ever, appropriate. More to the point in the present context, such an interpretation of these data would not articulate at all well with the respondents' subjective perceptions of their own temporal (in)consistencies on the four attributes.

TABLE III
SUMMARIES OF PERSONS-BY-OCCASIONS ANOVA FOR EACH OF FOUR ATTRIBUTES

Attribute	Source	df	SS	MS	F	p	Ω^2
A	Occasions	2	4.42	2.21	.94	ns	.01
	Persons	18	283.73	15.76	6.71	<.001	.76
	Resudual	36	84.62	2.35			
	Total	56	372.77				
B	Occasions	2	7.17	3.58	1.56	ns	.025
	Persons	18	194.27	10.79	4.69	<.001	.68
	Residual	36	82.77	2.30			
	Total	56	284.21				
C	Occasions	2	52.27	26.14	4.71	<.05	.12
	Persons	18	192.41	10.69	1.93	<.05	.43
	Residual	36	199.79	5.55			
	Total	56	444.47				
D	Occasions	2	3.63	1.82	.56	ns	.015
	Persons	18	112.36	6.24	1.91	<.05	.48
	Residual	36	117.74	3.27			
	Total	56	233.73				

The first hint in the data that this would prove to be the case came from the observation that subjective perceptions of temporal (in)consistency *varied* substantially across respondents for *all four attributes*. It will be recalled that subjective temporal (in)consistency on a given attribute was defined for each respondent in terms of the standard deviation of his/her three self-ratings on that attribute. Thus, a more precise way of stating the above is to say that the variance of those standard deviations was appreciable when computed across respondents for a single attribute (for Attributes A, B, C, and D, the respective variances were .50, .86, .67, and .86). These variances constitute prima facie evidence that the subjects did not perceive themselves as being equally consistent (or inconsistent) on *any one* of the attributes, the magnitudes of the aggregate statistical indices of (in)consistency notwithstanding.

It is possible, of course, that the obtained variability in the measures of subjective temporal (in)consistency reflects some inadequacy or peculiarity in the measures themselves rather than psychologically meaningful differences in the subjects' perceptions of their own temporal (in)consistencies on each attribute.

The results to be presented below, however, provide direct evidence that this is not the case.

As explained earlier, the findings obtained by Lamiell *et al.* (1980) indicated that with respect to subjective perceptions of internal consistency/coherence in behavior patterns, lay persons think in terms of a rationale that is essentially interactive in nature. Assuming that this would also be the case with respect to subjective perceptions of temporal (in)consistencies in the manifestation of particular attributes, the data of the present study were reanalyzed in accordance with the interactive measurement model represented by Eq. (5) (cf. Section II,C,2). The strategy here was to derive measures of temporal (in)consistency that could be interpreted at the level of the individual subject on an attribute-by-attribute basis. In turn, the utility of those measures would be evaluated by correlating them with the measures of subjective temporal (in)consistencies discussed previously.

As reference to the discussion of Eq. (5) will show, the application of the interactive measurement model to the S_{pao} values in Table II requires a specification of the extreme alternative scores ($S'_{pao\ max}$ and $S'_{pao\ min}$ values) that could possibly be obtained on each attribute, given the definition of the attributes, that is, given the procedure used to generate the S_{pao} values for that attribute. Given (a) the procedure used to score responses (V_{pio}) in the self-reported activity protocols, (b) the metric on which the subjective "relevance values" (R_{iao}) of the 18 activities were defined with respect to the four underlying attributes, and (c) the additive integration function implicit in the matrix multiplication procedure discussed above, it can easily be seen that $S'_{pao\ max}$ for a given attribute would be obtained for an activity protocol, indicating that all activities with positive relevance values on that attribute had been engaged in with maximum frequency (nine), while all items with negative relevance values on the attribute had been engaged in with minimum frequency (zero). Conversely, the $S'_{pao\ min}$ for a given attribute would be obtained for an activity protocol, indicating that all activities with positive relevance values on the attribute had been engaged in with minimum frequency (zero), while all activities with negative relevance values on the attribute had been engaged in with maximum frequency. Thus, the reader can verify (with reference to Table I) that the values of $S'_{pao\ max}$ and $S'_{pao\ min}$ for the four attributes assessed in the present study would be as shown in Table IV.

Using the values shown in Table IV, the S_{pao} values in Table II were rescaled according to Eq. (5). To illustrate this process, consider the S_{pao} values computed for Respondent 1 on Attribute A on each of the three measurement occasions. As shown in Table II, these values were 2.28, $-.76$, and 1.53. The differences between each of these values and $S'_{pao\ min}$ for Attribute A (-16.56) were, respectively, 18.84, 15.80, and 18.09. The length of the scale on which Attribute A was defined in the present study (i.e., $S'_{pao\ max} - S'_{pao\ min}$ for

TABLE IV
VALUES OF $S'_{\text{pao min}}$ AND $S'_{\text{pao max}}$ FOR EACH OF FOUR ATTRIBUTES

	Attribute			
	A	B	C	D
$S'_{\text{pao min}}$	−16.56	−16.11	−14.40	−15.84
$S'_{\text{pao max}}$	16.65	15.93	16.65	15.84

Attribute A) was 33.21. The ratios of the three differences defined above to this value are, respectively, .57, .48, and .54 (rounded to two decimals). These three values are assumed to provide interactive measures of Respondent 1 for Attribute A on each of three measurement occasions. That is, each of the scores is defined in terms of information obtained for that respondent on a given measurement occasion with respect to the set of empirical referents (self-reported activity frequencies and subjective relevance values) for one of the four attributes.

All of the remaining data in Table II were rescaled according to the procedures just described (with $S'_{\text{pao min}}$ and $S'_{\text{pao max}}$ changing across attributes). The results of this rescaling operation are provided in the left panel of Table V.[2]

On the basis of the I_{pao} values shown in Table V, the temporal (in)consistency with which each respondent manifested any given attribute was defined operationally in terms of the total Euclidean distance moved by a respondent on the attribute across measurement occasions. As applied to the data of the present study, this procedure can be formally expressed as follows:

$$C_{\text{pa.}} = \{[(I_{\text{pa1}} - I_{\text{pa2}})^2]^{1/2} + [(I_{\text{pa2}} - I_{\text{pa3}})^2]^{1/2}\} \qquad (6)$$

where $C_{\text{pa.}}$ refers to the (in)consistency of person p with respect to attribute a across the three measurement occasions: I_{pa1}, I_{pa2}, and I_{pa3} refer to the interactively defined measures of person p for attribute a on measurement Occasions 1, 2, and 3, respectively, and $[(I_{\text{pa1}} - I_{\text{pa2}})^2]^{1/2}$ and $[(I_{\text{pa2}} - I_{\text{pa3}})^2]^{1/2}$ refer to the Euclidean distances moved by person p on attribute a from measurement Occasion 1 to measurement Occasion 2, and from Measurement Occasion 2 to Measurement Occasion 3, respectively. By applying Eq. (6) to the data shown in the left panel of Table V, the reader can verify that the temporal (in)consistency

[2]The reader may note that since the values of $S'_{\text{pao min}}$ and $S'_{\text{pao max}}$ for any one attribute are, *in these data*, constant across both persons and occasions; the resulting I_{pao} values for any one attribute are simply linear transforms of the original S_{pao} values. It should be borne in mind, however, that the logic of interactive measurement does not *require* constancy in the values of $S'_{\text{pao max}}$ and $S'_{\text{pao min}}$ either across persons or over time, and in data sets where such constancy does not exist, the I_{pao} values generated by interactive measurement would *not* be linear transforms of the original S_{pao} values. The importance of this point will become more apparent in Section IV, where the problem of the "psychological situation" is discussed in some detail.

TABLE V
INTERACTIVELY DERIVED ATTRIBUTE MEASURES AND TEMPORAL (IN)CONSISTENCY VALUES

Person	Attribute	Interactive measures on occasion			Attribute-by-attribute temporal (in)consistencies	Overall temporal (in)consistencies
		1	2	3		
1	A	.57	.48	.54	.15	
	B	.49	.46	.43	.06	
	C	.34	.23	.43	.31	
	D	.49	.43	.50	.13	.38
2	A	.61	.66	.61	.10	
	B	.34	.36	.45	.11	
	C	.60	.59	.51	.09	
	D	.39	.56	.53	.20	.31
3	A	.45	.46	.51	.10	
	B	.40	.41	.37	.05	
	C	.49	.42	.36	.13	
	D	.43	.42	.39	.04	.16
4	A	.44	.46	.38	.10	
	B	.45	.46	.45	.02	
	C	.51	.54	.40	.17	
	D	.43	.47	.38	.13	.24
5	A	.60	.54	.65	.17	
	B	.40	.42	.34	.10	
	C	.51	.49	.58	.11	
	D	.47	.40	.41	.08	.26
6	A	.49	.44	.38	.11	
	B	.52	.57	.57	.05	
	C	.45	.41	.37	.08	
	D	.42	.47	.46	.06	.17
7	A	.57	.57	.59	.02	
	B	.27	.25	.26	.03	
	C	.51	.52	.53	.02	
	D	.49	.49	.49	.00	.05
8	A	.51	.47	.52	.19	
	B	.42	.56	.42	.28	
	C	.59	.40	.56	.35	
	D	.49	.46	.57	.14	.48
9	A	.53	.54	.48	.07	
	B	.45	.42	.44	.05	
	C	.46	.60	.35	.39	
	D	.53	.45	.53	.16	.43

(*continued*)

TABLE V—*Continued*

Person	Attribute	Interactive measures on occasion			Attribute-by-attribute temporal (in)consistencies	Overall temporal (in)consistencies
		1	2	3		
10	A	.59	.59	.52	.07	
	B	.38	.43	.56	.18	
	C	.54	.50	.30	.24	
	D	.44	.40	.38	.06	.32
11	A	.35	.39	.31	.12	
	B	.47	.49	.48	.03	
	C	.35	.42	.35	.14	
	D	.42	.46	.51	.09	.21
12	A	.46	.51	.41	.15	
	B	.45	.42	.48	.08	
	C	.51	.37	.40	.17	
	D	.51	.60	.59	.10	.30
13	A	.49	.40	.47	.16	
	B	.40	.43	.43	.03	
	C	.43	.40	.44	.07	
	D	.53	.54	.55	.02	.18
14	A	.58	.54	.46	.12	
	B	.49	.46	.47	.04	
	C	.42	.46	.45	.05	
	D	.56	.53	.43	.13	.20
15	A	.52	.48	.47	.05	
	B	.42	.47	.47	.05	
	C	.53	.41	.37	.15	
	D	.51	.44	.46	.09	.20
16	A	.48	.43	.63	.25	
	B	.38	.53	.50	.18	
	C	.44	.36	.32	.14	
	D	.43	.53	.55	.12	.41
17	A	.44	.40	.36	.08	
	B	.44	.40	.59	.23	
	C	.60	.62	.25	.39	
	D	.58	.49	.28	.30	.58
18	A	.56	.56	.54	.02	
	B	.42	.40	.35	.07	
	C	.48	.51	.47	.07	
	D	.49	.41	.37	.12	.17
19	A	.47	.48	.54	.07	
	B	.41	.41	.45	.04	
	C	.44	.43	.35	.09	
	D	.39	.39	.42	.03	.12

scores for the 19 respondents, computed attribute by attribute, are as shown in the middle panel of that table.[3]

In addition to the attribute-by-attribute temporal (in)consistency scores shown in the center panel of Table V, a single overall index of temporal (in)consistency was defined operationally for each of the 19 respondents in terms of the total Euclidean distance he/she moved in the four-dimensional space across measurement occasions. The general formula used to compute this overall consistency index for each respondent was

$$C_{\mathrm{p..}} = [\sum_{a=1}^{4} (I_{\mathrm{pa1}} - I_{\mathrm{pa2}})^2]^{1/2} + [\sum_{a=1}^{4} (I_{\mathrm{pa2}} - I_{\mathrm{pa3}})^2]^{1/2}$$

The overall temporal (in)consistency scores thus derived are shown in the last column of Table V.

For the specific purposes of the present study, the important question at this point was: How well, if at all, would the interactively derived measures of temporal (in)consistency shown in Table V correspond to measures of subjective temporal (in)consistency, as defined by the standard deviation of the respondents' ratings of their own activity protocols on the four criterion attributes? To address this question, the interactively derived temporal (in)consistency scores for each attribute [i.e., the values of $C_{\mathrm{pa.}}$ from Eq. (6)] were correlated with the measure of subjective temporal (in)consistency for that same attribute. In addition, the respondents' global self-ratings of psychological (in)consistency over time were correlated with the overall temporal (in)consistency index (i.e., the values of $C_{\mathrm{p..}}$), computed in the manner just discussed. The results of these analyses are shown in Table VI.

As can be seen in Table VI, all five of the obtained correlations were statistically significant in the expected direction. That is, for each of the four attributes, a measure of subjective temporal (in)consistency, derived directly from respondents' self-ratings on the attribute, was systematically related to the interactively derived measure of temporal (in)consistency on that same attribute as defined in terms of Eq. (6). In line with these findings, the .57 correlation in Table VI indicates that the measure of overall subjective temporal (in)consistency, defined directly in terms of respondents' subjective judgments, was systematically related to the interactively derived index of overall temporal (in)consistency, as defined in terms of the distances moved by the individual respondents through the four-dimensional attribute space over time.

Consistent with the major hypothesis of the present study, and with the results

---

[3]Euclidean distances along single dimensions are, of course, equivalent to simple absolute differences. However, the more generally applicable distance formula has been used here in order to reflect the more general view that (in)consistencies in personality might reasonably be represented in terms of distances moved by individuals in a "psychological space," undimensional or otherwise [cf. computation of overall (in)consistency index].

TABLE VI

CORRELATIONS BETWEEN INTERACTIVELY DERIVED TEMPORAL (IN)CONSISTENCIES AND SUBJECTIVE TEMPORAL (IN)CONSISTENCIES[a,b]

	Attribute			
	A	B	C	D
Correlation between standard deviation of self ratings and interactive measure of temporal (in)consistency (computed attribute-by-attribute)	.47	.52	.49	.67
Correlation between global subjective judgments of temporal (in)consistency and interactive measure of overall temporal (in)consistency		.57		

[a] All correlations based on $N = 19$.
[b] All correlations at or beyond .05 level of statistical significance.

obtained by Lamiell *et al.* (1980), the correlations shown in Table VI constitute direct empirical evidence that subjective perceptions of temporal (in)consistency in the manifestation of particular attributes cannot be understood adequately from the aggregate perspective that individual differences investigators have routinely brought to bear on such matters. More specifically, the evidence just presented reveals that (a) lay persons can differ substantially in subjective perceptions of their own (in)consistencies with respect to any given attribute even when over three-fourths of the total variance in a person-by-occasions matrix of attribute scores can be "explained" statistically in terms of the persons component (cf. the .76 omega-square ratio in Table III), *and* that (b) such differences in subjective perceptions of temporal (in)consistency are systematically related to differences *that can in fact be empirically detected* when (in)consistency is measured by an investigator on a case-by-case basis, rather than summarized in terms of some statistical index. Thus, when the omega-square ratios in Table III are juxtaposed with the interactive measurement values of Table V, it is obvious that any given individual could indeed be either consistent *or* inconsistent in *his/her* manifestation of a particular attribute irrespective of the magnitude of the statistical index of (in)consistency on the "IBM sheet" (Mischel, 1969). In short, by virtue of its individualized or "idiographic" level of analysis, the alternative approach to the question of temporal (in)consistency illustrated previously appears, in comparison with the aggregate level of analysis inherent in the traditional approach, to articulate more fully with subjective perceptions of that phenomenon.

The findings just reported are compatible with the general notion that the interactive measurement model has some utility as a formal representation of the manner in which subjective personality impressions are formulated. Those findings do not, however, speak directly to the question of the *relative* utility of that model, in comparison with the more traditional normative and ipsative models, for such purposes. That is, while it may be true that lay persons approach personality-relevant phenomena at the level of the individual, it is entirely possible they do so in a manner that can be equally—or better—represented in terms of the normative or ipsative models. The findings to be presented next, which were obtained in a study by the present author in collaboration with Mark A. Foss, Steven J. Trierweiler, and G. Michael Leffel, speak to this question.

C. Study III: Toward a Model of the Cognitions Underlying Subjective Personality Impressions

1. Data Collection

The procedure used in the present study was similar in many respects to that used in Study II. In this case, however, respondents did not provide criterion attribute ratings of their own self-reported activity patterns. Rather, each of 43 respondents was asked to rate, on a single criterion attribute, three activity protocols for each of 22 stimulus persons. These stimulus protocols were identical in their format to those used in Study II, and had been obtained from 22 undergraduate student volunteers using the same procedures used in Study II. The protocols, described as self-reported activity patterns obtained from 22 of their peers on three different occasions, were in turn presented to the respondents in the present study.

The 43 undergraduate students (22 males, 21 females) who served as subjects in this study were drawn from an introductory psychology course at the University of Illinois, and received extra credit toward their course grade in return for their cooperation. At the time of his/her participation, each subject was presented with the 22 sets of three activity protocols, asked to consider carefully the information in each protocol, and then to rate that protocol in terms of the degree to which it reflected one of four underlying attributes. Each subject therefore provided 66 criterion attribute ratings. For purposes of making these ratings, each subject was provided with response scales identical to those used in the previous study.

Of the total of 43 respondents, 11 rated the stimulus person protocols on criterion Attribute A ("Filling spare time, diversionary, or 'idle' vs Physically and/or mentally involved, or 'earnest' "), 10 on criterion Attribute B ("Hedonistic or oriented toward physical pleasure vs Nonhedonistic or not oriented toward physical pleasure''), 13 on criterion Attribute C (''Socially oriented vs Nonsocially oriented''), and 9 on criterion Attribute D (''Low in motor activity vs High in motor activity'').

In seeking to understand the data analyses of the present study, the reader will find it helpful to bear in mind that the central problem here is that of formally representing the cognitive rationale by which lay persons translate *covert judgments* about the behavior patterns of individuals into *overt ratings* on response scales. Stated otherwise, the primary objective of the analyses to be reported below was to shed light on what is, in effect, the subjective analog of the measurement model problem in personality research, as discussed in Section II,C.

2. Data Analysis and Results

The first step in analyzing the data of the present study was to define, for each of the 22 stimulus persons, an attributes-by-measurement occasions profile based on the criterion attributes ratings made by the respondents for each of that stimulus person's three activity protocols. These profiles, which will be referred to as ''subjective impression profiles,'' were constructed by computing the mean of the ratings made by a particular subgroup of the respondents in judging the degree to which a given stimulus person's occasion-o activity protocol reflected a particular criterion attribute.

For example, each stimulus person's Occasion 1 activity protocol had been rated by 11 of the respondents with respect to Attribute A. The ''subjective impression'' of each stimulus person on Occasion 1 with respect to Attribute A was therefore defined as the mean of those 11 ratings. Similarly, the mean of the ratings provided by the same 11 respondents for each stimulus person's Occasion 2 protocol defined the subjective impression of the latter with respect to Attribute A on Occasion 2. Finally, the mean of the ratings provided by the 11 respondents for each stimulus person's Occasion 3 protocol defined the subjective impression of that stimulus person with respect to Attribute A on Occasion 3.

Following the same procedure, the mean of the ratings provided by the second subgroup of respondents ($N = 10$) was used to define the subjective impression of each stimulus person on each occasion with respect to Attribute B. Finally, the third and fourth subgroup of respondents ($N = 13$ and $N = 9$, respectively) provided the ratings used to define the subjective impression of each stimulus person on each occasion with respect to Attributes C and D, respectively.

Before proceeding any further, two points should be made in connection with the subjective impression profiles. First, as originally planned, the present research called for each respondent to rate all 66 activity protocols on all four criterion attributes. This would have permitted the construction of subjective impression profiles based entirely on the ratings provided by single respondents. However, a pilot test of that procedure indicated that the total of 264 ratings required of each respondent was an overwhelming task within the time constraints imposed on the investigator's access to the respondents. Accordingly, the alternative data collection procedure used here, which required only 66 ratings by any one respondent, had to be adopted.

One consequence of this procedure is that what are here referred to as "subjective impression" profiles must, strictly speaking, be recognized as composite profiles, constructed on the basis of many respondents' ratings of each stimulus person. The constraints imposed by this fact on our interpretation of the findings will be further considered after these findings have been fully presented.

The second point to be made in connection with the subjective impression profile is that all criterion attribute ratings were numerically coded on a scale ranging from $-.50$ to $+.50$. This was accomplished by means of a simple linear interpolation of the original response scale, which ranged from 0 to 10. Scoring the subjective ratings in this manner did not, of course, affect the relative locations of the ratings on the response scales provided (which response scales, it should be understood, constitute the subjective analog of the y-axis in Fig. 2, presented earlier). The scoring procedure did, however, ensure that the numerical values ultimately entered in each subjective impression profile would be defined on a scale bounded at the extremes by $\pm.50$. The reasons for employing this coding scheme will become apparent as the discussion proceeds. For subsequent illustrative purposes, the subjective impression profile for Stimulus Person #1 derived in accordance with the procedures described previously is shown in Table VII.

Having constructed a subjective impression profile for each of the 22 stimulus persons, the next step in the data analysis was to derive—without reference to the criterion attribute ratings actually made by the respondents—empirical representations of the subjective impression profiles that *would have* been obtained *if* the cognitive rationale by which the subjects translated their judgments into response scale ratings could be formally represented in terms of the normative, ipsative, normative–ipsative, and interactive measurement models, respectively. Using the various indices of profile dissimilarity discussed by Cornbach and

TABLE VII
SUBJECTIVE IMPRESSION PROFILE FOR STIMULUS PERSON #1

Attribute	Occasion		
	1	2	3
A	.01	.00	.10
B	$-.10$	$-.28$	$-.28$
C	.09	.10	.18
D	$-.07$	$-.18$	$-.14$

Gleser (1953), these "alternative possible" subjective impression profiles were
then compared to the subjective impression profiles actually obtained. In this
way, it was possible to investigate the relative utilities of the various measurement models as formal representations of the cognitive process underlying the
formulation and expression of subjective personality impressions.

In order to construct the "alternative possible" subjective impression profiles
without reference to the criterion attribute ratings actually obtained, it was necessary to *estimate* the subjective *judgments* of the stimulus persons presumably
formulated by the respondents prior to making their ratings. As was the case in
Study II, it was assumed in the present study that the subjective judgments could
be estimated as though they had been formulated in terms of an intuitive or
implicit application of Eq. (1).

Since in the present study (a) the 18 activities shown in each stimulus person's
protocol, as well as the four criterion attributes rated, were identical to those of
Study II, and since (b) little between-person variation in the subjective "relevance values" of the activities vis-à-vis the four criterion attributes had been
found in Study II (cf. discussion of the INDSCAL analyses in Section III,B,2), it
was assumed that the activity coordinates reported in Table I would likewise
provide, for the respondents in the present study, an adequate empirical representation of the subjective R_{iao} values of Eq. (1).

The activity frequencies in the stimulus persons' protocols, defining the subjective V_{pio} component of Eq. (1), were scored in terms of the same 0–9 scheme
used in Study II, and estimates of the subjective S_{pao} values were computed
according to the matrix multiplication procedure previously described. In this
way, a complete stimulus persons-by-attributes-by measurement occasions (22 $\times$
4 $\times$ 3) matrix of S_{pao} values, similar to that shown in Table II, was generated. It
was to the 12 values in this matrix assigned to each stimulus person (four
attributes, three measurement occasions each) that the various measurement
models were applied, resulting in the scores used to construct the normative,
ipsative, normative–ipsative, and interactive profiles for each of the 22 stimulus
persons. The specifics of the procedures used to construct those profiles can
perhaps best be explained with reference to actual data.

Table VIII presents the S_{pao} values estimated for Stimulus Person #1 in
accordance with the procedures just explained. In order to apply the normative
measurement model to those data, one needs information about the S_{pao} values
estimated for other stimulus persons for the same attribute on the same measurement occasion. For this reason, the values of $\bar{S}_{.ao}$ and $SD_{.ao}$ in Eq. (2) (see
Section II,C,2) actually obtained from the data of the present study have been
provided in parentheses adjacent to each S_{pao} value in Table VIII. Given all of
the information in Table VIII, and applying the measurement model represented
by Eq. (2), the reader can verify that the normatively defined levels at which

TABLE VIII

SUBJECTIVE S_{pao} VALUES DEFINED FOR STIMULUS PERSON #1

	Measurement occasion					
	1		2		3	
Attribute	S_{pao}	$(\bar{S}_{.ao}, SD_{.ao})$	S_{pao}	$(\bar{S}_{.ao}, SD_{.ao})$	S_{pao}	$(\bar{S}_{.ao}, SD_{.ao})$
A	3.22	(.45, 2.72)	1.20	(.38, 2.33)	5.21	(.53, 2.95)
B	−3.77	(2.38, 2.08)	−2.74	(−1.99, 2.17)	−5.45	(−1.79, 2.02)
C	1.46	(.38, 2.38)	1.12	(.45, 2.56)	3.80	(.06, 2.90)
D	−1.05	(−1.43, 2.18)	−3.38	(−.72, 2.07)	−3.15	(−.20, 2.14)

Stimulus Person #1 would be said to have manifested the various attributes on the various measurement occasions are as indicated in Table IX.

In theory, of course, the scale on which z scores in profiles such as those represented in Table IX are defined ranges to infinity on both the positive and negative sides of zero. In practice, however, boundary conditions (cf. Budescu, 1980) are typically established for interpreting such data at the level of the individual by reexpressing z scores in terms of their corresponding areas under the normal curve. This is, for example, precisely the rationale underlying the computation of percentile scores or T scores, and a recent application of that rationale in empirical personality research can be found in Harris (1980).

In reexpressing the z scores of the present research in terms of their corresponding areas under the normal curve, information concerning the direction of deviation from the midpoint of the scale was retained. Thus, for example, the z score of $+1.02$ shown in Table IX was reexpressed as .35, the area under the normal curve between $z = .00$ and $z = +1.02$ (cf. Edwards, 1964, Table III). Similarly, the z score of $-.48$ in Table IX was reexpressed as $-.18$, the area under the normal curve between $z = .00$ and $z = -.48$. This procedure had the

TABLE IX

NORMATIVELY DERIVED z SCORES FOR STIMULUS PERSON #1

	Measurement occasion		
Attribute	1	2	3
A	1.02	.35	1.59
B	−.48	−.34	−1.81
C	.45	.26	1.29
D	.17	−1.29	−1.38

TABLE X

NORMATIVE, IPSATIVE, NORMATIVE–IPSATIVE, AND INTERACTIVE PROFILES FOR STIMULUS PERSON #1

Profile	Attribute	Occasion		
		1	2	3
Normative	A	.35	.14	.44
	B	−.18	−.13	−.46
	C	.17	.10	.40
	D	.07	−.40	−.42
Ipsative	A	.00	−.34	.34
	B	.13	.28	−.37
	C	−.18	−.25	.37
	D	.37	−.24	−.18
Normative–	A	.38	.29	.33
ipsative	B	−.39	−.04	−.34
	C	.10	.25	.28
	D	−.08	−.41	−.27
Interactive	A	.10	.03	.16
	B	−.10	−.08	−.17
	C	.01	.00	.09
	D	−.03	−.11	−.10

effect of establishing the boundaries for profiles defined in terms of z scores at ±.50. (It was in consideration of this fact that the previously described convention for scoring respondents' subjective ratings on the criterion attributes was adopted.) By applying this procedure to the data in Table IX, we arrived at the normatively defined profile for Stimulus Person #1 shown in Table X.

Returning now to the data in Table VIII, the values of $\bar{S}_{pa.}$ and $SD_{pa.}$ [cf. discussion of Eq. (3), Section II,C,2] were computed. As the reader can again verify, these values are, respectively, 3.21 and 2.00 for Attribute A, −3.99 and 1.37 for Attribute B, 2.13 and 1.46 for Attribute C, and −2.53 and 1.28 for Attribute D.[4] Using these values, and applying Eq. (3) in the appropriate manner, the set of ipsative z scores for Stimulus Person #1 was generated. Again reexpressing those z scores as areas under the normal curve, the ipsative profile for Stimulus Person #1 shown in Table X was obtained.

In accordance with our earlier discussion of what is here being referred to as the normative–ipsative measurement model, the normatively derived z scores shown in Table IX were used to compute the values of $\bar{Z}_{p.o}$ and $SD_{z,p.o}$ [cf.

---

[4]These values have been rounded to the nearest hundredth. Also, computation of the $SD_{pa.}$ values conformed to the procedure appropriate for estimating population parameters.

discussion of Eq. (4a), Section III,C,2]. The reader can verify that these values are, respectively, .29 and .62 for Measurement Occasion 1, $-.26$ and .75 for Measurement Occasion 2, and $-.08$ and 1.76 for Measurement Occasion 3 (cf. Footnote 4). Using these values, and applying Eq. (4a) in the appropriate manner, the normative–ipsative z scores for Stimulus Person #1 were computed. The reexpression of those z scores as areas under the normal curve yielded the normative–ipsative profile shown in Table X.

The last profile derived from the data in Table VIII was that constructed according to the interactive measurement model. Since the subjective V_{pio}, R_{iao}, and integration function components of Eq. (1) were, in the present study, the same as in Study II, it is perhaps apparent that the subjective $S'_{pao\ max}$ and $S'_{pao\ min}$ values used here were identical to those shown in Table V (see Section III,B,2). However, it is perhaps also apparent that by applying Eq. (5) to the data in Table VIII, the resulting I_{pao} values would have been defined on a scale bounded at the extremes by the values .00 and $+1.00$, a fact that would have undermined interpretations of the profile dissimilarity analyses to be discussed.

In order to circumvent this problem, the interactive measurement model was defined, for the purposes of the present analyses, as follows:

$$I_{pao} = (S_{pao} - S'_{pao\ mid})/(S'_{pao\ max} - S'_{pao\ min}) \qquad (5a)$$

where I_{pao}, S_{pao}, $S'_{pao\ max}$, and $S'_{pao\ min}$ are defined as previously, and $S'_{pao\ mid}$ is defined as $(|S'_{pao\ max}| + |S'_{pao\ min}|)/2$.

By using Eq. (5a) rather than Eq. (5) in the present study, it was possible to define each stimulus person's interactive profile in terms of values on a scale bounded at the extremes by $\pm.50$, thus rendering those profiles metrically comparable to all of the ones previously discussed. As applied to the data in Table VIII, Eq. (5a) yielded the interactive profile for Stimulus Person #1 shown in Table X. So as to facilitate an appreciation for the differences between the "pictures" of an individual that an investigator can create when different measurement models are applied, in turn, to a common set of "raw" S_{pao} values, the data from Table X have been presented graphically in Fig. 3.

The normative, ipsative, normative–ipsative, and interactive profiles for each of the remaining 21 stimulus persons were constructed in exact accordance with the procedures just explained. The four sets of 22 profiles thus obtained were then systematically compared to the subjective impression profiles in terms of the indices of profile dissimilarity discussed by Cronbach and Gleser (1953). As applied to the profiles of the present study, the manner in which these indices were computed is specified by the following equations:

$$D_x = \left[\sum_{a=1}^{4} \sum_{o=1}^{3} (X_{ao,s} - X_{ao,s'})^2 \right]^{1/2} \qquad (7)$$

$$D_{\mathrm{x}} = [n(\bar{X}_{\mathrm{x}} - \bar{X}_{\mathrm{s}'})^2]^{\frac{1}{2}} \tag{8}$$

$$D_{\mathrm{SH}} = \left[\frac{(D_{\mathrm{x}}^2 - D_{\mathrm{x}}^2)^{\frac{1}{2}} - (SC_{\mathrm{s}} - SC_{\mathrm{s}'})^2}{(SC_{\mathrm{s}})\,(SC_{\mathrm{s}'})}\right]^{\frac{1}{2}} \tag{9}$$

$$D_{\mathrm{SC}} = [(SC_{\mathrm{s}} - SC_{\mathrm{s}'})^2]^{\frac{1}{2}} \tag{10}$$

In these equations, D_{x} refers to the *overall* degree of dissimilarity between two profiles, $D_{\bar{x}}$ refers to differences in *elevation* between two profiles, D_{SH} to differences in *shape* between two profiles, and D_{SC} refers to differences in *scatter* between two profiles. The symbol X above refers to a particular entry in any given profile, with the subscripts a and o being defined as previously. The

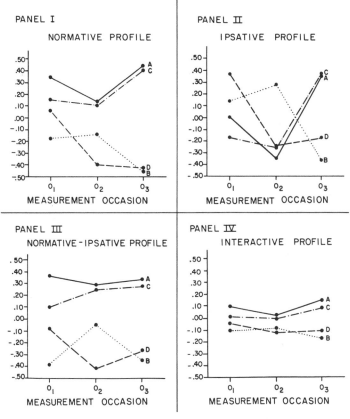

FIG. 3. Attributes-by-measurement occasions profiles for Stimulus Person #1 based on different measurement models.

symbols s and s' refer, respectively, to the source profiles (normative, ipsative, normative–ipsative, interactive, or subjective impression) from which corresponding X values have been taken for the purposes of any given comparison. The symbol n [see Eq. (8)] refers to the number of data points in a given profile (in this research, n was therefore always equal to 12). Finally, the symbol SC stands for the scatter of a given profile, and was defined as the standard deviation of the entries in that profile, divided by the square root of n (Cronbach & Gleser, 1953).

Given the data in Tables VII and X, and given the above discussion of the equations used to compute the dissimilarity indices, the reader can verify that the results of the analyses involving the various profiles for Stimulus Person #1 are as shown in Table XI.

Bearing in mind that the lower the value of any given dissimilarity index, the better the correspondence between two profiles in terms of that index, it can be seen in Table XI that, on all four dissimilarity indices, the interactively derived profile for Stimulus Person #1 corresponded better to the subjective impression profile than did any of the other three profiles. A summary of the findings obtained in this manner for the entire set of 22 stimulus persons is provided in Table XII.

Of particular importance in these findings is the fact that, with respect to the index of overall profile dissimilarity—that is, the index that incorporates all of the relevant features of profiles—the interactive profiles corresponded significantly better to the subjective impression profiles than did either the normative, ipsative, or normative–ipsative profiles. Although not reflected in Table XII, it is worth pointing out that there was not a single violation of this pattern anywhere in the data. That is, for each of the 22 stimulus persons, without exception, the D_x value obtained in the subjective impression vs interactive comparison was lower than the corresponding D_x values in the remaining comparisons.

Further inspection of Table XII suggests that the primary source of this pattern

TABLE XI
RESULTS OF PROFILE DISSIMILARITY ANALYSES FOR STIMULUS PERSON #1

Dissimilarity index	Comparison			
	Subjective impression vs normative	Subjective impression vs ipsative	Subjective impression vs normative–ipsative	Subjective impression vs interactive
D_x	.72	1.01	.72	.31
D_x	.17	.17	.21	.10
D_{SH}	.61	1.28	.68	.55
D_{SC}	.54	.45	.49	.18

TABLE XII
SUMMARY OF PROFILE DISSIMILARITY ANALYSES FOR 22 STIMULUS PERSONS[a]

	Comparison			
Dissimilarity index	Subjective impression vs normative	Subjective impression vs ipsative	Subjective impression vs normative–ipsative	Subjective impression vs interactive
D_x	$.85_\text{a}$	$.92_\text{a}$	$.88_\text{a}$	$.40_\text{b}$
D_x	$.27_\text{a}$	$.11_\text{b}$	$.12_\text{b}$	$.12_\text{b}$
D_SH	$.98_\text{a}$	1.12_a	1.02_a	1.04_a
D_SC	$.46_\text{a}$	$.54_\text{a}$	$.56_\text{a}$	$.19_\text{b}$

[a] Entries in Table XII are means, based on an $N = 22$. Within any row, entries with different subscripts differ statistically at or beyond .05 level of significance.

of findings was neither in the elevation nor in the shape components of the profiles, but instead in their respective *scatters*. An attempt will now be made to develop a possible theoretical explanation for these findings.

3. Discussion

It will be recalled from our earlier discussion that the rationales that underlie the normative, ipsative, and normative–ipsative measurement models share one very important feature. Specifically, all of those rationales are such that the meaningful interpretation of any single "raw" score (S_pao value) assigned to a given person for a particular attribute on a specific measurement occasion is derived by contrasting that score with, or placing it within the context of, other "raw" scores which actually exist in some larger data set, that is, S_pao values empirically obtained at other locations in the hypothetical persons-by-attribute-by-measurement occasions "data box" discussed by Cattell (1966). This fact is directly reflected in the $\bar{S}$ and SD components of Eqs. (2), (3), and (4a).

Under the terms of the normative measurement model, for example, the level at which the occasion o activity protocol for person p is said to reflect attribute a hinges in part on S_pao values located at other points along the persons dimension of the "data box." Similarly, under the terms of the normative–ipsative measurement model, the level at which the occasion o activity protocol for person p is said to reflect attribute a hinges (in addition to the above) on S_pao values located at other points along the attributes dimension of the "data box." Finally, under the terms of the ipsative model, the level at which person p's occasion o protocol is said to reflect attribute a hinges in part on S_pao values located at other points along the occasion dimension of the "data box."

As also explained earlier, the primary methodological difference between all of the above measurement models and the interactive model is that, under the terms of the latter, the meaningful interpretation of a single S_{pao} value does not necessarily involve—and in fact will rarely coincide with—any contrast between that value and other actually obtained S_{pao} values. Instead, the interpretation hinges entirely on a contrast between the obtained S_{pao} value and the extreme alternative values obtainable under whatever constraints have (necessarily) been imposed by the procedure used to generate the former. That is, the meaning of any single S_{pao} value emerges via a specification of the limitations unavoidably created (regardless of one's measurement model) *by the assessment procedure itself*. Thus, whether or not the values of $S'_{pao\ max}$ and $S'_{pao\ min}$ in Eqs. (5) and/or (5a) actually exist in a particular data set—indeed, whether or not they have ever been empirically obtained in *any* data set—has no bearing whatsoever on the interpretation of a particular S_{pao} value. Those extreme values are presumed to be relevant simply by virtue of the fact that they "fix" the endpoints (and thus the length) of the dimension used to represent the attribute being assessed, thereby providing an empirically specifiable context within which any given "raw" S_{pao} value can be rendered intelligible.

Now, precisely by virtue of their extremity, the values of $S'_{pao\ max}$ and $S'_{pao\ min}$ will rarely, if ever, actually be obtained in empirical research. As a direct consequence of this, an array of attribute measures derived by interpreting "raw" assessments with reference to such points will virtually always have less scatter than arrays of measures derived by interpreting "raw" assessments with reference to other, actually obtained "raw" assessments. It cannot be regarded as accidental, therefore, that the interactive profile shown in Panel IV of Fig. 3 has markedly less scatter than the other three profiles. Indeed, for all 22 stimulus persons in the present study, the scatter of the interactive profile was less than the scatters of the corresponding normative, ipsative, and normative–ipsative profiles.

In the light of this discussion, and given the evidence that with respect to the component of scatter the subjective impression profiles consistently corresponded better to the interactive profiles than to the normative, ipsative, or normative–ipsative profiles, one possible theoretical perspective on the nature of the judgments presumed to be reflected in the ratings used to construct the former begins to emerge.

Specifically, it is entirely possible that, given information about the activity pattern of a particular individual at a particular point in time, the lay person is capable of expressing a psychologically meaningful judgment about the level at which that activity pattern reflects a particular underlying attribute without any cognitive reference whatsoever to other judgments he/she may have made about (a) the levels at which that same attribute is reflected in the activity patterns of other individuals (as would be the case if the cognitive process were essentially normative in nature), (b) the levels at which that attribute is reflected in the activity patterns of that same individual on other occasions (as would be the case if the cognitive process were essentially ipsative in nature), or (c) the levels at which other attributes are reflected in the activity pattern of that same individual on the same occasion (as would be the case if the cognitive process were essentially normative–ipsative in nature). Instead, it is possible that, at the time at which such a judgment is made, it is psychologically meaningful to the lay person by virtue of a context provided by the *alternative possible* judgments he/she *might* have made about *that* individual with respect to *that* attribute on *that* occasion, had the available information about that individual assumed any one of a variety of alternative possible patterns. Those alternative possible patterns, and the alternative possible judgments that would coincide therewith, are presumed to be established, intuitively or implicitly, in the mind of the respondent on any particular judgment occasion by virtue of (a) the items of information about the individual that are available to (and considered by) the respondent, and (b) the way in which those items of information are construed by the respondent vis-à-vis the underlying attribute in question.

Items (a) and (b) refer, respectively, to the subjective analogs of the V_{pio} and R_{iao} components of any formal personality assessment procedure [cf. Eq. (1)]. Taking this perspective, one is led to the hypothesis that, in making judgments of the sort obtained in the present research, lay persons utilize those subjective V_{pio}s and R_{iao}s as a basis for "computing" subjective analogs of $S'_{pao\ max}$ and $S'_{pao\ min}$. These latter values would provide the rater with a cognitive context within which to express a psychologically meaningful judgment about any given activity protocol. More specifically, this hypothesis implies that, in placing a mark on a response scale so as to express his/her judgment (subjective S_{pao} value) of any single activity protocol, the subject does so in such a way that the position of that mark relative to the endpoints of the response scale corresponds to the "picture" in his/her head of the location of the subjective S_{pao} value relative to the subjective $S'_{pao\ max}$ and $S'_{pao\ min}$ values.

It is interesting to note that this theoretical explanation would account for the not uncommon finding in person perception/social judgment research that subjects generally avoid using the extremes of the response scales. From the present perspective, the explanation for this phenomenon would be that subjects rarely encounter "stimuli" that coincide with their subjective representations of the extremes of the response scales, and therefore that ratings at those extremes would rarely be "psychologically appropriate." Of more immediate connection with the present study, the theoretical explanation developed above would account for the findings with respect to the scatter components of the various profiles, and in turn the more general finding that, in terms of the overall dissimilarity index, the interactive profiles consistently corresponded better than did the normative, ipsative, or normative–ipsative ones to those derived from subjective ratings.

It is appropriate to reiterate here that the subjective impression profiles used in the present study cannot properly be taken to represent the subjective impressions of any single respondent. Consequently a more adequate test of the theoretical explanation developed above necessarily awaits further research, in which subjective impression profiles *are* defined entirely on the basis of ratings made by a single respondent. Only in this way can a cognitive process that is presumed, in theory, to transpire at the level of the individual be thoroughly investigated. It bears mentioning that research designed to meet this requirement is currently underway.

Recognizing the limitations of the present study, the findings reported here nevertheless provide at least preliminary support for the view that subjective personality impressions are formulated on the basis of a cognitive rationale that is more adequately represented in terms of the interactive measurement model than in terms of either the normative or ipsative models (or some combination thereof).

If personality investigators are going to be serious in the 1980s about attending to the cognitive processes of their subjects, then we are also going to have to consider seriously the possibility that those processes might not be most fruitfully studied, represented, or understood by research that is grounded (either implicitly or explicitly) in the logic of normative or ipsative measurement. Stated otherwise, we are going to have to entertain the possibility that the cognitive processes *we* have employed *as investigators*—by virtue of our normative and ipsative measurement models—might not coincide with the cognitive processes that our subjects bring to bear on the same phenomena. To the contrary, the findings of the present study suggest that concern with understanding our subjects' cognitive processes may require us to adopt an interactive measurement model. At a minimum, those findings indicate that this is an issue warranting further investigation.

IV. Overview and Conclusion

In the maze of equations and other technical aspects of the preceding section, it would perhaps be easy to lose sight of the major conceptual issues that have been of concern here. Thus, in concluding this article, it may be worthwhile to recapitulate its central themes, and to consider briefly some of the ramifications of the arguments that have been developed.

Our discussion began with an identification of three critical facets of the overriding metatheoretical objectives of the scientific study of personality: First, the discipline requires a viable framework for empirical personality *description*; second, given such a framework, programmatic personality research should be directed toward an understanding of the process of personality *development*; and third, the scientific study of personality seeks ultimately to establish general principles that contribute to an understanding of human behavior/psychological functioning *at the level of the individual*.

With this as a collective premise, it was then argued that the psychology of personality is in need of a viable alternative to all of the basic research strategies that currently dominate the field. More specifically, it was argued that, as useful as those various strategies might be for certain purposes, none of them adequately confronts the personality investigator's most fundamental problem: that of empirically describing the personality of any given individual. Failing in this regard, it is difficult to see how any of those strategies could prove adequate in terms of the personality investigator's remaining concerns, however useful those strategies might be for other purposes (e.g., those of differential psychology, cf. Lamiell, 1981).

Developing the above argument, it was explained that the inadequacies of all of the prevailing research strategies vis-à-vis the problem of empirical personality description stem from the same basic source: All of those strategies result in attempts to treat as a *statistical* problem what is actually a problem of *measurement*. Given the aggregate statistical indices generated within those strategies, it is, for all intents and purposes, never possible to infer how consistent or inconsistent **any** one individual has been in his/her manifestation of any one attribute over time or across situations. If it is agreed that this is precisely what an investigator must know in order to determine the relevance of any particular attribute to the description of any given individual's personality, then it follows that some alternative approach to that problem must be adopted.

In Section II,C, the formal properties of the alternative measurement models (normative, ipsative, and interactive) that could conceivably be brought to bear on the task of empirical personality description were discussed in detail. The discussion was concluded by noting that, since any one of the alternative measurement models could in principle be used as the basis for constructing attributes-by-measurement occasion profiles for single individuals, any one of those models could therefore be defended, in principle, as a formal approach to the problem of empirical personality description.

It should be noted here that, in constructing attributes-by-measurement occasions profiles for single individuals, an investigator would, in effect, be creating an empirical medium suitable for addressing questions regarding the process of personality development. Using time series research designs, for example, theoretically derived explanations for the emergence of, maintenance of, and changes in personality characteristics could be tested in such profile data *at the level of the individual*. To the extent that one's hypotheses were repeatedly confirmed in (theoretically relevant portions of) the profiles of single individuals, one would, in effect, be accumulating empirical support for general principles of personality, that is, principles that (a) would contribute to an understanding of the process of personality development, *and* (b) would have been tested at the level of the individual. In short, by approaching the problem of empirical personality description as a problem of measurement, an investigator would simultaneously be adopting an approach that would be at least *formally* consonant with the other two metatheoretical objectives of the scientific study of personality.

As emphasized in Section II,C, however, the fact that the alternative measurement models differ in their formal characteristics mandates an appreciation for the fact that the adoption of one model over the others *is not an atheoretical decision*. Quite to the contrary, in adopting one measurement model over another as a basis for the scientific study of personality, an investigator must seek to ensure that the formal properties of that model—and thus of the data it generates—are compatible with the formal aspects of his/her theoretical concerns. This, in turn, obviously requires that the latter be clearly articulated.

For example, the concerns of an investigator who claims to be interested, in theory, with the phenomenon of (in)consistency in "behavior" [or, more precisely, (in)consistency with respect to the sets of empirical referents for particular attributes] are not going to be well served within the constraints imposed by the adoption of a normative measurement model. The interpretable data yielded by applications of that model do not speak unambiguously to that phenomenon. They speak instead to the phenomenon of (in)consistency in *relative position in a group on commonly assessed attributes*, which is simply not the same thing (cf. Panels I and IV in Fig. 3). While most personologists undoubtedly recognize this distinction (cf. Lay, 1977; Magnusson & Endler, 1977b), its implications vis-à-vis the measurement model problem do not appear to be widely appreciated. Thus, investigators continue to discuss the phenomenon of (in)consistency or (in)stability in the "behavior" of individuals with reference to data which have not only been aggregated across persons, but which have also been generated in accordance with a measurement model that was inappropriate to begin with, *vis-à-vis the stated concerns*. If there is to be further progress in the scientific study of personality, then, as investigators in the field, we are going to have to become much more precise in the articulation of our theoretical concerns, and much more careful in distinguishing between those questions that our measurement models will and will not permit us to address.

The idiothetic perspective on the scientific study of personality is firmly grounded in the theoretical notion that the "kind of person" one is perceived to be (whether by oneself or by another) emerges out of considerations of the "sorts of things" one tends to do in cognitive contrast with the "sorts of things" one tends *not* to do but *could* do. Stated more generally, personality is a phenomenon based ultimately in accumulated information about an individual's actions, interpreted or rendered meaningful within a context provided by *the perception and construal of that individual's alternative possibilities for action*.

In the final analysis, the interactive measurement model proposed by Lamiell (1981) and applied in the research presented here is nothing more or less than a tool that enables one to articulate the theoretical notion just discussed in an explicit and systematic, that is, scientific way. It is the formal connectedness between the measurement model and the theoretical notion that establishes the former as appropriate for empirical research conducted in accordance with the latter.

It would obviously be premature to claim at this point that the idiothetic approach to the scientific study of personality has been shown to be more useful than are other possible approaches. There are, however, several conceptual and empirical considerations which suggest that, in the last analysis, this might well prove to be the case. In concluding this article, three of those considerations will be discussed. The first has to do with the enduring problem of determining which attributes shall be assessed in studying the personality of any given individual. The second has to do with the current problem of representing person–situation interactions in a dynamic rather than mechanistic way (cf. Magnusson & Endler, 1977b). The third consideration, and the one that is tied most directly to the empirical evidence presented earlier, has to do with the problem of exploring the interface of cognition and personality.

As regards the first of these problems, the idiothetic approach would, in contrast to the traditional "nomothetic" orientation, enable the personologist to dispense completely with the assumption that the attributes in terms of which any one individual is to be studied *must* be applicable to all (Nunnally, 1967) or at least some (Bem & Allen, 1974; Kenrick & Stringfield, 1980) other individuals. As is well known, those who have advocated a genuinely idiographic approach to the study of personality (most notably Gordon Allport) have steadfastly insisted that such an assumption is untenable, at least when it is made a priori. It is interesting to note in this connection that, when properly interpreted, the mass of correlational and (other) variance partitioning evidence available in the extant empirical literature of personality psychology constitutes an overwhelming indication that the idiographists have been correct on this matter all along. This comment undoubtedly warrants some amplification.

It has been noted several times in this article that, under most definitions of the concept of personality, the relevance of any particular attribute to a description of an individual's personality hinges in some way on the degree of consistency with which that individual manifests that attribute. It has also been explained that, with respect to the question of (in)consistency, all that can be reasonably safely inferred from the correlations, omega-square ratios, and generalizability coefficients thus far produced within the traditional nomothetic framework is that the individuals who have been assessed have not been *equally* (in)consistent in their manifestations of the vast array of attributes that have been measured. In combination, these two points lead directly to one conclusion: Research conducted within the nomothetic tradition has yet to yield a single personality attribute that can properly be claimed, in the light of existing evidence, to be *equally* applicable to a description of all of the individuals assessed in any given study.

It should be emphasized that there are only two conceivable ways around this conclusion. One would be to argue (and then document) that the deviations from unity of essentially all of the statistical indices referred to can be attributed entirely to measurement error, at least for certain attributes. The other would be to argue that the problem of determining whether or not a particular attribute is relevant to the description of an individual's personality does not, after all, have anything to do with the degree of consistency with which he/she manifests that attribute over time or across situations.

Pending a convincing development of one or both of these arguments, it should be clear that one's stance with respect to the assumption of universal applicability (Bem & Allen, 1974) ought no longer be regarded as simply a matter of theoretical or methodological preference. As paradoxical as it may seem, the available evidence relevant to that assumption, virtually all of which has been obtained from research conducted according to the nomothetic position, actually provides (when properly interpreted) massive and direct empirical support for the idiographic position.

Within the idiothetic framework, any subset of the 18,000 or so personality adjectives identified by Allport and Odbert (1936) could, in principle, be used to characterize the actions of a single individual at a given point in time. Which subset is in fact used will be directly dependent on the perception and construal of that individual's alternative possibilities for action at that point in time. For example, an individual's actions on a given occasion would be characterized as "friendly" if, on that occasion, he/she was observed engaging in actions construed by the characterizer as "friendly" when actions construed by the characterizer as "unfriendly" were perceived as viable alternative possibilities. Since, in idiographic or interactive measurement, a formal expression of the level at which the individual has manifested "friendliness" would be derived without reference to assessments made of other persons on that attribute, there would be no need to assume anything *one way or the other* about the relevance of that attribute to the study of any other person. In this sense, the adoption of the idiothetic approach over a nomothetic (or quasi-nomothetic) approach would be more consonant with the evidence just considered, indicating that the a priori assumption that a single attribute *must* be common to more than one individual is untenable.

The second problem to be taken up here in discussing the potential utility of the idiothetic framework derives from the need in contemporary personality psychology for a *dynamic* rather than mechanistic approach to studying person-situation interactions. As Magnusson and Endler (1977b) have so cogently stated, the need for such an approach derives from (a) the fact that, *in theory*, the interactionist views the person and the situations as being ''inextricably interwoven as part of the process within which behavior develops and is maintained'' (p. 22), and from (b) the recognition that existing models for interactional research cannot adequately represent this theoretical view. Thus did those authors state:

> The lack of adequate methodological tools for studying dynamic interactions is an obstacle for future research. The development of such methods is one of the most urgent needs in terms of providing us with more effective research on the person by situation interaction issue. (p. 25)

By adopting an idiothetic perspective, it becomes possible for one to envision how the study of the person and the situation could be inextricably interwoven *methodologically* as well as theoretically. In order to see this, it is necessary to understand that, from the idiothetic perspective, a *psychological situation* is defined as an *interval of time* (not necessarily a physical location) during which certain concepts dominate the perception and construal of one's alternative possibilities for action. For example, a ''competitive'' psychological situation would be defined as an interval of time during which the concept ''competitive vs noncompetitive'' dominates the perception and construal of the individual's alternative possibilities for action. Similarly, a ''love and affection'' situation (Rotter, 1955) would be defined as an interval of time during which the attribute ''affectionate vs nonaffectionate'' dominates the perception and construal of one's alternative possibilities for action.

In general, to the extent that the concepts dominating the construal of one's perceived alternative possibilities for action remain constant within a given interval of time, one would be said to remain in the same psychological situation. Conversely, to the extent that the concepts dominating the construal of one's perceived alternative possibilities for action change over time, one would be said to move from one psychological situation to another.

For the purpose of the present discussion, the most important aspect of this is its implication that, to empirically assess an individual's *psychological situation* within a given interval of time is to specify, for that individual, a set of perceived alternative possibilities for action, and to specify the underlying concepts or attributes in terms of which those alternative possibilities are construed or ''psychologically organized'' (Golding, 1977). These are, of course, precisely the variables that one specifies in the process of assessing *the person*, as formally represented, respectively, by the V_{pio} and R_{iao} components by Eq. (1). Thus, if one adopts the definition of the psychological situation offered by the idiothetic perspective, one can see that the information which provides the context for empirically measuring the person *is* the information used to empirically define the psychological situation. Thus does the assessment of the person become inextricably interwoven with the assessment of the psychological situation.

From the theoretical perspective of a dynamic interactionist, it is obviously reasonable to assume that, at any given point in time, the perception and construal of alternative possibilities for action could differ across persons being investigated. In other words, at any given point in time, the psychological situation may be different for different persons. Moreover, and virtually by definition of the term "dynamic," it seems reasonable to assume that the perception and construal of any one individual's alternative possibilities for action can change over time, i.e., that an individual can move through time from one psychological situation to another. Now, if an investigator wishes to be able to represent these theoretical dynamics empirically, then he/she must allow for the possibility that the V_{pio} and R_{iao} components of one's assessment procedures may have to be specified differently for different individuals, and for different measurement occasions within an individual. In other words, the investigator must be prepared to abandon a strict reliance on standardized assessment devices (Tyler, 1978), a development that would be anathema to current models for interactional research.

The reason for this is that the abandonment of standardized assessment devices would completely undermine the logic of normative and ipsative measurement on which the current models for interactional research are based. In the case of normative measurement, for example, the very sensibility of placing a psychological interpretation on the "raw" S_{pao} values assigned to one individual by contrasting it with the "raw" S_{pao} values assigned to other individuals is based on the assumption that *all* of the S_{pao} values have been generated from a common assessment device. Only in this way could observed differences between the scores possibly be said to represent psychological differences between persons rather than methodological differences between the procedures used to assess persons. Similarly in the case of ipsative measurement, the very sensibility of placing a psychological interpretation on the "raw" S_{pao} value assigned to an individual on one occasion by comparing it with the "raw" S_{pao} values assigned to that same person on other occasions is based on the assumption that all of the S_{pao} values have been generated from the same assessment device. Only in this way could any observed differences between the scores possibly be said to represent psychological changes in the person over time, rather than methodological changes in the procedures used to assess the person over time.

In interactive measurement, the interpretation of a single S_{pao} value does not require reference to any other S_{pao} values. For this reason, the sensibility of applying the interactive model to "raw" S_{pao} values is in no way affected by the abandonment of standardized assessment devices. Indeed, a distinguishing feature of interactive measurement is that, by virtue of the specification of $S'_{pao\ max}$ and $S'_{pao\ min}$ values for each individual on each measurement occasion, any effects attributable to the assessment procedure are "automatically" incorporated into the computation of interpretable I_{pao} values. Thus, any single I_{pao} value is *always* understood to express the level at which an individual's actions reflect a given attribute *within the constraints necessarily imposed* by specifying

the V_{pio}, R_{iao}, and integration function of Eq. (1). The theoretical interpretation of this is that the I_{pao} values generated by interactive measurement have the
empirically specified constraints imposed by the psychological situation "built
in."

It was undoubtedly in consideration of the point just developed that Cattell
(1944) described interactive measurement as follows:

> It is measurement in terms of the actual physical and biological effects of behavior, usually,
> in test situations, *within a restricted framework defined by the test*. It recognizes the oneness of
> the organism-environment and pays tribute to the oft-forgotten fact that a trait is never resident
> only in the organism but is a *relation* between the organism and environment. (p. 293,
> emphasis added)

In the light of the foregoing, it is here suggested that, by adopting the idiothetic framework for personality research, investigators might simultaneously be
adopting a framework which is capable of representing *methodologically* the
oneness of the organism–environment, that is, the *theoretical* notion that persons
and situations are "inextricably interwoven."[5]

The final matter to be discussed here brings us back to a consideration of the
empirical findings presented in Section III. It will be recalled that the relevance
of those findings derives from the problem of reconciling the traditional
metatheoretical concerns of personality theory with the emergent concern in
contemporary personality psychology of understanding the cognitive processes
of the subjects of our inquiry, that is, the manner in which *our subjects* think
about their own and one anothers' personalities.

Consider collectively, the results of the three studies discussed provide a
strong indication that subjective personality impressions are grounded in a cognitive process that cannot be represented adequately within the constraints imposed
by the various research strategies that to date have dominated the scientific study
of personality. More specifically, those results indicate that the subjective
perspective on personality-relevant phenomena is neither (a) captured by the
aggregate perspective that the aforementioned strategies have led to, nor, when
the issues are framed at the level of the individual, (b) adequately represented in
terms of the normative and/or ipsative measurement models on which those

---

[5]Cattell's (1944) reference to the "actual physical and biological effects of behavior" reflects his
conviction that scientifically adequate interactive measures could be developed only in what he called
"dimensions of the external world," that is, only within "behavioral" data. He patently rejected the
possibility of scientifically adequate interactive measurement within the more abstract realm of what
he called "introspective" data, which would presumably include data constituted of subjective
ratings of persons with respect to *underlying attributes* of behavior [cf. Fiske's (1979) distinction
between the "two worlds" of psychological phenomena]. Indeed, Cattell labeled attempts at interactive measurement in the introspective realm as "false absolute" or "false interactive," and decreed
that true interactive measurement in the introspective realm was "impossible in the absence of ESP"
(p. 294). However, the results of Study III would seem to contraindicate this view.

strategies are based. Instead, the evidence presented indicates that subjective personality impressions are grounded in a rationale that is essentially interactive in nature.

By no means should this be taken as an argument that one's subjective personality impressions are impervious either to information gleaned from observing the actions of other persons or to that contained in the memory or anticipation of one's own actions at other points in time. The problem is not one of determining whether or not subjective impressions of self and others are influenced by interpersonal (normative) and/or intrapersonal (ipsative) factors. Clearly they must be. The problem is: How—precisely—are such influences to be conceptualized theoretically and, therefore, represented empirically?

From the idiothetic perspective, information available to the individual from normative and/or ipsative sources is viewed, in theory, as input into one's perception and construal of alternative possibilities for action. Thus, my observation of what others do, my memory of what I have done in the past, and, indeed, my anticipation of what I might do in the future can all influence my perception of what I *could* be doing at present. Moreover, sociocultural and developmental factors can certainly influence the manner in which I construe my perceived behavioral alternatives vis-à-vis certain underlying qualities or attributes.

Methodologically speaking, this theoretical perspective leads to the view that the influence of what might be regarded as normative and ipsative factors on subjective personality impressions should be formally represented in terms of the subjective V_{pio} and R_{iao} of Eq. (1), as they are the components of the methodological framework used to represent the perception and construal of alternative possibilities for action. Within that framework, however, it is maintained that once those components have been defined, one has all the information one needs in order to specify the context within which one's actions at a given point in time are interpreted. That is, the intelligibility of any resulting characterization of one's actions [represented by the subjective S_{pao} component of Eq. (1)], does not require reference to characterizations one might actually have made about other persons, or about oneself at other points in time. It hinges instead on an awareness of the characterizations one might have made, under the circumstances, had one's actions been other than they were (Rychlak, 1976; Tyler, 1978).

It is one thing to say that subjective impressions of self and others are influenced by normative and/or ipsative factors. It is quite another thing to claim or simply assume that the cognitive process underlying the formulation and expression of such impressions can be adequately studied, represented, and understood in terms of the formal properties of normative and/or ipsative measurement. The findings obtained in Study III strongly suggest that that cognitive process cannot be so represented, and may in fact be more adequately represented in terms of the formal properties of interactive measurement. Thus, those findings suggest that the potential utility of the idiothetic framework might extend well beyond its formal compatibility with the long-standing metatheoretical concerns of the scientific study of personality. In addition, and by virtue of its reliance on interactive rather than normative or ipsative measurement, the idiothetic framework might well provide the most viable means of bridging the gap between investigators' conceptions of their subjects, and their subjects' conceptions of themselves and one another. At the very least, it is to be hoped that the issues raised by the evidence considered herein would be given serious attention by any personologist who is genuinely committed to empirical exploration at the interface of cognition and personality.

References

Allport, G. W. *Personality: A psychological interpretation*. New York: Holt, 1937.

Allport, G. W. The general and the unique in psychological science. *Journal of Personality*, 1962, **30**, 405-422.

Allport, G. W. Traits revisited. *American Psychologist*, 1966, **21**, 1-10.

Allport, G. W., & Odbert, H. S. Trait-names: A psycholexical study. *Psychological Monographs*, 1936, No. 211.

Anderson, N. H. Averaging vs. adding as a stimulus combination rule in impression formation. *Journal of Experimental Psychology*, 1965, **70**, 394-400.

Anderson, N. H., & Shanteau, J. Weak inference with linear models. *Psychological Bulletin*, 1977, **84**, 1155-1170.

Argyle, M., & Little, B. R. Do personality traits apply to social behavior? *Journal for the Theory of Social Behavior*, 1972, **2**, 1-35.

Baldwin, A. L. Personal structure analysis: A statistical method for investigating the single personality. *Journal of Abnormal and Social Psychology*, 1942, **37**, 163-183.

Baldwin, A. L. The study of individual personality by means of the intraindividual correlation. *Journal of Personality*, 1946, **14**, 151-168.

Beck, S. J. The science of personality: Nomothetic or idiographic? *Psychological Review*, 1953, **60**, 353-359.

Bem, D. J., & Allen, A. On predicting some of the people some of the time: The search for cross-situational consistencies in behavior. *Psychological Review*, 1974, **81**, 506-520.

Bem, D. J., & Funder, D. C. Predicting more of the people more of the time: Assessing the personality of situations. *Psychological Review*, 1978, **85**, 485-501.

Berman, J. S., & Kenny, D. A. Correlational bias in observer ratings. *Journal of Personality and Social Psychology*, 1976, **34**, 263-273.

Birnbaum, M. H. Reply to the devil's advocates: Don't confound model testing and measurement. *Psychological Bulletin*, 1974, **81**, 854-859. (a)

Birnbaum, M. H. The nonadditivity of personality impressions. *Journal of Experimental Psychology*, 1974, **102**, 543-561 (Monograph). (b)

Block, J. Some reasons for the apparent inconsistency of personality. *Psychological Bulletin*, 1968, **70**, 210-212.

Block, J. *Lives through time*. Berkeley, Calif.: Bancroft, 1971.

Block, J. Advancing the psychology of personality: Paradigmatic shift or improving the quality of research? In D. Magnusson & N. S. Endler (Eds.), *Personality at the crossroads: Current issues in interactional psychology*. Hillsdale, N.J.: Erlbaum, 1977. Pp. 37-68.

Block, J. *Some enduring and consequential structures of personality*. Paper presented at "Explorations in Personality—78," Michigan State University, East Lansing, November 17, 1978.

Bowers, K. S. Situationism in psychology: An analysis and a critique. *Psychological Review*, 1973, **80**, 307–336.

Budescu, D. V. Some new measures of profile dissimilarity. *Applied Psychological Measurement*, 1980, **4**, 261–272.

Campbell, D. T., & Fiske, D. W. Convergent and discriminant validation by the multitrait-multimethod matrix. *Psychological Bulletin*, 1959, **56**, 81–105.

Carlson, R. Where is the person in personality research? *Psychological Bulletin*, 1971, **75**, 203–219.

Carroll, J. D., & Chang, J. Analysis of individual differences in multidimensional scaling via an N-way generalization of "Eckart-Young" decomposition. *Psychometrika*, 1970, **35**, 238–319.

Cattell, R. B. Psychological measurement: Normative, ipsative, interactive. *Psychological Review*, 1944, **51**, 292–303.

Cattell, R. B. *The scientific analysis of personality*. Baltimore: Penguin, 1965.

Cattell, R. B. (Ed.) *Handbook of multivariate experimental psychology*. Chicago, Ill.: Rand McNally, 1966.

Cronbach, L. J. Beyond the two disciplines of scientific psychology. *American Psychologist*, 1975, **30**, 116–127.

Cronbach, L. J., & Gleser, G. Assessing similarity between profiles. *Psychological Bulletin*, 1953, **50**, 456–473.

D'Andrade, R. G. Trait psychology and componential analysis. *American Anthropologist*, 1965, **67**, 215–228.

Dawes, R. M., & Corrigan, B. Linear models in decision-making. *Psychological Bulletin*, 1974, **81**, 95–106.

Edwards, A. L. *Experimental design in psychological research*. (Revised edition). New York: Holt, 1964.

Ekehammar, B. Interactionism in personality from a historical perspective. *Psychological Bulletin*. 1974, **81**, 1026–1048.

Endler, N. S. The case for person-situation interactions. *Canadian Psychological Review*, 1975, **16**, 12–21.

Endler, N. S., & Magnusson, D. (Eds.) *Interactional psychology and personality*. New York: Wiley, 1976. (a)

Endler, N. S., & Magnusson, D. Toward an interactional psychology of personality. *Psychological Bulletin*, 1976, **83**, 956–974. (b)

Epstein, S. The stability of behavior: I. On predicting most of the people much of the time. *Journal of Personality and Social Psychology*, 1979, **37**, 1097–1126.

Epstein, S. The stability of behavior: II. Implications for research. *American Psychologist*, 1980, **35**, 790–806.

Eysenck, H. J. The science of personality: Nomothetic! *Psychological Review*, 1954, **61**, 339–342.

Falk, J. Issues distinguishing idiographic from nomothetic approaches to personality theory. *Psychological Review*, 1956, **63**, 53–62.

Fiske, D. W. Can a personality construct be validated empirically? *Psychological Bulletin*, 1973, **80**, 89–92.

Fiske, D. W. The limits for the conventional science of personality. *Journal of Personality*, 1974, **42**, 1–11.

Fiske, D. W. *Strategies for personality research*. San Francisco: Jossey-Bass, 1978. (a)

Fiske, D. W. Cosmopolitan constructs and provincial observations: Some prescriptions for a chronically ill specialty. In H. London (Ed.), *Personality: A new look at metatheories*. New York: Wiley, 1978. Pp. 21–43. (b)

Fiske, D. W. Two worlds of psychological phenomena. *American Psychologist*, 1979, **34**, 733–739.

Funder, D. C. The "trait" of assigning traits: Individual differences in the tendency to trait ascription. *Journal of Research in Personality*, 1980, 14, 376–385.

Gaito, J. Measurement scales and statistics: Resurgence of an old misconception. *Psychological Bulletin*, 1980, **87**, 564–567.

Goldberg, L. R. Simple models or simple processes? Some research on clinical judgments. *American Psychologist*, 1968, **23**, 483–496.

Goldfried, M. R., & Kent, R. N. Traditional versus behavioral personality assessment: A comparison of methodological and theoretical assumptions. *Psychological Bulletin*, 1972, **77**, 409–420.

Golding, S. L. Flies in the ointment: Methodological problems in the analysis of the percentage of variance due to persons and situations. *Psychological Bulletin*, 1975, **82**, 278–288.

Golding, S. L. The problem of construal styles in the analysis of person-situation interactions. In D. Magnusson and N. S. Endler (Eds.), *Personality at the crossroads: Current issues in interactional psychology*. Hillsdale, N.J.: Erlbaum, 1977. Pp. 401–407.

Golding, S. L. Toward a more adequate theory of personality: Psychological organizing principles. In H. London (Ed.), *Personality: A new look at metatheories*. New York: Wiley, 1978. Pp. 69–95.

Harris, J. G., Jr. Nonvalidation and idiovalidation: A quest for the true personality profile. *American Psychologist*, 1980, **35**, 729–744.

Hartshorne, H., & May, M. A. *Studies in the nature of character*. Vol. I. *Studies in deceit*. New York: Macmillan, 1928.

Hase, H. D., & Goldberg, L. R. Comparative validity of different strategies of constructing personality inventory scales. *Psychological Bulletin*, 1967, **67**, 231–248.

Hirschberg, N. A correct treatment of traits. In H. London (Ed.) *Personality: A new look at metatheories*. New York: Wiley, 1978. Pp. 45–68.

Hogan, R., DeSoto, C. B., & Solano, C. Traits, tests, and personality research. *American Psychologist*, 1977, **32**, 255–264.

Holt, R. Individuality and generalization in the psychology of personality. *Journal of Personality*, 1962, **30**, 377–404.

Jackson, D. N., & Messick, S. Individual differences in social perception. *British Journal of Clinical and Social Psychology*, 1963, **2**, 1–10.

Kelly, G. A. *The psychology of personal constructs*. New York: Norton, 1955.

Kenrick, D. T., & Stringfield, D. O. Personality traits and the eye of the beholder: Crossing some traditional philosophical boundaries in the search for consistency in all of the people. *Psychological Review*, 1980, **87**, 88–104.

Kim, M. P., & Rosenberg, S. Comparison of two structural models of implicit personality theory. *Journal of Personality and Social Psychology*, 1980, **38**, 375–389.

Kleinmuntz, B. *Personality measurement: An introduction*. Homewood, Illinois: The Dorsey Press, 1967.

Lamiell, J. T. On the utility of looking in the "wrong" direction. *Journal of Personality*, 1980, **48**, 82–88.

Lamiell, J. T. Toward an idiothetic psychology of personality. *American Psychologist*, 1981, **36**, 276–289.

Lamiell, J. T., Foss, M. A., & Cavenee, P. On the relationship between conceptual schemes and behavior reports: A closer look. *Journal of Personality*, 1980, **48**, 54–73.

Lay, C. Some notes of the concept of cross-situational consistency. In D. Magnusson & N. S. Endler (Eds.), *Personality at the crossroads: Current issues in interactional psychology*. Hillsdale, N.J.: Erlbaum, 1977, pp. 143–146.

Lay, C., & Jackson, D. N. Analysis of the generality of trait-inferential relationships. *Journal of Personality and Social Psychology*, 1969, **12**, 12–21.

Levy, L. *Conceptions of personality: Theories and research*. New York: Random House, 1970.

London, H. (Ed.) *Personality: A new look at metatheories*. New York: Wiley, 1978. (a)

London, H. Personality: Paradigms and politics. In H. London (Ed.), *Personality: A new look at metatheories*. New York: Wiley, 1978. Pp. 153–166. (b)

Magnusson, D., & Endler, N. S. (Eds.) *Personality at the crossroads: Current issues in interactional psychology*. Hillsdale, N.J.: Erlbaum, 1977. (a)

Magnusson, D., & Endler, N. S. Interactional psychology: Present status and future prospects. In D. Magnusson & N. S. Endler (Eds.), *Personality at the crossroads: Current issues in interactional psychology*. Hillsdale, N.J.: Erlbaum, 1977. Pp. 3–35. (b)

McGowan, J., & Gormly, J. Validation of personality traits: A multicriteria approach. *Journal of Personality and social Psychology*, 1976, **38**, 492–503.

Mehrabian, A., & O'Reilly, E. Analysis of personality measures in terms of basic dimensions of temperament. *Journal of Personality and Social Psychology*, 1980, **38**, 492–503.

Mischel, W. *Personality and assessment*. New York: Wiley, 1968.

Mischel, W. On continuity and change in personality. *American Psychologist*, 1969, **24**, 1112–1118.

Mischel, W. Toward a cognitive social learning reconceptualization of personality. *Psychological Review*, 1973, **80**, 252–283.

Mischel, W. On the future of personality measurement. *American Psychologist*, 1977, **32**, 246–254.

Mischel, W. On the interface of cognition and personality: Beyond the person-situation debate. *American Psychologist*, 1979, **34**, 740–754.

Mulaik, S. A. Are personality factors raters' conceptual factors? *Journal of Consulting Psychology*, 1964, **28**, 506–511.

Norman, W. T. On estimating psychological relationships: Social desirability and self report. *Psychological Bulletin*, 1967, **67**, 273–293.

Nunnally, J. C. *Psychometric theory*. New York:McGraw-Hill, 1967.

Passini, F. T., & Norman, W. T. A universal conception of personality structure? *Journal of Personality and Social Psychology*, 1966, **4**, 44–49.

Pervin, L. A. *Current controversies and issues in personality*. New York: Wiley, 1978.

Phares, E. J., & Lamiell, J. T. Personality. In M. R. Rosenzweig & L. W. Porter (Eds.), *Annual review of psychology* (Vol. 28). Palo Alto, Calif.: Annual Reviews, 1977. Pp. 113–140.

Rosenberg, S., Nelson, C., & Vivekananthan, P. S. A multidimensional approach to the structure of personality impressions. *Journal of Personality and Social Psychology*, 1968, **9**, 283–294.

Rosenberg, S., & Sedlak, A. Structural representations of implicit personality theory. In L. Berkowitz (Ed.), *Advances in experimental social psychology* (Vol. 6). New York: Academic Press, 1972.

Rosenzweig, S. The place of the individual and of idiodynamics in psychology: A dialogue. *Journal of Individual Psychology*, 1958, **14**, 3–20.

Rotter, J. B. The role of the psychological situation in determining the direction of human behavior. In M. R. Jones (Ed.), *Nebraska Symposium on Motivation*. Lincoln, Nebraska: University of Nebraska Press, 1955. Pp. 245–269.

Rychlak, J. F. Personality theory: Its nature, past, present and—future? *Personality and Social Psychology Bulletin*, 1976, **2**, 209–224.

Rychlak, J. F. *A philosophy of science for personality theory*. Boston, Mass.: Houghton, 1968.

Sanford, N. Personality: Its place in psychology. In S. Koch (Ed.). *Psychology: A study of a science* (Vol. 5). New York: McGraw-Hill, 1963.

Schneider, D. J. Implicit personality theory: A Review. *Psychological Bulletin*, 1973, **79**, 294–309.

Sechrest, L. Personality. In M. R. Rosenzweig & L. W. Porter (Eds.), *Annual Review of Psychology* (Vol. 27). Palo Alto, Calif.: Annual Reviews, 1976. Pp. 1–27.

Shweder, R. A. How relevant is an individual differences theory of personality? *Journal of Personality*, 1975, **43**, 455–484.

Shweder, R. A. Likeness and likelihood in everyday thought: Magical thinking in judgments about personality. *Current Anthropology*, 1977, **18**, 637-648. (a)

Shweder, R. A. Illusory correlation and the MMPI controversy. *Journal of Consulting and Clinical Psychology*, 1977, **45**, 917-924. (b)

Shweder, R. A. Illusory correlation and the MMPI controversy: Reply to some of the allusions and elusions in Block's and Edwards' commentaries. *Journal of Consulting and Clinical Psychology*, 1977, **45**, 936-940. (c)

Shweder, R. A. Factors and fictions in person perception: A reply to Lamiell, Foss, and Cavenee. *Journal of Personality*, 1980, **48**, 54-73.

Shweder, R. G., & D'Andrade, R. G. Accurate reflection or systematic distortion? A reply to Block, Weiss, & Tborne. *Journal of Personality and Social Psychology*, 1979, **37**, 1075-1084.

Shweder, R. A., & D'Andrade, R. C. The systematic distortion hypothesis. *New Directions for Methodology of Social and Behavioral Science*, 1980, **4**, 37-58.

Stephenson, W. *The study of behavior: Q-technique and its methodology.* Chicago, Ill.: Univ. of Chicago Press, 1953.

Tyler, L. Toward a workable psychology of individuality. *American Psychologist*, 1959, **14**, 75-81.

Tyler, L. *Individuality: Human possibilities and personal choice in the psychological development of men and women.* San Francisco: Jossey-Bass, 1978.

Wegner, D. M., & Vallacher, R. R. *Implicit psychology: An introduction to social cognition.* London and New York: Oxford Univ. Press, 1977.

Wiggins, J. S. *Personality and prediction: Principles of personality assessment.* Reading, Mass.: Addison-Wesley, 1973.

Wiggins, N. Individual differences in human judgments: A multivariate approach. In L. Rappoport & D. A. Summers (Eds.), *Human judgment and social interaction.* New York: Holt, 1973. Pp. 110-142.

Zanna, M. P., Olson, J. M., & Fazio, R. H. Attitude-behavior consistency: An individual difference perspective. *Journal of Personality and Social Psychology*, 1980, **38**, 432-440.

PROGRESS IN EXPERIMENTAL PERSONALITY RESEARCH, VOLUME 11

FACT AND ARTIFACT IN TRAIT PERCEPTION: THE SYSTEMATIC DISTORTION HYPOTHESIS[1]

Richard A. Shweder

COMMITTEE ON HUMAN DEVELOPMENT
UNIVERSITY OF CHICAGO
CHICAGO, ILLINOIS

I. Introduction: The Systematic Distortion Hypothesis

The systematic distortion hypothesis states that our beliefs about personality structure tend to be inaccurate with respect to how attitudes, affects, and behaviors covary (see D'Andrade, 1965, 1973, 1974; Shweder, 1972, 1973, 1975, 1977a, 1977b, 1977c, 1979a, 1980a; Shweder & D'Andrade, 1979, 1980). The

---

[1]This article is a revision and synthesis of sections of two unpublished manuscripts entitled "Fact and Artifact in Personality Assessment: The Influence of Conceptual Schemata on Individual Difference Judgments," and "Attributional Illusions in Psychological Theory: The Forsaken Quest for an Individual Difference Theory of Personality." The article also draws on formulations and materials in Shweder (1972, 1975, 1979a), and Shweder and D'Andrade (1979, 1980). Responsibility for the views set forth here, however, is entirely my own.

main idea is that, under the memory conditions characteristic of most lay and scientific personality assessments, judges either infer correlational structure from a general model of conceptual association, or find conceptually associated memory items easier to retrieve. In other words, *inferences* about personality contain a systematic bias in that propositions about "what is like what" are substituted for propositions about what is likely, and *memory* for personality relevant events contains a systematic bias in that attitudes, affects, and behaviors that are conceptually associated (e.g., "aggression" and "dominance," "disagrees" and "criticizes") are recalled as if they covaried. The Chapmans have labeled this effect "illusory correlation" (Chapman, 1967; Chapman & Chapman, 1967, 1969).

The systematic distortion hypothesis concerns the limitations of our current knowledge of personality syndromes. Personality syndrome is interpreted here as a package of correlated affective, attitudinal, and behavioral characteristics. Personality syndromes are sometimes referred to as global traits, underlying factors, or general dimensions. "Introversion" is an example of a postulated syndrome; the syndrome is postulated with the expectation that the correlational structure of individual differences across comparable contexts will reveal a discriminated cluster of positively correlated attributes, including "prefers to work alone," "slow to make friends," "daydreams at meetings." The personality psychology literature is rich in postulated syndromes: the "dependent" child (seeks help, seeks reassurance, seeks attention, seeks physical proximity); the "paranoid" adult (hostile, suspicious, grandiose); the "permissive" mother (feeds her children on demand, refrains from physical punishment, accepts nudity, tolerates masturbation). Hundreds of postulated syndromes extant in the literature could be cited: "ego-strength," "Machiavellianism," "anxiety," "psychoticism," "ascendency," "altruism."

One implication of the systematic distortion hypothesis is that one cannot trust evidence of personality syndromes derived from memory-based assessment procedures (inventories, rating forms, questionnaire interviews). And, since most evidence in support of proposed personality syndromes is of this memory-based type, a second implication is that the very idea that people have global traits consisting of covarying behaviors may be illusory, the product of a widespread human tendency to rely on similarity and conceptual proximity for estimating cooccurrence probability (Tversky & Kahneman, 1974).

An explicit, contemporary version of the systematic distortion hypothesis was first advanced by D'Andrade in 1965. An earlier, exemplary formulation can be found in Newcomb (1929, 1931). A cognate formulation can be found in Mulaik (1964). Since 1965 the hypothesis has been sympathetically received in some quarters (Mischel, 1968, 1973; Berman & Kenny, 1976; Fiske, 1978; Ebbesen & Allen, 1977, 1979; Cooper, 1981; Gara & Rosenberg, 1981; Mirels, n.d.; Nisbett, 1980; Borman, 1982) and criticized in others (Block, 1977; Block, Weiss, & Thorne, 1979; Epstein, 1979; Jackson, Chan, & Stricker, 1979; Lamiell, Foss,

& Cavenee, 1980). Replies to criticism can be found in Shweder (1977b, 1979a, 1980a) and Shweder and D'Andrade (1979).

Unfortunately, for the sake of scientific progress, the systematic distortion hypothesis seems to be easily misunderstood, apparently lending itself to hyperbolic formulations that detract from rational debate and are unlikely to produce pertinent empirical investigations. Indeed, anyone so unfortunate as to read only the literature critical of the systematic distortion hypothesis might well come away with the misbegotten notion that the hypothesis denies the existence of personality, claims that raters make ratings ignorant of ratees, or hypothesizes a social process in which people interact with each other in a linguistic fantasy world!

The systematic distortion hypothesis also seems to generate a good deal of resistance. Global trait concepts (dominant, aggressive, friendly, dependent, etc.) are deeply entrenched in most natural languages and in lay personality theory (see Shweder, 1972; White, 1980; Shweder & Bourne, 1981, for cross-cultural evidence). Many readers probably subscribe to the widespread assumption that natural language categories and implicit personality theory would not persist unless they were more or less valid. Indeed, there are even some contemporary theories of category formation which argue that lay categories are basically encodings of "real world" correlational structures (Rosch, 1975; Rosch & Mervis, 1975; Rosch, Mervis, Gray, Johnson, & Boyes-Braem, 1976). Thus, any hypothesis that would *deny* that our beliefs about correlational structure are more or less accurate summaries of the actual "relative frequencies of joint occurrences of various personality attributes and behavioral dispositions in other persons" (Passini & Norman, 1966, p. 47) has some explaining to do.

The aim of this article is to eliminate misunderstandings and, hopefully, to overcome resistance (also see Shweder, 1979a, 1980 ; Shweder & D'Andrade, 1979). The systematic distortion hypothesis shall be described and a corpus of studies supporting the hypothesis shall be reviewed. The implications of the hypothesis shall be enumerated with special reference to personality structure and implicit personality theory. Throughout the article pauses are taken to anticipate possible misunderstandings.

II. The Systematic Distortion Hypothesis: Testing the Hypothesis

The systematic distortion hypothesis asserts that judges on personality inventories, interpersonal checklists, and questionnaire interviews unwittingly substitute a preexisting model of conceptual association for a description of correlational structure. Thus, the correlational structure of ratings replicates preexisting beliefs about what is like what with little sensitivity to the correlational structure of actual behavior.

One way to test the systematic distortion hypothesis is to collect conceptual association judgments, memory-based ratings, and observational evidence on an equivalent set of attitudinal, affective, or behavioral variables. By a conceptual association judgment I mean a direct judgment of "similarity in meaning" between pairs of descriptive terms or phrases, a derived measure of conceptual proximity based on common associates in a free association task, or the relative number of predications common to the pairs of terms or phrases being judged (see, e.g., Szalay & Deese, 1978). A summary of the conceptual association judgments among all possible pairs of variables in a set of attitudinal, affective, or behavioral variables shall be referred to as a "conceptual association matrix." By observational evidence I mean a reliable, reasonably objective, "on-line" record made at the time of observation. Such records will be referred to as "immediate scorings," and a summary of the intercorrelations in immediate scorings among all possible pairs of variables in a set of attitudinal, affective, or behavioral variables shall be referred to as an "actual behavior matrix." By memory-based ratings I mean the type of judgment characteristic of personality assessment instruments such as the MMPI, the California Q-Sort, or the Brief Psychiatric Rating Scale. Judges are asked to abstract and summarize their previous observations of themselves or others on a set of attitudinal, affective, or behavioral variables. The intercorrelations in memory-based ratings among all possible pairs of variables in a set of attitudinal, affective, or behavioral variables shall be referred to as a "rated behavior matrix."

The systematic distortion hypothesis predicts that the correlational structure of variables in rated behavior matrices is unlike that of equivalent variables in actual behavior matrices, yet replicates the patterning of conceptual association judgments among those same variables in conceptual association matrices. In other words, what correlates with what in memory-based ratings tells us more about preexisting ideas of what is like what than about what correlates with what in actual behavior. This predicted pattern of results is illustrated in Fig. 1.

The data presented in Fig. 1 are from a videotape study conducted by R. G. D'Andrade and reported in Shweder and D'Andrade (1980). The subset of data presented in Fig. 1 is selected for illustrative purposes only. In the study reported in Shweder and D'Andrade, 30 minutes of videotaped interaction among four members of a white, middle-class California family were analyzed using 11 categories of interpersonal behavior (6 of these categories are selected for illustration in Fig. 1).

Three observers conducted on-line immediate scorings of behavioral acts using the 11 categories. The mean reliability coefficient across all 11 categories for percentage of act across actors was .75. These immediate scorings were used to construct an actual behavior matrix for all pairs of 11 categories.

Twenty raters viewed the 30-minute videotape and then gave summary ratings of each actor on each category using a 7-point scale. Raters were asked "how much does [so-and-so] do the following [for example, "criticize"]?" These

Conceptual association matrix
(similarity of meaning judgments averaged across 10 judges)

	Ad	In	Su	Qu	Cr	Di
Advise		76	88	-04	-08	-36
Inform			64	-12	-12	-28
Suggest				-16	-28	16
Question					44	72
Criticize						44
Disagree						

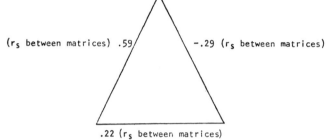

(r_s between matrices) .59 / \ -.29 (r_s between matrices)

.22 (r_s between matrices)

	Ad	In	Su	Qu	Cr	Di
Advise		42	51	24	10	05
Inform			37	14	00	-10
Suggest				11	13	-02
Question					12	-01
Criticize						59
Disagree						

	Ad	In	Su	Qu	Cr	Di	
		00	00	00	67	33	Advise
			-33	33	-33	00	Inform
				33	33	-67	Suggest
					-33	-67	Question
						00	Criticize
							Disagree

Rated behavior matrix
(mean τ coefficients averaged
over 20 memory-based raters)

Actual behavior matrix
(τ coefficients for behavior
percentage averaged across immediate
on-line scorings
of three reliable observers)

FIG. 1. The systematic distortion hypothesis. Degrees of correspondence (r_s) between correlational structures derived from similarity of meaning judgments (conceptual association matrix), memory-based ratings (rated behavior matrix), and immediate scorings (actual behavior matrix). Subset of data from videotape study (Shweder & D'Andrade, 1980) selected to illustrate typical pattern of findings.

memory-based ratings were used to construct a rated behavior matrix for all pairs of 11 categories.

Ten judges made similarity of meaning judgments for all pairs of lexical labels for the 11 interpersonal behavior categories. Judgments were made on a scale running from +100 ("identical in meaning") to −100 ("completely opposite in meaning"). These similarity of meaning judgments were used to construct a conceptual association matrix for all pairs of 11 categories.

The conceptual association matrix, the rated behavior matrix, and the actual behavior matrix were compared directly with each other by correlating over the parallel cells of each pair of matrices. This is one way of asking whether the correlational structure of each matrix reveals the same information about what goes with what across individual differences in conduct.

Using all 11 categories the correspondence between the conceptual association matrix and the rated behavior matrix was substantial ($r = .75$), while that between the rated behavior matrix and the actual behavior matrix ($r = .22$) and the actual behavior matrix and the conceptual association matrix ($r = .00$) was either weak or nonexistent. For the subset of six categories selected for illustrative purposes in Fig. 1, the measures of intermatrix correspondence are .59, .22, and −.29, respectively. Across seven different tests of intermatrix correspondence (D'Andrade, 1974; Shweder, 1975, 1977a; Shweder & D'Andrade, 1980), the mean intermatrix correlation between conceptual association matrices and rated behavior matrices has been .75, the mean intermatrix correlation between rated behavior matrices and actual behavior matrices has been .25, and the mean intermatrix correlation between actual behavior matrices and conceptual association matrices has been .26.

What has been discovered is the pattern of results predicted by the systematic distortion hypothesis: (a) Conceptual associations among event descriptors (e.g., "disagrees" and "criticizes") do not parallel the correlational structure of actual behavior (e.g., "disagrees" and "criticizes" are uncorrelated; see Fig. 1), at least not across individual differences in conduct as immediately scored; (b) the correlational structure of rated behavior does not parallel the correlational structure of actual behavior; and (c) the correlational structure of rated behavior does parallel our lay model of conceptual associations among event descriptors.

The overall pattern of results lends itself to the interpretation that memory-based reports about the correlational structure of individual differences are really reflections of a preexisting lay model of conceptual association, and that conceptual association is a poor index of cooccurrence likelihood in the real world.

A noteworthy distinguishing feature of actual behavior matrices vs rated behavior matrices and conceptual association matrices is the relative absence of neat syndromes, global traits, or simple main effects in actual behavior matrices, and the striking presence of these broad underlying factors in conceptual association and rated behavior matrices. Thus, in Fig. 1, for example, the conceptual association matrix displays a neat differentiation of two "styles" of interpersonal behavior, viz. advise, inform, suggest vs question, criticize, disagree. That clean partitioning of behavioral traits blurs slightly in the rated behavior matrix but is still detectable, while in the actual behavior matrix one is hard-pressed to retrieve any underlying general factors. It is as if the celestial mind of man conceives of pure global types which the mundane world of behavior refuses to instantiate.

As the reader can see, there are three pieces to the pattern of evidence required to support the systematic distortion hypothesis. Each shall now be considered in turn.

A. THE FIT BETWEEN CONCEPTUAL ASSOCIATION MATRICES AND RATED BEHAVIOR MATRICES

Personality researchers share with other scientists the image of the world as "a scene of recurrent kinds of events and changes which exemplify certain regular connections" (Hart, 1961, p. 184). In keeping with this image, a major goal for personality researchers has been to devise a parsimonious set of syndromes, traits, factors, or dimensions (e.g., egoistic vs altruistic, extroverted vs introverted) for predicting individual differences in one context from knowledge of individual differences in another one. In other words, personality researchers *qua* taxonomists have sought to construct categories which summarize regularities in behavior and enable them to make relatively valid inductive generalizations (e.g., children who "offer help" are children who "make suggestions," "people who like parties" are "people who introduce themselves to strangers"). In the quest for an adequate personality classification, correlational structure has been a central concern (see Gilmour, 1937, 1951; Sokal & Sneath, 1963).

Perhaps the most fundamental criterion for evaluating a scientific classification is that it be "founded on attributes which have a number of other attributes correlated with them" (Gilmour, 1937, p. 1040), or, said alternatively, whatever the scheme of classification there must be a number of true and relevant statements which can be made regarding its constituent categories (e.g., "dependent" children are more likely than other children to seek help from peers, seek attention from adults, cling to their mothers' apron strings).

Correlational structure has been a central concern of personality researchers (e.g., Cattell, 1946; Sears, Maccoby, & Levin, 1957; Norman, 1963; Block, 1965; Overall, Hollister, & Pichot, 1967; Bales, 1970). Most personality taxonomies are the product of a data reduction process in which a relatively large number of individual difference attributes (e.g., self-reliance, responsibility, assertiveness) are sorted into a relatively small number of underlying syndromes, traits, or factors (e.g., character strength). Typically, trait equivalence and difference are determined by the extent to which sets of attributes covary, or said alternatively, by the extent to which knowledge of one attribute (e.g., he's "self-reliant") enables one to make valid predictions about other attributes (e.g., he's probably "responsible," "assertive"), and vice versa.

It is noteworthy that "impressive" personality taxonomies (e.g., LaForge & Suczek, 1955; Norman, 1963; Block, 1965; Smith, 1967; Wiggins, 1978) have been constructed almost entirely out of patterns of response covariation on memory-based checklists, inventories, and questionnaires. By an impressive taxonomy I mean one that is both parsimonious (e.g., a 30-item checklist is reduced to three underlying global traits) and valid (i.e., from knowledge of a subject's response to one item on the checklist one can draw inferences about how the subject responded to other items on it, and those inferences, using probabilistic criteria, turn out to be true). It is also noteworthy that most of the memory-based taxonomies extant in the personality literature can be reproduced by asking a handful of respondents to judge the degree of conceptual association (e.g., "similarity of meaning") of the items on the checklist, inventory, or questionnaire.

The underlying taxonomic structure of most memory-based personality classifications can be replicated from conceptual association (or similarity of meaning) judgments without having to rate anyone's personality. Table II illustrates this point with special reference to Bales' three-factor classification of personality and interpersonal behavior in small groups.

Bales' three-factor classification ("power," "likeability," and "task-orientation") was first induced from the correlational structure of hundreds of individual difference variables on 60 subjects who participated in 12 five-person groups. Most of Bales' measures were memory-based, including three personality inventories (MMPI, Cattell's 16 PF test, and Thurstone's temperament test) and ratings by peers and outside observers. Bales then devised a 26-item interpersonal rating form to diagnose personality and classify group members in his three-dimensional scheme. The 26 items are listed in Table I.

Shweder (1975) analyzed the correlational structure of a rated behavior matrix for the 26 items in Table I and compared it with the correlational structure of a conceptual association matrix for the same items. The rated behavior matrix was derived from the peer ratings of members of a self-analytic group, and was scaled in three-dimensional space (MDSCALE) (see Table II). The conceptual association matrix was derived from sorting task data where judges were asked to place items "similar in meaning" together in the same pile. Pairs of items appearing in the same pile across judges received higher conceptual association scores. The resulting conceptual association matrix was also scaled in three-dimensional space (MDSCALE) (see Table II). The rated behavior matrix was compared to the conceptual association matrix by determining the extent to which the two scaling solutions yielded identical spatial coordinates for three dimensions. This comparison is also shown in Table II.

Table II lists the three-dimensional spatial coordinates for the 26 items (Table I) in both rated behavior and the preexisting conceptual association model of judges. The two classifications of the items are quite similar, as indicated by rank–order correlations (r_s) of .86, .88, and .70 between the three rated behavior

TABLE I

BALE'S 26-ITEM RATING FORM FOR PERSONALITY AND INTERPERSONAL BEHAVIOR[a]

1. Resentful
2. Admired
3. Dominating
4. Speaks like an autocratic authority
5. Devaluates himself
6. Makes others feel he admires them
7. Especially addressed when others have serious opinions about which they want confirmation
8. Stands for the most conservative ideas and beliefs of the group
9. Rejects religious belief generally
10. Liked
11. Feels that others are generally too conforming to conventional social expectations
12. Always tries to speak objectively
13. Thinks of himself as entertaining
14. Warm and personal
15. Accepts failure and withdrawal for himself
16. Identifies himself with the underprivileged
17. Demands pleasure and gratification
18. Believes that equality and humanitarian concerns for others are very important
19. Introverted
20. Believes it is necessary to sacrifice the self for higher values
21. Assumes responsibility for task leadership
22. Receives a lot of interaction from others
23. Valuable for a logical task
24. Feels that his individual independence is very important
25. Personally involved in the group
26. Passively withholds cooperation

[a] Adapted from Bales (1970).

dimensions, on the one hand, and the three corresponding conceptual association dimensions, on the other. Conceptual association judgments yield patterns of interitem proximity similar to the correlational structure of rated behavior.

Most personality classifications derived from memory-based assessment procedures can be reproduced from conceptual association judgments. To date the following memory-based personality classifications have been successfully retrieved using conceptual association techniques.

1. Factor-analytic classification of personality adjectives, as given in Norman (1963). See D'Andrade (1965) and Mulaik (1964).

2. Leary grid organization of interpersonal behavior, as given in LaForge and Suczek (1955). See D'Andrade (1965).

3. Factor-analytic classification of personality and interpersonal behavior, as given in Bales (1970). See Shweder (1972, 1975).

TABLE II

Bales' Three Dimensions of Personality and Interpersonal Behavior[a]

Item number	Power		Likeability		Task-orientation	
	Conceptual dimension	Rating dimension	Conceptual dimension	Rating dimension	Conceptual dimension	Rating dimension
1	−.38	.01	−.89	−.99	−.12	−.44
2	.18	.34	.74	.71	.27	.30
3	.71	.77	−.82	−.54	.06	.13
4	.63	.65	−1.00	−.71	−.05	.21
5	−1.13	−.99	−.06	.12	−.18	−.43
6	−.18	−.15	.89	1.06	−.00	−.00
7	.62	.66	.41	.31	.49	.36
8	.43	−.34	−.68	−.78	.29	.67
9	−.09	.03	−.44	−.12	.30	−.96
10	.65	−.01	.89	1.00	−.27	.20
11	−.23	.16	−.53	−.53	−.66	−.73
12	.00	−.02	.21	−.02	.95	1.00
13	.65	.64	.00	−.13	−.46	−.65
14	.38	−.10	1.04	1.03	−.36	−.18
15	−1.22	−1.14	−.09	−.46	.16	−.48
16	−.71	−.72	−.22	.36	−.71	−.41
17	.45	.51	−.55	−.78	−.48	−.43
18	−.29	−.41	.61	.80	−.38	−.01
19	−1.12	−1.28	−.26	−.15	.38	.17
20	−.70	−.46	−.09	.42	−.48	.49
21	.79	.75	.06	.02	.20	.44
22	.73	.79	.85	−.03	.16	.09
23	.28	.47	.45	.42	.92	.66
24	−.05	.34	−.83	−.75	.18	.24
25	.34	.40	1.11	.64	.00	−.05
26	−.76	−.90	−.78	−.90	−.19	−.19
r_s of conceptual dimension and rating dimension	.86		.88		.70	

[a] Conceptual association and memory-based rating dimensions compared. MDSCALE spatial coordinates.

4. Factor-analytic classification of maternal personality, as given in Sears *et al*. (1957). See Shweder (1975).

5. Correlation matrices for Bales Interaction Process Analysis categories used as rating scales, as given in Borgatta, Cottrell, and Mann (1958) and in Mann (1959). See D'Andrade (1974).

6. Partial correlation matrix for observers rating extroversion–introversion in boys, as given in Newcomb (1929). See Shweder (1975, 1977a).

7. The Alpha factor of the MMPI, as given in Block (1965). See Shweder (1977a, 1977b).

8. The common-factor structure of the Murray Needs from five personality tests as given in Fiske (1973) and in Huba and Hamilton (1976). See Ebbesen and Allen (1977).

9. Syndrome clusters from the Brief Psychiatric Rating Scales, as given in Overall *et al.* (1967). See Shweder and D'Andrade (1980).

10. Trait clusters of personality adjectives, as given in Rosenberg, Nelson, and Vivekananthan (1968). See Gara and Rosenberg (1981).

11. Factor-analytic classification of California Q-set variables, as given in Block *et al.* (1979). See Block *et al.* (1979).

The results of all these studies are remarkably uniform: the correlational structure of rated behavior matrices and the personality taxonomies retrieved from rated behavior matrices closely resemble a model of conceptual associations preexisting in the minds of raters.

The fit between conceptual association matrices and rated behavior matrices is a necessary but not sufficient piece of the evidence required to support the systematic distortion hypothesis. It is necessary because the hypothesis claims that the correlational structure of memory-based ratings is a reflection of judges' preexisting models of conceptual association but it is not sufficient because the fit between conceptual association matrices and rated behavior matrices is also consistent with an alternative "accurate reflection" hypothesis. As noted in Shweder and D'Andrade (1979, p. 1076), this alternative hypothesis "asserts that ordinary folk learn or develop 'implicit personality theories' that summarize and preserve the empirical covariation of behavior across individual differences in conduct. According to this [accurate reflection] hypothesis, people use empirically valid implicit personality theories in making conceptual similarity judgments, thereby accurately reporting the intercorrelations of behaviors." Advocates of the accurate reflection hypothesis include Passini and Norman (1966), Block *et al.* (1979), and Jackson *et al.* (1979).

What are conceptual association matrices all about? What are subjects telling us when they judge two personality descriptors (e.g., aggressive/dominant) similar in meaning? According to the systematic distortion hypothesis (Shweder & D'Andrade, 1979, p. 1081), similarity of meaning judgments are based on the relative number of predications common to the two terms being judged. There are many types of true things one can say about particular pairs of terms, for example, that both behaviors referred to by the terms make one (e.g.) angry, that the referred-to behaviors follow each other in a sequence, or share common characteristics. According to the systematic distortion hypothesis, similarity of meaning judgments vary directly with the ease with which subjects bring these predications to mind, and most of the truths which subjects bring to mind in making similarity of meaning judgments reveal little about the likelihood that the behaviors covary across individual differences in conduct. In contrast, according to the accurate reflection hypothesis, similarity of meaning judgments are more or less accurate probabilistic summaries of the actual correlational structure of individual differences.

Are similarity of meaning judgments reports about noncorrelational conceptual associations (systematic distortion hypothesis) or are they accurate summaries of correlational structure (accurate reflection hypothesis)? There are at least three methods for choosing between these two interpretations of conceptual association matrices.

One method is to elicit detailed introspective accounts of the reasoning that produces a similarity of meaning judgment. Ask subjects what they were thinking of when they judged (e.g.) "self-esteem" and "leadership" or "aggression" and "dominance" more similar in meaning than "pretentious" and "reclusive." Research by Shweder (1977c) suggests that ordinary folk have great difficulty with correlational reasoning (also see Smedslund, 1963; Ward & Jenkins, 1965; Jenkins & Ward, 1965; Crocker, 1981), and rely instead on semantic relationships other than correlation in making a similarity of meaning judgment (also see Shweder, 1972.)

Some pairs of terms, for example, "hostile" and "warm," are judged dissimilar in meaning either because the judge cannot imagine applying both terms to the same *act,* or because the two terms evoke opposed connotations (re: Osgood, Suci, & Tannenbaum, 1957). Those two types of semantic exclusions, of course, tell us nothing about whether people who tend to engage in more "hostile" acts than others are also less likely than others to engage in "warm" acts.

Other pairs of terms, for example, "aggression" and "dominance," are judged similar in meaning because they are sequentially linked segments in a common "script" (re: Abelson, 1976), viz. "fighting to get ahead in a hierarchy." This type of conceptual association, a scripted sequential dependency, again tells us little about individual differences, that is, whether people who exercise their authority more than others also tend to behave more aggressively.

Still other pairs of terms, for example, "self-esteem" and "leadership," are judged similar in meaning because they coexist as elements in an idealized behavioral type. Indeed many subjects estimate that there are far more "people with self-esteem" in the population than there are leaders, a base-rate estimate consistent with the view that most people with self-esteem are *not* leaders. However, subjects do not think of base-rates (see Lyon & Slovic, 1976) when they judge "self-esteem" and "leadership" similar in meaning. Instead, they think of Franklin Delano Roosevelt, John Kennedy, or some other embodiment of our culture's portrait of an ideal leader.

A good deal more work must be done on the diverse forms of conceptual association underlying similarity of meaning judgments. Two coding schemes for classifying types of conceptual associations have been proposed by Flavell and Stedman (1961) and Casagrande and Hale (1967) (see also D'Andrade, 1974). The very preliminary work reported in Shweder (1972, 1977c) suggests that similarity of meaning judgments have much to do with sequential scripting, shared denotations and connotations, shared effects, and part–part and part–whole relationships, and rather little to do with a process of correlational reasoning across individual differences in conduct.

Free associational methods (e.g., Szalay & Deese, 1978) provide a second way to choose between systematic distortion and accurate reflection interpretations of similarity of meaning judgments. The systematic distortion hypothesis predicts that direct pairwise similarity of meaning judgments should be reproducible from free associational data. That is, pairs of personality terms judged more similar in meaning should display more common associates on free associational tasks, and measures of conceptual proximity derived from free associational data should correlate with scaled judgments of likeness in meaning. The accurate reflection hypothesis makes no such prediction. Indeed, if similarity of meaning judgments are merely accurate reports of the intercorrelations among behaviors, free associational data should tell us little about what is like what in the minds of subjects.

No one has yet tried to replicate direct pairwise similarity of meaning judgments for personality terms using free associational techniques. Successful replications have been performed with terms from other domains (Szalay & Deese, 1978, pp. 116–120).

Gara and Rosenberg (1981), however, have elicited semantic feature descriptions for each of 20 personality adjectives. Subjects were asked, "What would lead you to label a person _____?" Two conceptual association matrices were derived using two different measures of interitem feature sharing, and these "shared feature" based conceptual association matrices were compared to a conceptual association matrix derived from direct similarity of meaning judgments. The two intermatrix correlations were .61 and .72. D'Andrade (1974) and Shweder (1977c) have argued that conceptual association matrices reflect a variety of types of conceptual relationships, including shared semantic features. In line with this observation, Gara and Rosenberg's (1981) work suggests that feature sharing is an important part, but only one part, of the story. For other techniques for deriving conceptual association matrices see Stefflre, Reich, and McClaren-Stefflre (1971) and D'Andrade, Quinn, Nerlove, and Romney (1972).

There is a third way to choose between systematic distortion vs accurate reflection interpretations of similarity of meaning judgments. According to the systematic distortion hypothesis, conceptual associations (shared features, scripted sequential dependencies, common effects, part–part relationships, etc.)

are poor indices of covariation relationships across individual differences in conduct. In contrast, the accurate reflection hypothesis holds that conceptual association matrices are reflections of implicit personality theories that summarize and preserve the empirical correlational structure of behaviors across personalities. To choose between the two hypotheses one need only compare, using the same items, the interitem similarity structure of conceptual association matrices with the interitem correlational structure of actual behavior matrices. To date comparisons with seven data sets have been performed (D'Andrade, 1974; Shweder, 1975, 1977a; Shweder & D'Andrade, 1980). For the most part, these comparisons support the systematic distortion hypothesis. Conceptual association matrices are weakly related to actual behavior matrices.

B. THE DISCREPANCY BETWEEN CONCEPTUAL ASSOCIATION MATRICES AND ACTUAL BEHAVIORAL MATRICES

There are relatively few behavior observational studies in the personality literature, probably because memory-based rating techniques (inventories, questionnaires, etc.) are so much easier to administer, score, and analyze. There are also relatively few multimethod studies in the personality literature, despite Campbell and Fiske's (1959) now "ancient" warning of the hazards of single method research. To test the systematic distortion hypothesis adequately, it is necessary to compare the correlational structure of equivalent sets of personality variables across conceptual association matrices, rated behavior matrices, and actual behavior matrices. Between D'Andrade (1974), Shweder (1975, 1977a), and Shweder and D'Andrade (1980), seven relevant data sets have been either located or generated. Two data sets each come from Borgatta et al. (1958), Mann (1959), and Newcomb (1929). One data set comes from Shweder and D'Andrade (1980).

All these data sets are multimethod sets, utilizing both behavior observational techniques and memory-based ratings. The behavior observational evidence varies from on-line videotape codings (Shweder & D'Andrade, 1980) to immediate scorings of the stream of behavior (Mann, 1959) and "daily records" (Newcomb, 1929) where observers were instructed to note the presence or absence of a type of behavior as soon after its occurrence as possible. For the Shweder and D'Andrade (1980) data, the interscorer reliability coefficients for 11 categories averaged .75. For the Newcomb data (1929), the odd- vs even-day reliability coefficient for 26 categories averaged .78. For the Mann (1959) data, a single observer did the scoring alone, but had been precalibrated to an interobserver reliability criterion of .90 on a majority of categories. Reliabilities in the Borgatta et al. (1958) study are more difficult to assess with precision on the basis of the published data (see Shweder & D'Andrade, 1979). Hopefully, this article will entice some readers to generate new multimethod data sets appropriate for testing the systematic distortion hypothesis.

As noted earlier, the accurate reflection hypothesis advocated by Passini and Norman (1966) and Jackson *et al.* (1979) has not fared well in direct comparisons of conceptual association matrices with actual behavior matrices. Across seven tests the average correlation between conceptual association matrices and actual behavior matrices is .26. The range is from −.05 to .51. With regard to the Newcomb data, where the accurate reflection hypothesis has its best showing, there is an average intermatrix correlation of .38 between the conceptual association matrices of each of 10 judges, on the one hand, and the actual behavior matrix of Newcomb's observers (Shweder, 1977a). Yet even this modest degree of fit should probably be discounted since the "immediate scorings" in the Newcomb data were not always "on-line," and were probably themselves subject to modest degrees of systematic distortion in the direction of preexisting conceptual associations.

Overall, similarity of meaning judgments do not seem to reflect empirically valid implicit personality theories; our preexisting models of what is like what do not seem to parallel closely the actual correlational structure of individual differences in conduct. "Aggression" and "dominance" or "criticism" and "disagreement" (e.g.) may associate in our minds but not in the organization of personality.

C. The Discrepancy between Rated Behavior Matrices and Actual Behavior Matrices

The systematic distortion hypothesis states that the broad syndromes, global traits, underlying factors, and general dimensions retrieved from memory-based rating data (inventories, questionnaires, etc.) tell us more about preexisting, noncorrelational patterns of conceptual association (semantic feature sharing, scripted sequential dependencies, common effects, etc.) than about what correlates with what across individual differences in conduct. In Section II,A I briefly reviewed the ever-growing body of evidence that rated behavior matrices replicate preexisting associative connections among personality descriptors. In Section II,B I noted that what evidence does exist suggests that conceptual associations among personality descriptors are only weakly related to the actual correlational structure of individual differences. The obvious implication is that rated behavior correlations also tell us little about what correlates with what in the structure of personality. Indeed, across the seven multimethod data sets mentioned earlier, the average correlation between rated behavior matrices and actual behavior matrices was .25 (D'Andrade, 1974; Shweder, 1975, 1977a; Shweder & D'Andrade, 1980).

As we have seen, the systematic distortion hypothesis requires evidence on the relationship between three types of data matrices. The ideal way to test the hypothesis is to have raters observe behavior in which what actually correlates with what across ratees is unrelated, or opposed, to what associates with what in the preexisting conceptual association scheme of raters. Will the interitem correlational structure of the (subsequently rated) rated behavior matrix replicate the interitem proximity structure of the preexisting conceptual association matrix, as predicted by the systematic distortion hypothesis, or will it correspond to the interitem correlational structure of the actual behavior matrix?

One such test can be found in Shweder's (1975) reanalysis of Newcomb's (1929) study of extroversion and introversion in the behavior of boys at summer camp. In one part of the reanalysis, Shweder (1975, pp. 464–466) deliberately selected 33 pairs of items (e.g., "speaks with confidence of his own abilities"– "spends more than an hour a day alone") to ensure that conceptual association scores would be radically inconsistent with actual behavior correlations. Each of the 33 item pairs either associated in the minds of judges and was not positively correlated in actual behavior, *or* did not associate in the minds of judges and did positively correlate in actual behavior. In effect, over the 33 pairs of items, the degree of correspondence between what correlated with what in actual behavior and what associated with what in the minds of raters was set at −.36. The interitem proximity structure of preexisting conceptual associations was in radical conflict with the interitem correlational structure of observed individual differences. Under these manipulated circumstances, what happened to the interitem correlational structure of memory-based ratings? Memory-based ratings of what correlated with what replicated the interitem proximity structure of preexisting conceptual associations ($r = .84$) and were insensitive to the interitem correlational structure of observed behavior ($r = -.27$). Similar results have been reported by Chapman and Chapman (1967, 1969).

In the study just described, Shweder preset, at $r = -.36$, the discrepancy between interitem conceptual associations and interitem actual behavior correlations. Under naturally occurring conditions, the fit between conceptual association matrices and actual behavior matrices seems to vary between approximately .00 and .50, and the validity of rated behavior matrices varies accordingly (D'Andrade, 1974; Shweder, 1975, 1977a; Shweder & D'Andrade, 1980).

To summarize, rated behavior matrices tell us more about diverse noncorrelational forms of conceptual association in the minds of raters than about what actually correlates with what across personalities, and these conceptual association clusters can be most easily discovered by simply asking a handful of subjects "what is like what," without any reference to anyone's behavior.

Does that mean that raters are blind, that we live in a linguistic fantasy world, or that personality doesn't exist? Perhaps it is time for a "first cut" at some potential misunderstandings.

D. POTENTIAL MISUNDERSTANDINGS: A FIRST CUT

There are many ways to misunderstand the systematic distortion hypothesis. Some of these misunderstandings will now be addressed.

1. Raters Are Not "Blind"

It would be a mistake to conclude that raters are typically ignorant of the persons rated, that their responses are fabricated, or that they are typically insensitive to the intensity of a signal. Indeed, most raters know a lot about the person rated and they can bring to mind some combination of recalled incidents and prior attributions. It is not what raters know that gets them into trouble, but rather the inferences they are prepared to draw starting from retrieved knowledge that is probably unrepresentative, on the one hand, and ending with generalizations that follow pathways of conceptual association rather than probabilistic association, on the other.

The point of the systematic distortion hypothesis is not that *particular* rater judgments are characteristically inaccurate. Indeed, in the Newcomb (1929) data, ratings for *single* variables correlated in the .40–.50 range with measures derived from daily records. The real point is that (a) raters are far from perfect and, when raters do make errors, their errors are *systematically biased,* not random; (b) the typical memory-based personality rating situation requires the rater to abstract and summarize a mass of observations from hours, days, weeks, or months of observation on multiple categories that vary in their base rates and cue frequencies—numerous opportunities for error and, thus, systematic bias, occur; and (c) 20 or 30% error variance on particular items is probably enough to support moderate size, illusory interitem correlations. The systematic distortion hypothesis does not imply that raters are insensitive to a signal or only see what they expect to see!

2. "How People Classify," Not "Who Gets Classified How"

To understand the systematic distortion hypothesis one must honor the distinction between "classification" and "identification." Following Sokal (1974), classification can be defined as "the ordering or arrangements of objects into groups or sets on the basis of their relationships" (hence, the concern for correlational structure); identification can be defined as "the allocation or assignment of additional unidentified objects to the correct class, once such classes have been established by prior classification." The systematic distortion hypothesis is concerned with "how people classify" (classifications), not "who gets classified how" (identifications) (D'Andrade, 1965).

Classification and identification are different cognitive activities. Scientific classifications are designed to summarize the relationships among variables ("things that are hot" are "things that hurt," people who are "friendly" are "not aggressive") (Gilmour, 1937) and thus help us make valid inductive generalizations. But, as Hakel (1971) notes, sharing a structure of intervariable inferences among personality variables (classification) does not necessarily standardize agreement on the personality attributes that apply to ratees (identification). "Two raters might have identical patterns of trait intercorrelations and show no agreement [on whether such-and-such rating category applies to such-and-such ratee] ($r = .00$) or even perfect disagreement ($r = -1.00$)." The systematic distortion hypothesis is concerned with the scientific status (internal homogeneity and external validity) of the categories into which people are classified (e.g., introversion: hesitant to speak before a group, does not like parties, prefers to work alone) not with the question whether Aunt Sally is an "introvert."

III. The Systematic Distortion Hypothesis and Personality Structure

The systematic distortion hypothesis is a critique of the validity of personality classifications induced from memory-based personality ratings, implicit personality theory, or conceptual association judgments. The hypothesis implies that if one were to eliminate error and systematic bias from memory-based personality data, one would not discover global traits, broad syndromes, or general factors, but rather a complex of context-dependent truths, person by situation by response mode statistical interaction effects, and unstable intercorrelations among events, or alternatively said, that which is accurate in personality ratings would not support a global trait approach to individual differences in conduct.

A. THE GLOBAL TRAIT MODEL

A global trait theory of personality is an explanatory theory of a particular kind. It sets as its goal the reduction of the complexity and diversity of individual differences over time and context to a limited set of underlying forces in terms of which individuals may be said to differ regularly, a limited set of "more or less stable internal factors that make one person's behavior consistent from one time to another, and different from the behavior other people would manifest in comparable situations" (Child, 1968, p. 83).

A global trait theory is successful if its categories can be applied to make the diversity of individual differences appear consistent across situations, response modes, and time. Global trait theorists commit themselves to each of the following claims.

1. People differ in their behavior in comparable situations. (*Note:* the comparability of the situations in which differences in behavior are observed is crucial. Global trait theorists are not interested in why some people talk more in debating clubs than other people talk in libraries.)

2. Within any given situation there are behaviors which distinguish people from one another, and there are behaviors which do not distinguish people from one another. That is to say, investigators can separate behaviors typical of the situation, things anyone would do "under the circumstances," from the be-

haviors with respect to which individual *differences* are observed *in that situa-tion*. The fact that (e.g.) some students take notes during a lecture while others do not *is* grist for the mill of the global trait theorist. The fact that all students sit down in their seats during the lecture is *not* grist for the mill of the global trait theorist.

3. For any given person there are two sets of behaviors. One set consists of those individual difference behaviors that are characteristic of a particular person in the situations in which his or her behavior has been observed. The other set consists of those individual difference behaviors observed in the situations in which his or her behavior has been observed that are not characteristic of the person's behavior (i.e., behavior characteristic of other people's behavior in those situations).

4. The behaviors in both sets can be shown to be reducible to a relatively small set of theoretical categories which reveal the broad underlying generality of behavioral differences. For example, think of all the diverse behaviors (walks alone, tends to depression, easily hurt, worries over possible misfortune, reads a lot, suspicious of the motives of others, attends to details, daydreams, avoids talking before a group) that are theoretically equated and unified by the single underlying category, "introversion."

The first three propositions listed are endorsed by all individual difference theorists, and remain uncontroversial. The fourth proposition, however, is dis-tinctive of global trait theorists, and that is where the arguments begin (e.g., Mischel, 1968, 1973; Raush, Dittmann, & Taylor, 1959; Moos, 1969; Shweder, 1973, 1979a; Nisbett, 1980).

Global trait theorists seek to reduce the diversity of individual differences in behavior to a limited number of underlying factors (proposition 4). This is done empirically by detecting redundancies in the correlational structure of individual difference variables across response modes (the extroverted person is more likely to talk, make friends, and lend his possessions), and situations (the extroverted person is more likely to make friends at a party and in the dormitory). For the most part, the correlational redundancies among personality variables required to support global trait theory have been retrieved from response patterns on memory-based instruments. Child psychologists concerned with child-rearing practices speak of mothers who are "permissive" and point to a redundant cluster of correlated scales on a socialization questionnaire (e.g., Sears *et al.*, 1957). Clinical psychologists concerned with psychopathology speak of persons who are "ego-resilient" and point to a correlated pattern of scales on the MMPI (Block, 1965). Let us depart for a moment from this tradition of constructing personality taxonomies out of test responses, especially since what we are dis-cussing is systematic bias in memory-based procedures.

Presumably, personality researchers became interested in rating and inventory behavior not because they were interested in this type of behavior per se, but rather because it promised to be a cheap indicator or proxy for what they were really interested in, namely, the way people differ from one another in their feelings, thoughts, and actions across more important and relevant settings than the personality test context.

What type of classification of individual differences would we construct if we restricted ourselves to the data that really interest us, viz., reasonably systematic and reliable ongoing records of actual conduct across various response modes and naturalistic situations? Would we induce global traits, broad underlying factors, and generalized dimensions of individual difference? The answer is not favorable for global trait theory.

B. THE FAILURE OF THE GLOBAL TRAIT MODEL

The systematic distortion hypothesis challenges us to construct a model of personality structure with data from on-line records of conduct instead of memory-based assessment procedures. When one shifts methods from memory-based measures to behavioral observational techniques, one discovers that the world of individual differences is not organized in the way envisioned by global trait theorists. Individual differences exist (propositions 1–3), of course, but they do not seem to generalize widely across similar response modes or situations.

There are relatively few homogeneous multiitem clusters (e.g., dependent: seeks help, seeks attention, seeks physical proximity) that can be induced from behavior observational data on individual differences. Most personality researchers who collect data using on-line, immediate scoring techniques tend to discover complex person by response mode by situation statistical interaction effects. The observed set of individual difference behaviors characteristic of most persons (see Section III,A, proposition 3) looks (e.g.) as follows: speaks well in public, slow to make friends, prefers to work alone, sociable at parties. Such sets of behavior are not easily reducible to a small set of underlying global traits. Stated alternatively, when individual differences are observed across theoretically similar response modes (e.g., seeks attention, seeks help), and across naturally occurring situations (e.g., at home and at school), hypothesized global traits (e.g., "dependency," "assertiveness," "risk-taker") typically account for no more than 10% of the diversity of individual differences. The financial "risk-taker" is not the social "risk-taker," and the child who seeks help is not typically the one who seeks physical nearness (see, e.g., Newcomb, 1929; Raush *et al.*, 1959; Raush, Farbman, & Llewellyn, 1960; Sears, 1963; Longabaugh, 1966; Mischel, 1968; Moos, 1969; Slovic, 1972; Shweder, 1973, 1979a; Whiting & Whiting, 1975, p. 163; Cronbach, 1975; Yarrow & Waxler, 1976; Fiske, 1978).

Our ability to predict individual differences is substantially augmented if response mode and context are taken into account. One implication of this fact is that scientific personality taxonomies cannot be directly borrowed from the global abstract trait lexicon of implicit personality theory (e.g., "dependent," "friendly," "honest," "responsible"). Since high-order statistical interaction effects (time, place, response mode, dyad, etc.) prevail, scientific personality classifications must concretely specify the response mode and the contextual conditions under which correlational patterns can be expected to be found. Indeed, from a behavior observational point of view, one should probably not speak of "children who are dependent," but rather of "children who seek attention," on the one hand, and "children who seek physical nearness," on the other. And, if one were to find subsequently that "children who seek attention from their mothers in the playground" are not more likely than other children to "seek attention from their mothers at home," one would again want to revise one's taxonomic categories by writing in more context (reference to time, place, personnel, etc.).

The systematic distortion hypothesis challenges us to confirm global trait personality taxonomies with systematically collected, reliable, on-line behavior observational evidence. When Newcomb tried this in 1929, he discovered that individual difference variables that should have correlated according to global trait theory were no more significantly intercorrelated in actual behavior than a random selection of variables. Shweder (1973) discovered a similar thing in an examination of reported behavior observational intercorrelations among various indicators of "nurturance" and "egoism." Global trait categories like "nurturance" generate a theoretical expectation that (e.g.) children who "offer help" more than others are more likely than others to "make responsible suggestions" and less likely than others to "seek help." An examination of on-line data collected by L. Minturn (reported in Longabaugh, 1966) found little support for these theoretical expectations.

Global trait predictions generally have not fared well in the confrontation with behavior observational evidence. Therefore, one goal of global trait theorists probably cannot be realized, viz., to derive a parsimonious taxonomy that will enable them to predict validly individual differences in one context and response mode from knowledge of individual differences in another context or response mode. As Raush et al. (1960) remark, it is the "idiosyncratic" or "interactive" effects, "the particular meaning that a particular situation has for a particular person that is the major determinant of behavior." Memory-based ratings incline to the nomothetic; behavior observational evidence inclines to the idiographic.

C. POTENTIAL MISUNDERSTANDINGS: A SECOND CUT

There are many ways to misunderstand what has just been said about personality structure and the systematic distortion hypothesis. Some of these potential misunderstandings will now be addressed.

1. Personality Does Exist

The systematic distortion hypothesis does not deny the existence of trait dispositions. It does deny the existence of global traits, as retrieved from memory-based assessment procedures. The issue is not whether traits or individual differences exist, but rather how widely they generalize. We may well live in a world where an internally homogeneous, stable trait disposition is the tendency for middle-aged men to get angry when extravagantly dressed middle-aged women cut in front of them in line, but that regularity in someone's conduct may tell us little about whether he is more likely than others to get angry when contradicted in an argument at a scientific meeting.

2. Situationalism Is No Alternative to Personality Theory

The idea that global traits do not exist and that individual differences are narrowly context-dependent does not imply that situation or context is all there is to behavior. That would be tantamount to denying the existence of individual differences within situations, which would be ridiculous. Moreover, it is probably the case that, just as personality dispositions are context-dependent, situational influences are person-dependent (e.g., Raush et al., 1959; Moos, 1969). The way situations differ in their ability to elicit certain kinds of behaviors (e.g., cooperation, aggressiveness) typically depends on which person is involved. Statistical interaction effects are multiple necessary conditions (Kelley, 1972). Broad "main effects" are relatively rare for situations as well as persons.

3. There's More to Personality than Global Traits

The systematic distortion hypothesis does not presuppose that the only legitimate goal for personality researchers is to predict individual differences in one context from knowledge of individual differences in other contexts. The aims of the nomothetic taxonomist are not coincidental with the goals of personality research. Indeed, idiographic, clinical insight often involves an appreciation of unique context–person–response mode interactions and the acquired (and possibly unconscious) meanings of specific stimuli for specific persons (see Shweder, 1980b). There is more to personality than global traits.

4. Factor Analysis Is a Fine Thing

It would be a misunderstanding of the systematic distortion hypothesis to conclude that factor analysis, multidimensional scaling, and other statistical procedures for arriving at global multiitem categories are of limited usefulness in the study of human conduct. The implications of the systematic distortion hypothesis are restricted to personality classification per se, that is, the way individuals differ from each other across a variety of response modes and contexts as revealed by immediate scorings of conduct. It is quite possible there are global factors or dimensions that can be induced from behavioral records when one switches from studying individual differences to studying the way behaviors correlate across units such as dyads, behavioral episodes, and groups (see Shweder, 1972, 1973).

5. There Are No "Immaculate Perceptions"

The systematic distortion hypothesis is a critique of the validity of item–item correlational structures retrieved from memory-based personality ratings. The validity of rated behavior matrices is called into question by comparing their correlational structure to that of immediate, on-line scorings of conduct. The appeal to behavior observational evidence does not imply that theory, interpretation, and judgment should be banished from personality research, nor does it suggest that immediate, on-line scorings of conduct are "immaculate perceptions." The two critical assumptions made by advocates of the systematic distortion hypothesis are (a) what on-line scorers mean by (e.g.) "criticizes," or any other coding category is not different from what memory-based raters mean by the same category; and (b) reliable on-line scorings are a closer approximation of the correlational structure of actual behavior than are memory-based ratings.

On-line scorings are not interpretation-free; behavior is not self-describing. There are many ways to "code" behavior—each coding scheme transforms a behavioral event into a theory-laden significance. Is behavior to be described in terms of muscle twitches or actor intentions? If intentions are to be inferred, how much context should the coder appeal to in inferring the intention? Should the coder appeal to the outcome of the act, its effects on others, the actor's stated goals, events from earlier that day, earlier that year, or perhaps events prior to the actor's own recall (e.g., events from the first few years of life that unconsciously motivate the coded event)? Different coding schemes "translate" the stream of behavior in different ways. The systematic distortion hypothesis assumes only that whatever coding scheme is used, on-line scorers speak the same "language" as memory-based raters.

6. Some People Do Have Global Traits

The systematic distortion hypothesis implies that, given most global trait categories or factors (e.g., dependent vs self-reliant, egotistical vs altruistic), most people will mix together in their behavior items that should not go together from the point of view of the trait category. This implication does not deny that some people display global generality. Indeed, it may also be the case that for any particular person one or more aspects of his or her personality are characterized by global generality. The main difficulty emphasized by the systematic distortion hypothesis is that, from a *nomothetic* point of view, one can predict too few of the people too much of the time (*pace* Bem, 1974).

7. Aggregation Is Not the Answer

The idea of a global trait (e.g., extroversion) is that individual differences generalize widely across similar response modes (talkative, energetic, organizes activities) and across comparable situations for equivalent response modes (talks to his wife at dinner, talks to his or her colleagues at faculty meetings). The systematic distortion hypothesis states that memory-based evidence of internal homogeneity among trait indicators cannot be trusted, and that behavior observational evidence will not reveal the pattern of interitem correlations necessary to support the global trait concept.

Do global traits emerge from aggregated behavior observational evidence? Data are aggregated or pooled primarily to compensate for a "noisy" channel (measurement error due to faulty instruments), or to amplify a weak signal. Most of the observational evidence referred to in this article is derived from data aggregated over several occasions (see Nisbett, 1980, for a review). Newcomb's (1929) data, for example, are derived from 24 days of observation with odd- vs even-day reliabilities of .78. For obvious reasons, however, the data are aggregated across repeated occasions, but not across similar response modes or equivalent response modes for different situations. According to the systematic distortion hypothesis, similar response modes and equivalent response modes for different situations are not sufficiently intercorrelated to support the idea that people have global traits consisting of covarying behaviors. To aggregate data across similar response modes and across different situations would be tantamount to canceling by methodological fiat precisely those statistical interactions of person–situation–response mode that are embarrassing to the global trait concept (see Mischel & Peake, 1981).

IV. The Systematic Distortion Hypothesis and Implicit Personality Theory

Within personality psychology there are two widespread beliefs about implicit personality theory. The first belief is that ordinary language dictionary entries for personality and interpersonal behavior (e.g., industrious, honest, cooperative, dependent) are lexical labels for quasi-scientific categories. The descriptors in our everyday lexicon are often appropriated into academic discourse as though they were inductive summary formulas about personality dispositions which had utility in predicting future events and minimizing surprise (Brown, 1965, p. 612). The trait lexicon as a whole is often viewed as a "coding system" for "packaging" information about the correlational structure of individual difference variables (Cattell, 1943; Bruner, Shapiro, & Tagiuri, 1958; Passini & Norman, 1966; Jackson *et al.*, 1979). Utilizing this ordinary language lexicon as a coding system, ordinary folk are thought to develop more or less accurate implicit personality theories about what correlates with what across individual differences in conduct (e.g., people who are ''self-reliant'' are also ''responsible'').

The second prevalent belief in personality psychology is that if our ordinary language coding scheme yields inaccurate knowledge about what goes with what in personality, then ordinary language terms (e.g., self-reliant, aggressive, friendly, responsible, dependent) are either linguistic artifacts of no genuine importance, or should disappear from the language. I am doubtful of both beliefs.

One implication of the systematic distortion hypothesis is that ordinary language trait terms for describing personality and interpersonal behavior are too undifferentiated, too global to be scientifically useful. Individual differences are not stabilized and packaged at the abstract level of ''dependent,'' ''honest,'' and ''hostile,'' but rather at concrete levels such as ''tends to seek help when adults are around,'' ''cheats at poker,'' or ''gets irritated if evidence for global traits cannot be retrieved from behavior observational evidence.'' A scientifically useful coding scheme for personality differences must be sufficiently differentiated to encode individual differences by means of response mode descriptors (e.g., ''seeks help'') and situational descriptors (e.g., ''from male adults'').

The inferences one can draw from our ordinary trait lexicon are not useful for predicting future events and minimizing surprise. It does not follow, however, from this implication of the systematic distortion hypothesis, that our ordinary trait lexicon has no important function in human affairs, or is a linguistic artifact on the wane. It does not follow because there is no reason to postulate that ordinary language terms have evolved to serve only the goals of inductive science, no reason to assume that the activities in which trait descriptors play a part in everyday life are only scientific activities, and no reason to reduce the uses of language to the aims of science. Our trait lexicon may well serve important functions other than summarizing and encoding correlational structure.

A. THE USES OF A TRAIT LEXICON: SCIENTIFIC VS NONSCIENTIFIC FUNCTIONS

When are ordinary language trait terms actually used? At what types of occasions is personality trait talk to be found? For the moment these questions cannot be answered with any confidence; we know little about the way our trait lexicon is actually used in everyday life. Thus, I can only speculate and look forward to future research.

What little do we know about the scientific and nonscientific uses of our ordinary trait lexicon? A priori, one can imagine nonscientific functions. Most trait terms can be used as adjectives of appraisal communicating either approval (''thrifty'') or critical evaluation (''stingy''). Trait terms can be used to inspire conduct ("be courageous"), to proscribe conduct ("stop being so dependent"), or to influence the way others will feel about or react to a person ("he's dishonest"). Given the diverse functions of language—the rhetorical, the persuasive, the regulatory, the symbolic—there seems to be no a priori reason to assume that trait terms evolved to serve scientific functions exclusively.

There are other reasons to doubt that our ordinary trait lexicon evolved as a scientific coding scheme. Ordinary folk do not need global trait terms to describe one another's personalities and do not always use global terms. In one cross-cultural study of free descriptions of personality, for example, Shweder and Bourne (1981) discovered that 46% of American descriptors and 20% of Oriya (Indian) descriptors are unqualified global trait attributions. Eighty percent of Oriya descriptors (and 54% of American descriptors) referred to either response mode ("she shouts profanities") or context ("she brings cakes for my children on festival days"), and this despite the fact that the Oriya language is rich in global trait descriptors and Oriya informants are capable of generating global trait terms. It is by no means obvious that interpersonal *description* in everyday life is typically executed at the abstract level of our trait lexicon.

Moreover, ordinary folk do not typically *explain* one another's conduct by means of our personality trait lexicon. For example, in one quasi-naturalistic study, Lewis (1978) asked informants to explain why someone in their immediate environment was doing whatever he or she was doing. Lewis discovered that less than 5% of everyday explanations of conduct (why is he out jogging today?) is in global trait form (e.g., "he's compulsive"). He discovered that everyday explanations for actions are typically goal-oriented (e.g., "he's studying because he has an exam tomorrow) and everyday explanations for emotions are typically situationalist—emotions are thought to be externally elicited, not voluntarily willed (e.g., "she's feeling nervous because the highway is covered with ice"). Global personality trait explanations seem to be relatively rare in everyday life.

When is our global trait lexicon utilized? More research has to be done before this question can be answered with any confidence. Speculating, I would hold out "personnel selection" as the paradigmatic "language game" within which global trait terms are bandied about. By "personnel selection" I mean any occasion that requires justifying the allocation of individuals to positions in social groups and social networks.

Members of functioning social groups must answer certain perennial questions about the recruitment of members, the selection of leaders, and the formation of bonds of intimacy, cooperation, and sharing. Who's in and who's out? Who's up and who's down? Who's close and who's distant? (Schutz, 1967; Bales, 1968, 1970). All of us, as members of collectivities, routinely make decisions about who should be accepted, promoted, retained, confided in, allied with, delegated responsibility, etc. These are the personnel selection decisions of everyday life.

My speculation suggests that around such decisions global personality trait talk plays a major part (in gossip, recommendations, formal decision making, etc.). This should be true in all societies, but especially so in a voluntaristic, individualistic culture where entrenched values make it reprehensible to accept, promote, embrace, or befriend on the basis of family connections, birthright, caste, color, etc. Thus, it is not surprising that underlying group structure, role perception, and personality attribution is a universal semantic space for conveying messages about hierarchy-subordination and solidarity-conflict (Bales, 1970; Shweder, 1972; Kirk & Burton, 1977; White, 1980), a common semantic space that makes it possible to "map" personality trait labels (assertive, self-esteem, self-reliant) onto social positions (e.g., "leader").

Why should personnel selection be carried on with terms from our global trait lexicon? One conceivable answer is that global trait attributions predict role performance. Perhaps information about peer or interviewer impressions coded in global trait terms (self-reliant, responsible, honest) reduces uncertainty about how people will conduct themselves as leader, friend, ally, subordinate, etc. There is not much convincing evidence to encourage us in this view.

Global trait attributions are notoriously unreliable. Indeed, merely to attain respectable split-half interobserver reliabilities from lay observers using our global trait lexicon as a coding scheme one must pool the attributions of approximately eight observers (Smith, 1967), a procedure rarely followed in everyday life. Pairwise interobserver reliabilities seem to range from .15 to .35 (Hakel, 1971; Fiske, 1978). Indeed, Bourne (1977) discovered that pairs of observers of the same person agreed only about 20% of the time in their attributive selection of global trait labels. Observers of two different people agreed 16% of the time. The difference in amount of agreement, two observing one and two observing two, was not significant.

Moreover, role performance is probably quite sensitive to "treatment effects" (Einhorn & Hogarth, 1978; Einhorn, 1980). Those who are accepted, selected as leaders, made intimates, etc., are given opportunities and treated in ways withheld from those who are rejected, kept at a distance, etc. It is much easier to be cooperative when someone holds out a hand. It remains to be seen whether the allocation of people to social positions, solely on the basis of the global trait impressions of three or four peers, yields significantly more effective leaders, cooperative allies, loyal employees, etc., than a selection procedure among qualified recruits based on a random number table or astrological chart. My suspicion is that the results would not justify a heavy investment in the attributive use of our global trait lexicon.

Thus, I am led to consider a second conceivable answer to the question: Why should personnel selection be carried on with terms from our global trait lexicon? Perhaps personality trait talk serves a symbolic function, not a predictive one. Perbaps personnel selection is a gloss for an expressive ritual in which we say something with words and action about our cultural values, concepts of the person, and views of man in society (for a discussion of expressive rituals, see Shweder, 1981). If groups are to function, decisions must be made about how to distribute individuals to positions in social groups and networks. But, if interobserver reliability is low, interitem correlations among indicators of the "same" global trait are weak, and treatment effects are substantial, it is conceivable that, apart from gross screening, *from a predictive point of view*, almost any selection device will do. Note, however, that not any selection device will do from a *symbolic point of view*.

The principles we use to allocate individuals to social roles express something about our values, goals, and view of the "person." A culture like our own, deeply committed to the axiom or premise that society derives its authority from the consent of autonomous and unique individuals, takes an interest in the search for an underlying, stable core character, and has reason to subscribe to the fiction that personality fits the role (see Selby, 1974, 1975, for an alternative, Zapatec view). Neither a random number table nor a geneological tree are the right kind of symbol for the image of man enshrined in our culture. Indeed, some of the best predictors of role performance, race, religion, and sex are ignored because they imply social classifications symbolically offensive to our axiomatic notions of justice, personal achievement, and individualism.

It should be reemphasized that much of what has just been said is speculation designed to encourage future research. One central point, however, should not be lost in the midst of this speculation: Ordinary language global trait terms are not necessarily labels for scientific categories. Our global trait lexicon may serve functions other than packaging information about the correlational structure of individual differences in conduct.

It is hoped that the implication of this point is also clear: The persistence of global trait categories in ordinary language may be unrelated to issues of truth or falsity. One should not expect trait terms to go away simply because they fail to yield valid predictions about what correlates with what across personalities, nor should one doubt that our trait lexicon fails to yield valid predictions simply because it has not gone away.

B. POTENTIAL MISUNDERSTANDINGS: A THIRD CUT

There are a number of ways to misunderstand what has been said about lexical categories, the scientific and nonscientific functions of language, and implicit personality theory. Some of these potential misunderstandings will now be addressed.

1. Global Trait Terms Are Not Linguistic Artifacts

The systematic distortion hypothesis does not imply that our ordinary language lexicon of global trait terms (e.g., responsible, dependent) comprises merely labels for deficient scientific categories or linguistic artifacts of no importance. It is certainly true that in the hands of some personality trait theorists our ordinary language trait lexicon has been appropriated for scientific use, for which it is probably deficient. It is also true that ordinary folk sometimes use global trait terms for interpersonal description, although global trait terms are rarely used to explain behavior. However, language serves many functions: descriptive, prescriptive, rhetorical, persuasive, regulatory. Although global trait categories are poor scientific categories this does not mean that our trait lexicon has no important place in our culture.

2. Language Does Not Correspond to Reality

The systematic distortion hypothesis implies that the various referents (e.g., seeks help, seeks attention, seeks proximity) of a global trait term (e.g., dependent) do not typically hang together, empirically cohere, or intercorrelate across personalities; likeness is not paralleled by cooccurrence likelihood. Some critics of the systematic distortion hypothesis treat this implication as a denial of a premise they take to be self-evident, viz. that words are related to, or correspond to, things in reality. The language–reality correspondence assumption is probably widespread. Before debating its implications for the systematic distortion hypothesis it may be useful to clarify what it means. Upon examination, the notion of language–reality correspondence seems to me to be a premise without promise.

The idea that words are related (or correspond) to things in reality is an empty notion, until one specifies the particular way words are supposed to be related to things in reality. It is necessary to be specific because there are obviously many ways words are not related to things in the world—many ways in which the idea of language–reality correspondence is plainly false. No one, for example, would ask how the world is spelled (see Goodman, 1960), nor would anyone suggest that the sequential order of words in a sentence is paralleled by some sequential order of the things mentioned by the words in a sentence, nor would anyone suggest that big words (e.g., "microorganism") are names for big things. So, in what way are words related to things in reality?

It is, of course, quite undeniable that words are related to things in the world in at least one sense: Words *are* things in the world. But that is a trivial point.

Words are also related to things in the world in a second sense: Words *refer* to things in the world, although some of the things in the world they refer to are other words, symbols, and representations. If all words have reference, then some of the things they refer to must be other words, symbols, and representations. This qualification is necessary if one is to explain the *difference* in meaning of such terms as "poo-poo," "feces," and "shit," all of which refer to the same nonlinguistic thing in the world, or the difference in meaning of terms such as "elf," "centaur," and "unicorn," all of which refer to nothing except perhaps things in the world like descriptions, stories, or drawings of "elves," "centaurs," and "unicorns" (see Goodman, 1949, 1968).

Not much follows, however, from the fact that words have reference. Certainly it does not follow that the things referred to by words are like the words themselves or correspond to them. A knee, for example, is part of a body. Does it follow that the word "knee" is part of the word "body"?

But, perhaps I have missed some subtlety in the apparently naive premise that language corresponds to reality. Fortunately, the claims of the systematic distortion hypothesis are less subtle: (a) There are many true things one can say about pairs of behavioral descriptors (e.g., the behaviors referred to by the descriptors have overlapping reference, the behaviors follow one another in a script, the behaviors are both parts of an image of a behavioral type, the behaviors are pleasant, sexy, and powerful); (b) most of the true things one can say about pairs of behaviors reveal little about the joint probability of occurrence of the behaviors across personalities; and (c) judges on memory-based assessment procedures confuse one set of truths (likeness, sequential dependency, part–part, common effect, etc.) with a second set (i.e., cooccurrence likelihood).

Fortunately, the distinction between likeness and likelihood is honored by most of us, even when, in our less vigilant moments, we slip into the careless assumption that language corresponds to the world. For if language and conceptual associations did imitate reality, we would not have to observe behavior at all. Face validity would guarantee internal and external validity. That would be very strange, indeed. Unfortunately, that seems to be what has happened in the personality psychology literature. Sets of items that have face validity conceptually associate in the minds of raters. Raters report correlational structures that replicate their preexisting associative networks, thereby producing illusory evidence of internal and external validity. Propositions about likeness are confused with propositions about cooccurrence likelihood. Ideas become reality.

3. Ordinary Folk Do Have Valid Social Knowledge

The systematic distortion hypothesis raises doubts about our knowledge of correlational structure and suggests that our correlational beliefs are not always in rapport with the contingent structure of our environment. The hypothesis does not imply, however, that we lack valid social knowledge or that valid correlational beliefs about individual differences are necessary for successful adaptation in a social environment.

The concept of correlation is a formal operational one (Inhelder & Piaget, 1958); it calls for a comparison of two conditional probabilities. Recent research suggests that normal, intelligent adults are disinclined to formal operational thinking (Wason & Johnson-Laird, 1972; Tversky & Kahneman, 1974) and have difficulty processing correlation-relevant information (Smedslund, 1963; Ward & Jenkins, 1965; Shweder, 1977c; Shweder & D'Andrade, 1980). It seems to me that one implication of this research is that many adaptive processes do not require formal operational thinking, and may only require limited intellectual skills. In everyday social life, one can get quite far with the ability to imitate, to notice things that are contiguous in time or space, to recognize things one has seen before, and to estimate relative frequencies. Valid correlational thinking may not be a requisite for social adaptation.

Ordinary folk do possess valid social knowledge and much of the social knowledge they possess requires relatively low-level, mundane inference abilities. Some of this knowledge is episodic and script-like (Schank & Abelson, 1977; Forgas, 1979); we know the social routines and sequential steps for "going to the restaurant," "greeting a friend," "interviewing a prospective employee," or we know how to find out about the routine (e.g., "buying a house"). Some of the knowledge is repetitive and context-specific; we know how so-and-so behaved last time under such-and-such circumstances (past behavior predicts future behavior), and we know the kinds of things so-and-so wants and how to manipulate them to get him or her to do what we want (context-specific knowledge of "reinforcers"). There is no reason to assume that our potential for adaptive behavior must be derived from some supposed formal operational ability. The context-specific intellectual demands of everyday social life may not be very great.

V. Conclusion: From Likeness to Likelihood

The systematic distortion hypothesis casts doubt on the belief that people have global personality traits consisting of multiitem covarying behaviors. The hypothesis implies that individual differences are not organized in the way envisioned by global trait theorists. According to the systematic distortion hypothesis, individual differences do not generalize very widely, that is, there are few empirically homogenous multiitem categories (e.g., "altruistic," "dependent," "extroverted") that can be induced from the interitem correlational structure of behavior observational data on individual differences.

The systematic distortion hypothesis states that judges on memory-based personality assessment instruments (inventories, rating forms, questionnaires) either infer correlational structure from a general model of conceptual association, or find conceptually associated memory items easier to retrieve. Conceptual proximity is utilized as a guide for estimating cooccurrence probability, thereby replicating a preexisting associative network that has little to do with what correlates with what across personalities. Likeness is substituted for likelihood. Thus, according to the systematic distortion hypothesis, correlational clusters (i.e., global traits) derived from memory-based procedures cannot be treated as accurate reflections of the empirical correlational structures of behavior.

The systematic distortion hypothesis challenges us to anchor our claims about the organization of individual differences in the firmer ground of reliable, on-line behavioral observational evidence. There would, of course, be little point in utilizing data-gathering techniques which require that we engage in the arduous and time-consuming enterprise of observing, immediately recording, and coding a heavy dose of behavioral occurrences, *if* we could rely on raters to abstract and summarize the essentials from masses of behavioral events. Unfortunately, human memory and inference are subject to many influences, one of which is the structure of conceptual associations among the descriptors we use to assess behavior. Years of saved time are no consolation for invalid results.

References

Abelson, R. P. Script processing in attitude formation and decision making. In J. S. Carroll & J. W. Payne (Eds.), *Cognition and social behavior*. Hillsdale, N.J.: Erlbaum, 1976.

Bales, R. F. Interaction process analysis. *International Encyclopedia of the Social Sciences*, 1968, **7**, 465–471.

Bales, R. F. *Personality and interpersonal behavior*. New York: Holt, 1970.

Bem, D. On predicting some of the people some of the time. *Psychological Review*, 1974, **81**, 506–520.

Berman, J. S., & Kenny, D. A. Correlational bias in observational ratings. *Journal of Personality and Social Psychology*, 1976, **34**, 263–273.

Block, J. *The challenge of response sets*. New York: Appleton, 1965.

Block, J. An illusory interpretation of the First Factor of the MMPI: A reply to Shweder. *Journal of Consulting and Clinical Psychology*, 1977, **45**, 930–935.

Block, J., Weiss, D. S., & Thorne, A. How relevant is a semantic similarity interpretation of personality ratings? *Journal of Personality and Social Psychology*, 1979. **37**, 1055–1074.

Borgatta, E. F., Cottrell, L. S., & Mann, J. H. The spectrum of individual interaction characteristics: An interdimensional analysis. *Psychological Reports*, 1958, **4**, 275–319.

Borman, W. C. Personality research and performance appraisal. In F. Landy & S. Zedeck (Eds.), *Performance measurement*. Hillsdale, N.J.: Erlbaum, 1982, in press.

Bourne, E. Can we describe an individual's personality? Agreement on stereotype versus individual attributes. *Journal of Personality and Social Psychology*, 1977, **35**, 863–872.

Brown, R. *Social psychology*. New York: Free Press, 1965.

Bruner, J., Shapiro, D., & Tagiuri, R. The meaning of traits in isolation and combination. In R. Tagiuri & L. Petrullo (Eds.), *Person perception and interpersonal behavior*. Stanford, Calif.: Stanford Univ. Press, 1958.

Campbell, D. T., & Fiske, D. W. Convergent and discriminant validation by the multitrait-multimethod matrix. *Psychological Bulletin*, 1959, **54**, 24–31.

Casagrande, J. B., & Hale, K. L. Semantic relationships in Papago folk-definitions. In D. Hymes (Ed.), *Studies in southwestern ethnolinguistics*. The Hague: Mouton, 1967.

Cattell, R. B. The description of personality: Basic traits resolved into clusters. *Journal of Abnormal and Social Psychology*, 1943, **38**, 476–506.

Cattell, R. B. *Description and measurement of personality*. New York: World Book, 1946.

Chapman, L. J. Illusory correlation in observational report. *Journal of Verbal Learning and Verbal Behavior*, 1967, **6**, 151–155.

Chapman, L. J., & Chapman, J. P. Genesis of popular but erroneous psychodiagnostic observations. *Journal of Abnormal Psychology*, 1967, **72**, 193–204.

Chapman, L. J., & Chapman, J. P. Illusory correlation as an obstacle to the use of valid psychodiagnostic signs. *Journal of Abnormal Psychology,* 1969, **74,** 271-280.

Child, I. L. Personality in culture. In E. F. Borgatta & W. W. Lambert (Eds.), *Handbook of personality theory and research.* Chicago, Ill.: Rand McNally, 1968.

Cooper, W. H. Ubiquitous halo. *Psychological Bulletin,* 1981, **90,** 218-244.

Crocker, J. Judgment of covariation by social perceivers. *Psychological Bulletin,* 1981, **90,** 272-292.

Cronbach, L. J. Beyond the two scientific disciplines of scientific psychology. *American Psychologist,* 1975, **30,** 116-127.

D'Andrade, R. G. Trait psychology and componential analysis. *American Anthropologist,* 1965, **67,** 215-228.

D'Andrade, R. G. Cultural constructions of reality. In L. Nader & T. W. Maretzki (Eds.), *Cultural illness and health.* Washington, D.C.: American Anthropological Association, 1973.

D'Andrade, R. G. Memory and the assessment of behavior. In T. Blalock (Ed.), *Social measurement.* Chicago, Ill.: Aldine-Atherton, 1974.

D'Andrade, R. G., Quinn, N., Nerlove, S. B., & Romney, A. K. Categories of disease in American-English and Mexican-Spanish. In A. K. Romney, R. N. Shepard, & S. B. Nerlove (Eds.), *Multidimensional scaling* (Vol. 2). New York: Academic Press, 1972.

Ebbesen, E. B., & Allen, R. B. *Further evidence concerning Fiske's question: "Can personality constructs ever be validated?"* Unpublished manuscript, 1977. (Available from E. B. Ebbesen, Department of Psychology, University of California at San Diego, La Jolla, Calif. 92037.)

Ebbesen, E. B., & Allen, R. B. Cognitive processes in implicit trait inferences. *Journal of Personality and Social Psychology,* 1979, **37,** 471-488.

Einhorn, H. J. Overconfidence in judgment. In R. A. Shweder (Ed.), *Fallible judgment in behavioral research, New directions for methodology of social and behavioral science,* (Vol. 4). San Francisco: Jossey-Bass, 1980.

Einhorn, H. J., & Hogarth, R. M. Confidence in judgment: Persistence of the illusion of validity. *Psychological Review,* 1978, **85,** 395-416.

Epstein, S. The stability of behavior: I. On predicting most of the people much of the time. *Journal of Personality and Social Psychology,* 1979, **37,** 1097-1126.

Fiske, D. W. Can a personality construct be validated empirically? *Psychological Bulletin,* 1973, **80,** 89-92.

Fiske, D. W. *Strategies for personality research.* San Francisco: Jossey-Bass, 1978.

Flavell, J. H., & Stedman, D. J. A developmental study of judgments of semantic similarity. *The Journal of Genetic Psychology,* 1961, **98,** 279-293.

Forgas, J. P. *Social episodes: The study of interaction routines.* New York: Academic Press, 1979.

Gara, M. A., & Rosenberg, S. Linguistic factors in implicit personality theory. *Journal of Personality and Social Psychology,* 1981, **41,** 450-457.

Gilmour, J. S. L. A taxonomic problem. *Nature (London),* 1937, **139,** 1040-1042.

Gilmour, J. S. L. The development of taxonomic theory since 1851. *Nature (London),* 1951, **168,** 400-402.

Goodman, N. On likeness of meaning. *Analysis,* 1949, **10,** 1-7.

Goodman, N. The way the world is. *Review of Metaphysics,* 1960, **14,** 44-66.

Goodman, N. *Language of art.* New York: Bobbs-Merrill, 1968.

Hakel, M. D. Similarity of post-interview trait rating intercorrelations as a contributor to interrater agreement in a structured employment interview. *Journal of Applied Psychology,* 1971, **55,** 443-448.

Hart, H. L. A. *The concept of law.* London and New York: Oxford Univ. Press, 1961.

Huba, G. J., & Hamilton, D. L. On the generality of trait relationships: Some analyses based on Fiske's paper. *Psychological Bulletin,* 1976, **83,** 868-875.

Inhelder, B., & Piaget, J. *The growth of logical thinking from childhood to adolescence.* New York: Basic Books, 1958.

Jackson, D. N., Chan, D. W., & Sticker, L. J. Implicit personality theory: Is it illusory? *Journal of Personality,* 1979, **47,** 1–10.

Jenkins, H. M., & Ward, W. C. Judgment of contingency between responses and outcomes. *Psychological Monographs,* 1965, **79,** 1–17.

Kelley, H. H. Causal schemata and the attribution process. In E. E. Jones *et al.* (Eds.), *Attribution: Perceiving the causes of behavior.* Morristown, N.J.: General Learning Press, 1972.

Kirk, L., & Burton, M. Meaning and context: A study of contextual shifts in meaning of Maasai personality descriptions. *American Ethnologist,* 1977, **4,** 734–761.

LaForge, R., & Suczek, R. F. The interpersonal dimension of personality: III. An interpersonal checklist. *Journal of Personality,* 1955, **24,** 94–112.

Lamiell, J. T., Foss, M. A., & Cavenee, P. On the relationship between conceptual schemes and behavior reports: A closer look. *Journal of Personality,* 1980, **48,** 54–73.

Lewis, P. *Levels of explanations in everyday life.* Unpublished manuscript, Committee on Human Development, University of Chicago, 1978.

Longabaugh, R. An analysis of the cross-cultural study of children's social behavior. *The structure of interpersonal behavior: A cross-cultural analysis.* (Final Report: Research Project No. s-106). Cornell University, 1966.

Lyon, D., & Slovic, P. Dominance of accuracy information and neglect of base rates in probability estimation. *Acta Psychologica,* 1976, **40,** 287–298.

Mann, R. D. *The relation between personality characteristics and individual performance in small groups.* Unpublished doctoral dissertation, University of Michigan, 1959.

Mirels, H. L. *Inferential illusions, inferential typicality, and the organization of self-reports.* Unpublished manuscript, Ohio State University (n.d.).

Mischel, W. *Personality and assessment.* New York: Wiley, 1968.

Mischel, W. Towards a cognitive social learning reconceptualization of personality. *Psychological Review,* 1973, **80,** 252–283.

Mischel, W., & Peake, P. In search of consistency: Measure for measure. In M. P. Zanna, E. T. Higgins, & C. P. Herman (Eds.), *Consistency in social behavior.* Hillsdale, N.J.: Erlbaum, 1981.

Moos, R. H. Sources of variance in responses to questionnaires and in behavior. *Journal of Abnormal Psychology,* 1969, **74,** 405–412.

Mulaik, S. A. Are personality factors raters' conceptual factors? *Journal of Consulting Psychology,* 1964, **28,** 506–511.

Newcomb, T. M. The consistency of certain extrovert-introvert behavior patterns in 51 problem boys. *Contributions to Education,* 1929, 382.

Newcomb, T. M. An experiment designed to test the validity of a rating technique. *Journal of Educational Psychology,* 1931, **22,** 279–289.

Nisbett, R. E. The trait construct in lay and professional psychology. In L. Festinger (Ed.), *Retrospections on social psychology.* London and New York: Oxford Univ. Press, 1980.

Norman, W. T. Toward an adequate taxonomy of personality attributes: Replicated factor structure in peer nomination personality ratings. *Journal of Abnormal and Social Psychology,* 1963, **67,** 574–583.

Osgood, C. E., Suci, G. J., & Tannenbaum, P. H. *The measurement of meaning.* Urbana, Ill.: Univ. of Illinois Press, 1957.

Overall, J. E., Hollister, L. E., & Pichot, P. Major psychiatric disorders: A four-dimensional model. *Archives of General Psychiatry,* 1967, **16,** 146–151.

Passini, F. T., & Norman, W. T. A universal conception of personality structure? *Journal of Personality and Social Psychology,* 1966, **4,** 44–49.

Raush, H. L., Dittmann, A. T., & Taylor, T. J. Person, setting, and change in social interaction. *Human Relations,* 1959, **12,** 361–377.

Raush, H. L., Farbman, I., & Llewellyn, L. G. Person, setting and change in social interaction II: A normal control study, *Human Relations,* 1960, **13,** 305-332.

Rosch, E. Universals and cultural specifics in human categorization. In R. W. Brisling, S. Bochner, & W. J. Lonner (Eds.), *Cross-cultural perspectives on learning.* New York: Wiley, 1975.

Rosch, E., & Mervis, C. B. Family resemblances: Studies in the internal structure of categories. *Cognitive Psychology,* 1975, **7,** 573-605.

Rosch, E., Mervis, C. G., Gray, W. D., Johnson, D. M., & Boyes-Braem, P. Basic objects in natural categories. *Cognitive Psychology,* 1976, **8,** 382-439.

Rosenberg, S., Nelson, C., & Vivekananthan, P. S. A multidimensional approach to the structure of personality impressions. *Journal of Personality and Social Psychology,* 1968, **9,** 283-294.

Schank, R., & Abelson, R. *Scripts, plans, goals and understanding.* Hillsdale, N.J.: Erlbaum, 1977.

Schutz, W. *Joy.* New York: Grove Press, 1967.

Sears, R. R. Dependency motivation. In M. R. Jones (Ed.), *Nebraska symposium on motivation.* Lincoln: Univ. of Nebraska Press, 1963.

Sears, R. R., Maccoby, E. E., & Levin, H. *Patterns of child rearing.* New York: Harper, 1957.

Selby, H. A. *Zapotec deviance.* Austin: Univ. of Texas Press, 1974.

Selby, H. A. Semantics and causality in the study of deviance. In M. Sanches & B. G. Blount (Eds.), *Sociocultural dimensions of language use.* New York: Academic Press, 1975.

Shweder, R. A. Semantic structures and personality assessment. (Doctoral dissertation, Harvard University, 1972). (University Microfilms No. 72-29, 584)

Shweder, R. A. The between and within of cross-cultural research. *Ethos,* 1973, **1,** 531-543.

Shweder, R. A. How relevant is an individual difference theory of personality? *Journal of Personality,* 1975, **43,** 455-484.

Shweder, R. A. Illusory correlation and the M.M.P.I. controversy (commentaries by Jack Block and Allen Edwards). *Journal of Consulting and Clinical Psychology,* 1977, **45,** 917-924. (a)

Shweder, R. A. Illusory correlation and the M.M.P.I. controversy: Author's reply to some of the allusions and elusions in Block's and Edwards' commentaries. *Journal of Consulting and Clinical Psychology,* 1977, **45,** 936-940. (b)

Shweder, R. A. Likeness and likelihood in everyday thought: Magical thinking in judgments about personality. *Current Anthropology,* 1977, **18,** 637-648. (c)

Shweder, R. A. Rethinking culture and personality theory. Part I: A critical examination of two classical postulates. *Ethos,* 1979, **7,** 255-278. (a)

Shweder, R. A. Rethinking culture and personality theory. Part II: A critical examination of two more classical postulates. *Ethos,* 1979, **7,** 279-311. (b)

Shweder, R. A. Factors and fictions in person perception: A reply to Lamiell, Foss and Cavenee. *Journal of Personality,* 1980, **48,** 74-81. (a)

Shweder, R. A. Rethinking culture and personality theory. Part III: From Genesis and typology to hermeneutics and dynamics. *Ethos,* 1980, **8,** 60-94. (b)

Shweder, R. A. Anthropology's romantic rebellion against the enlightenment: Or, there's more to thinking than reason and evidence. Presented at the Annual Meeting of the American Association for the Advancement of Science, January 5, 1981, Toronto, Canada.

Shweder, R. A., & Bourne, E. Does the concept of the person vary cross-culturally? In A. J. Marsella & G. White (Eds.), *Cultural conceptions of mental health and therapy.* New York: Reidel, 1982.

Shweder, R. A., & D'Andrade, R. G. Accurate reflection or systematic distortion? A reply to Block, Weiss and Thorne. *Journal of Personality and Social Psychology,* 1979, **37,** 1075-1084.

Shweder, R. A., & D'Andrade, R. G. The systematic distortion hypothesis. In R. A. Shweder (Ed.), *Fallible judgment in behavioral research. New directions for methodology of social and behavioral science, No. 4.* San Francisco: Jossey-Bass, 1980.

100   RICHARD A. SHWEDER

Slovic, P. Information processing, situation specificity, and the generality of risk-taking behavior. *Journal of Personality and Social Psychology,* 1972, **22,** 128–134. (b)

Smedslund, J. The concept of correlation in adults. *Scandinavian Journal of Psychology,* 1963, **4,** 165–173.

Smith, G. M. Usefulness of peer ratings of personality in educational research. *Educational and Psychological Measurement,* 1967, **27,** 967–984.

Sokal, R. R. Classification: Purposes, principles, progress, prospects. *Science,* 1974, **185,** 1115–1123.

Sokal, R. R., & Sneath, P. H. A. *Principles of numerical taxonomy.* San Francisco: Freeman, 1963.

Stefflre, V., Reich, P., & McClaren-Stefflre, M. Some eliciting and componential procedures for descriptive semantics. In P. Kay (Ed.), *Explorations in mathematical anthropology.* Cambridge, Mass.: MIT Press, 1971.

Szalay, L. B., & Deese, J. *Subjective meaning and culture: An assessment through word associations.* Hillsdale, N.J.: Erlbaum, 1978.

Tversky, A., & Kahneman, D. Judgment under uncertainty: Heuristics and biases. *Science,* 1974, **185,** 1124–1131.

Ward, W. C., & Jenkins, H. M. The display of information and the judgment of contingency. *Canadian Journal of Psychology,* 1965, **19,** 231–241.

Wason, P. C., & Johnson-Laird, P. N. *Psychology of reasoning.* London: Batsford, 1972.

White, G. Conceptual universals in interpersonal language. *American Anthropologist,* 1980, **82,** 759–781.

Whiting, B. B., & Whiting, J. W. M. *Children of six cultures.* Cambridge, Mass.: Harvard Univ. Press, 1975.

Wiggins, J. S. A psychological taxonomy of trait-descriptive terms: The interpersonal domain. *Journal of Personality and Social Psychology,* 1978, **37,** 395–412.

Yarrow, M. R., & Waxler, C. Z. Dimensions and correlates of prosocial behavior in young children. *Child Development,* 1976, **47,** 118–125.

THE THEORY OF COGNITIVE ORIENTATION: WIDENING THE SCOPE OF BEHAVIOR PREDICTION

Hans Kreitler and Shulamith Kreitler

DEPARTMENT OF PSYCHOLOGY
TEL AVIV UNIVERSITY
RAMAT AVIV
TEL AVIV, ISRAEL

I. Introduction

The theory of cognitive orientation (CO) was developed originally to clarify and conceptualize our ideas about the nature and function of the cognitive determinants of human behavior. Although initiated by clinical observations, the aim was merely understanding and explanation. The first experiments were designed to test some hypotheses concerning the role of content variables in the evocation and guidance of molar behavior. However, the further we wandered along this path, zigzagging between conceptualization and experimentation, the more frequently prediction of behavior and manipulation of cognitive contents were required. The former was used for convincing ourselves of the validity of our assumptions, the latter for studying causal relations. Even in our book, "Cognitive Orientation and Behavior" (1976), we presented the experiments primarily as confirming evidence, amended by some casual remarks about practical applications.

Only during the last few years have we and our collaborators begun to look beyond the purely theoretical contribution into domains of practical importance. It has become increasingly clear that prediction of behavior is of great importance not merely from the viewpoint of the theory but also for the practice and application of psychology in different domains. Moreover, predicting behavior may be beneficial both for the subject and for those who are concerned with how the subject will behave. Hence, the emphasis placed on predicting different behaviors in the studies generated by the CO theory in recent years.

However, as may be expected, the range of research has broadened into different branches, chief among which are the following: replications of previous predictions of behavior on new samples, and sometimes new dependent variables, in order to examine the stability and reliability of the findings; predictions of new types of behavior in order to extend the predictive potential of the theory and to examine its utility in domains of practical importance and with regard to abnormal samples; testing of new means for improving the predictive ability of the theory; research into developmental aspects; studies of different theoretical processes as named by the theory and development of new theoretical applications designed to promote the development of the theory itself; and studies focusing on modifying cognitive contents in order to attain expected modifications in molar behaviors. The studies described in this article relate to all these branches of recent research except the last type, which will be published separately (S. Kreitler & H. Kreitler, 1981).

Neither the experiments nor a recent contribution to problems in personality can be properly understood, however, without some working knowledge of the underlying CO theory. In the present context this implies some familiarity with the essential processes, the sequence of their occurrence and operation, and their underlying concepts. Yet, it requires neither information about all the psychological and physiological details involved, nor about the relations of various concepts to similar concepts developed by other investigators. All these can be found in H. Kreitler and S. Kreitler (1972a, 1976). Therefore, in our presentation of the theory (Sections II and III), we will concentrate on the essentials and largely forego discussion of background material and references to the work of others.

II. Cognitive Orientation Theory: The Submolar Level

A. MEANING AND ORIENTATION

In line with system theory, we regard living organisms as open systems that process energy and information. However, a great part of this information, indeed, the very information dealt with in the domain of human information processing, cannot be adequately characterized and quantified in terms of the reductionistic concepts and measures of information theory. Information theory is not sufficiently sensitive to meanings because "the amount does not specify the content, value, truthfulness, exclusiveness, history or purpose of the information" (G. Miller, 1953, p. 3; also Bar-Hillel, 1955; Cherry, 1957). "Meaning is the significance of information to the system that processes it" (J. Miller, 1965, pp. 193–194), not the amount of excluded alternatives, as postulated by information theory.

Going a step further, we maintain that meaning is the guiding agent of human behavior. The basic tenet of the CO theory is that human behavior, whether initiated by external or internal stimulation, is guided by the orientative aspects of cognition. Cognition is defined as the meaning-processing subsystem within the organism, that is, the subsystem that grasps, produces, elaborates, assigns, and manipulates meanings. It is the cognitive system, namely meanings and operations with meaning, that decides the course of action.

Two conditions have to be met in order to turn this declaration into a theory that can be used for explaining, predicting, and modifying behavior and that is amenable to empirical verification or falsification: (a) An instrument or an operational theory is required that would liberate meaning from its rather esoteric state by allowing for satisfactory characterization and quantification of meaning far beyond what was achieved by the previous limited attempts (e.g., Deese, 1965; Osgood, Suci, & Tannenbaum, 1958); and (b) A theory is required that accounts for the sequence of events and processes intervening between input stimulation and behavior output.

We feel that our theory of meaning and the theory of CO live up to these requirements. The relation between these two theories is imbalanced in that the theory of meaning is completely independent, while the CO theory cannot do without using some of the major concepts of the meaning theory. In other words, in the context of this article the theory of meaning is subservient to the CO theory and, therefore, will not be presented in full detail (H. Kreitler & S. Kreitler, 1976, chap. 2; S. Kreitler & H. Kreitler, 1983, in preparation). Instead, we will merely summarize those concepts and processes of meaning that are absolutely essential for understanding CO processes and required for the prediction of human molar behavior.

Meaning is defined as a *referent-related pattern of meaning values along 22 meaning dimensions*. A *referent* is anything to which meanings are assigned, for example, a stimulus, a situation, a word, a flash of light, a visceral signal, a memory item, an image. *Meaning value* is the smallest cognitive unit that lends meaning to a referent. For example, if the referent is a visual sensation, the notion "[it] is red" or merely "red" is a meaning value. Being a referent or being a meaning value is not a permanent status but an ad hoc function. A meaning value can be used as a referent (e.g., "it is black"; "black is beautiful"), and an already meaningful referent can serve as a meaning value. A *meaning dimension* is an abstracted aspect of content, the concept common to all the meaning values along this dimension. Originally (S. Kreitler, 1965; S. Kreitler & H. Kreitler, 1968) we regarded meaning dimensions merely as coding devices, but we have since learned that they are active agents involved not only in identification and coding of input but also in memory retrieval and problem solving (S. Kreitler & H. Kreitler, 1983, in preparation). Table I presents the 22 meaning dimensions, each one illustrated by a short example. It also shows other aspects of meaning, namely, the different types of relation and different forms of relation between a referent and its meaning value(s), as well as the two modes of meaning. Meaning values may be expressed verbally, gesturally, by drawings, movements, sounds, by pointing out objects or situations, and so on. It is obvious that meaning values may vary in veridicality.

In spite of the importance attached to meaning, the CO theory is not semantic but psychodynamic. Its subject matter is not meaning but rather evocation and cognitive guidance of behavior as well as prediction and modification of be-

TABLE I
Major Variables of the Meaning System

Meaning variable	Definition
Dimensions	
Contextual allocation	Superordinate concept or structure to which the referent belongs: eye— is an organ; is a part of the body
Range of Inclusion	Items that the referent includes as parts or members of the class(es) it designates: body—includes hands and feet; plant—includes flowers, trees
Function, purpose, or role	Functions of the referent or uses to which it is often put: house—serves for living
Action and potentialities for action	Actions that the referent does or could do, or that are done with it, to it: man—works and dreams
Manner of occurrence or operation	Stages, processes, acts, instruments involved in the occurrence or operation of the referent: eating—bringing food into the mouth, munching it, and swallowing
Antecedents and causes	The necessary and/or sufficient conditions for the referent's existence or operation: accident—happens because of too fast or too slow driving
Consequences or results	Consequences that derive directly or indirectly from the referent's existence or operation: hunger—eating
Domain of application	The items to which the referent is usually applied, with which it interacts: humid—applies to climate or washing; love—applies to people, animals, life
Material	The material of which the referent is made: cloth—made of synthetic fibers
Structure	The structure or organization of the referent and the interrelations of its parts: society—has a hierarchical, pyramidal organization
State and possible changes in state	The actual or potential state of the referent and the changes that could occur in it under specified conditions: snow—melts in heat; man—can become unwell
Weight and mass	The referent's weight, estimated or measured: baby—weighs 3–5 pounds
Size	Size of the referent, estimated or measured: virus—tiny
Quantity	The referent's quantity, estimated or measured: woman—slightly above 50% of the population
Locational qualities	The referent's place in absolute or relative terms: sun—in a side-branch of the galaxy
Temporal qualities	The time at which the referent exists or existed, its duration: happiness—lasts for seconds
Possession and belongingness	The referent's possessions and to whom it belongs: Mr. X—the owner of plant Y; TV—owned by companies and in some countries by the state
Development	The referent's ontogenetic or phylogenetic development, its forerunners, personal history, professional curriculum: U.N.—established in 1945; since then has become formally stronger and actually weaker

(continued)

TABLE I—*Continued*

Meaning variable	Definition
Sensory qualities	Sensory qualities characteristic of or perceivable by the referent: visual, auditory, gustatory, kinesthetic, internal.
Feelings and emotions	Feelings and emotions evoked or felt by the referent: exam—evokes anxiety; Mr. Z.—incapable of love
Judgments, opinions, and evaluations	Judgments, opinions, and evaluations concerning the referent or held by the referent: murder—inhuman
Cognitive qualities	Cognitive qualities and actions of the referent or concerning it: Mr. P.—very bright, reminds me of my brother
Forms of relation	
Assertion	Positive relation between a meaning value and a referent: room—is small
Denial or negation	Negation of relation between a meaning value and a referent: room—is not big
Mixed assertion and negation	The meaning value is related to the referent only sometimes, partly, or mildly: film—sometimes exciting
Conjunctive	Two or more meaning values are stated as essential: sky—both blue and above
Disjunctive	One, two, or more meaning values are stated as essential: table—either it is square or round
Double negation	Neither of the stated meaning values applies to the referent: Car X—neither safe nor comfortable
Types of relation	
Attributive	Specifying certain attributes as qualities of the referent. The relation
Substance-quality	between referent and meaning value is like that between a substance and its qualities: house—large
Actional	The relation between referent and meaning value is like that between a doer and its actions: inflation—increases insecurity
Comparative	The meaning values are related to the referent through the intermediation of another meaning value or referent.
Similarity (including identity)	The intermediation is based on similarity: sea—like the sky
Dissimilarity (including contrast)	The intermediation is based on dissimilarity: sea—unlike the soil
Complementa-riness	The intermediation is based on a complementary relation: father—has a son; son—has a father
Relational	The intermediation is based on a relational relation: avenue—broad street
Exemplifying–illustrative	The meaning values are related to the referent as examples
Exemplify-ing instance	The example is an instance such as an event, an object, a person: evil—war

(continued)

TABLE I—*Continued*

Meaning variable	Definition
Exemplify-ing situation	The example is a situation, an image: trust—a child looking up to his or her mother
Exemplify-ing scene	The example is a scene with dramatic and dynamic elements
Metaphoric-symbolic	The meaning values are related to the referent in a mediated, non-conventional manner
Interpretation	The meaning values are abstract and interpretative: life—the unknowable known
Metaphor	Imaginal meaning values are related interpretatively to a relatively more abstract referent: life—like a stream of fresh water
Symbol	Meaning values are related to the referent metaphorically and also include contrasting elements that are resolved through the image: love—a fire that creates and destroys
Modes of meaning	
Lexical (interpersonally shared) meaning	Includes the attributive and comparative types of relation
Symbolic (personal-subjective) meaning	Includes the exemplifying-illustrative and metaphoric-symbolic types of relation

havior. Its central concept is the essentially nonmechanistic term "orientation." Orientation, as we understand it, implies that behavior above the level of spinal reflexes is not determined by external and internal forces but is evoked and steered by orientative acts that consist in the comparison and the elaboration of meanings assigned to the representations of what are traditionally regarded as external and internal determinants of behavior. Expressed more directly, orientation predates behavior, notwithstanding its possible enrichment by behavioral feedbacks. This role of orientation is made possible by the potential *orientativeness* of meaning values in general and specific meaning constellations in particular (see Section III,B). The primary task of the CO theory is to describe and explain in theoretical and descriptive terms the processes between input and output of behavior, emphasizing mainly human molar behavior.

B. THE LOWEST LEVEL OF COGNITIVE FUNCTIONING

It is a fascinating paradox that Pavlov's work on conditioning, on the one hand, enabled behaviorists to discredit cognitive research successfully, but on the other hand, led to the experimental demonstration that forming a conditioned response presupposes a cognitively geared reflex that Pavlov himself enthusiastically regarded as the source of science and culture. He first called it the "what-is-it" reflex but later the orienting reflex (1927). The orienting reflex (OR) is a matrix of specific autonomic, electroencephalographic, sensory, and motor responses that, although not always concomitantly activated, should be regarded as a holistic reaction (Anokhin, 1958) cortically shaped, directed, and integrated (Sokolov, 1963, p. 15). It differs from defensive and adaptive reactions (Lynn, 1966, p. 10) as well as from arousal, with which it shares some characteristics (Johnson, 1968; Mackworth, 1969). Pavlov claimed that the OR is elicited by every new stimulus, but further research demonstrated that its antecedents include—besides novelty—surprise, incongruity, complexity, and indistinctiveness of the input (Berlyne, 1960, pp. 243–246). According to Sokolov (1963), an OR is induced whenever a fresh input deviates from the hitherto prominent "neuronal model" of former, as well as of extrapolated (i.e., expected), stimulation.

Many researchers (e.g., Bykov, 1958; Sokolov, 1963; Pribram, 1971) distinguish between two stages of the OR. The first consists of subcortically integrated autonomic and motor changes that maximize sensory functioning. The second, largely cortically integrated, already includes reactions of the exploratory type. Clearly distinguishable from mere arousal, the OR is assigned several functions beyond its role in the elicitation of conditioning. In Sokolov's terms (1963, p. 683), it is a "regulator which corrects an extrapolation, influencing the way new information is secured, selected, transmitted, and handled." In line with Pavlov, Berlyne (1965) and many others regard the OR as the cradle of cognitive functioning.

However, these researchers overlook two important aspects. Determining whether a stimulus is new or significant presupposes and requires some rudimentary cognitive functioning. Hence, cognitive functioning cannot itself be the result of the OR (H. Kreitler & S. Kreitler, 1970). Moreover, applying cognitive means for establishing or improving orientation is an innate tendency evidenced by the OR and its early appearance in life (Graham & Jackson, 1970; Jeffrey, 1968). The rudimentary cognitive means are the acts of meaning assignment required for distinguishing between familiar and unfamiliar inputs.

In sum, a rudimentary act of meaning assignment predates the orienting reflex and, hence, is a requirement for reacting to any input to the cognitive subsystem. In other words, orientation by cognitive means is, at least in humans, an elementary function.

C. PRIMARY INPUT ELABORATION AND OUTPUT SELECTION

The representation of every externally or internally elicited input to the cognitive system is first checked against the representation of the immediately preceding stimulation (Sokolov's "neuronal model") preserved in short-term memory. The check merely registers change according to the match–mismatch criterion that may vary across subjects and situations. If no change is found, hitherto ongoing processing continues. In case mismatch is registered "meaning action," a primary procedure for input identification, is set in operation in order to determine to which one of four alternatives the input pertains:

1. The input is a signal for a defensive or an adaptive reflex, or for a conditioned response.
2. The input is a signal for molar action and, hence, stands in need of a more elaborate clarification of its meaning than is warranted by meaning processes on this primary level.
3. The input is known to be irrelevant to the present situation.
4. The input does not pertain to alternative 1, 2, or 3 because it is new or particularly significant, according to specific criteria. Thus, it serves as a signal for the exploratory reaction provided by the OR, which may in turn provide sufficient meaning for identifying the input as the signal for alternative 1, 2, or 3.

The examination of these alternatives, which is probably sequential, requires a simple procedure of meaning assignment called "meaning action." Meaning action is the most rudimentary application of the meaning system, limited in the use of meaning dimensions, types of relations, and number of meaning values. Elicited by every input, meaning action is virtually continuous. Using the hitherto dominant neuronal model as a standard, it first determines match–mismatch, thus applying the comparative type of relation. Only in case of mismatch are meaning dimensions activated for the retrieval of meaning values and their assignment to the input. For example, when the activated meaning dimension is Sensory Qualities, the retrieved meaning value(s) could be "hot," perhaps the signal for a defensive reflex, or "red, bright, round," thus identifying a conditioned traffic signal. The meaning values must not be verbally coded and may not reach full consciousness.

By applying the microgenetic technique, we found that subjects use primarily two meaning dimensions (Sensory Qualities and Locational Qualities) for the initial identification of visual stimuli (S. Kreitler & H. Kreitler, 1977; 1982b, in preparation). The extremely short reaction times indicate preselection of particular meaning dimensions due either to innate predispositions or to prior experience. However, meaning action is not necessarily restricted to one or two meaning dimensions and two or three meaning values. It is an unfolding process. Alternative 2, for example, requires more meaning than alternative 1, and so on. Formally, we regard meaning action as terminated when one of the actions indicated by alternatives 1, 2, and 3 has been taken. Actually, it may develop into a higher form of meaning assignment that will be discussed in Section III,A.

Since meaning action guides the step-by-step unfolding process of initial input identification, it is an integral part of perception. There is no justification to separate strictly the early input analysis in terms of physical characteristics, such as tone of voice, from a later analysis in terms of meaning, as suggested by Broadbent (1958) in contrast to Treisman (1969). Even unattended sensory information undergoes an analysis in terms of meaning (Moray, 1969; Norman, 1969). However, the analysis is not exhaustive to the extent suggested by J. A. Deutsch and D. Deutsch (1963). Frequently, the intermediate output of meaning action, sometimes even a single meaning value, may cause a shift in attention to other aspects of the input or may even bring about the cessation of further analysis. Thus, meaning action solves the well-known problem of how to know what to attend to before knowing what the stimulus is.

Again, we regard meaning action as completed if action indicated by alternative 1, 2, or 3 can be taken directly or indirectly, owing to further information that has been derived from the perception improving components of the OR (i.e., alternative 4). Indeed, on this level there is no elaborate decision making, but an almost automatic selection between meaning bound alternatives, each of which has its preestablished behavioral program for guiding the output action.

III. Cognitive Orientation Theory: Determinants of Molar Behavior

A. MEANING GENERATION

The distinction between a level of submolar behavior and a level of molar behavior is more classificatory than factual. If we start at the output of molar behavior and trace its elicitation backward to primary input elaboration, the process appears to be an unbroken chain of cognitive operations. However, when starting with the input and describing, step-by-step, the increasingly complex operations in the different ensuing phases, one is likely to encounter a discontinuity, in that the process often terminates after primary input elaboration, with or without ensuing defensive, adaptive, or conditioned responses. Moreover, the operations of primary input elaboration and those involved in the elicitation of molar behavior differ so markedly in their complexity that it is appropriate to distinguish between two levels, notwithstanding the merely gradual increase in complexity.

The transition from the level of submolar behavior to that of molar behavior occurs if one of three conditions is met: (a) when, in spite of improved perception due to the OR, the input has not been identified sufficiently to inhibit the OR; (b) when the input has been identified as a signal for an adaptive, defensive, or conditioned response but this response proves to be insufficient for coping with the input; and (c) when, according to initial meaning, the stimulus is known or interpreted as a signal for a complex behavioral sequence, i.e., molar behavior.

The transition to the molar level is brought about by activating more comprehensive and elaborate processes of meaning assignment which we call "meaning generation." The referent of meaning generation is not only the input as such but also the meaning assigned to the input in the course of meaning action. Whereas the meaning values stemming from meaning action are mere denotations, the meaning values of meaning generation are frequently concepts. As compared with meaning action, in meaning generation more meaning dimensions—potentially all 22—are used, and a greater variety of types of relation, as well as forms of relation, is applied. The comprehensive meaning resulting from meaning generation includes not only meaning values of the lexical mode but also of the personal mode and, hence, is more orientative in regard to future action. Following Pavlov's terms, if meaning action is designed to answer the question "What is it?", the task of meaning generation can be characterized by imagining that it answers the question "What does it mean, and what does it mean to me and for me?". Finally, whereas the result of meaning action determines which of the four alternatives mentioned (Section II,C) is pertinent, the comprehensive meaning resulting from meaning generation constitutes the material that guides a particular kind of retrieval from long-term memory—the retrieval of four kinds of beliefs that are required for determining what kind of action should be undertaken. In other words, the mostly implicit, but sometimes also explicit, question "What am I to do?" can be regarded as terminating the phase of meaning generation.

B. BELIEFS, ORIENTATIVENESS, AND THE FOUR COGNITIVE ORIENTATION COMPONENTS

Beliefs are of paramount importance for the formation of behavioral intents and the ensuing molar behavior. Therefore, it is necessary to clarify our concept of belief before discussing the orientative function of beliefs and their role in experimental prediction and modification of human behavior.

We define belief as a cognitive unit that consists of at least two meaning values related to each other either by a third meaning value or by a syntactic device (e.g., children play games; humans breathe; they are here). The relation may appear in all the forms and types of relation listed in our meaning system (Table I). We regard beliefs not as behaviors or dispositions to behaviors but as cognitive units that are potentially orientative with regard to behavior. There are no restrictions on the object, source, foundation, or informational support of the meaning values that comprise a belief, nor on the contents, source, rationality, logical consistency, commonness, salience, foundation, and, most importantly, on the veridicality of the belief itself. The belief may be conscious, merely accessible to consciousness, or unconscious. It can be expressed or conceived in verbal or nonverbal form. It may be permanent, may have only an enduring core, may be retrieved from long-term memory and adjusted to a particular situation, or may be produced ad hoc and afterward forgotten. It is embedded in the multidimensional network of other similar or dissimilar, conforming or contradictory beliefs and usually belongs to more than one belief hierarchy that may promote its retrieval (for a detailed comparison of our belief concept with other definitions of belief and attitude, see H. Kreitler & S. Kreitler, 1976, pp. 80–86; for studies concerning the size and psychological reality of the belief unit, see H. Kreitler & S. Kreitler, 1976, pp. 365–377, and this article, Section XII).

Beliefs differ from meaning values in many respects. The two most important differences are the following. First, a meaning value as such has no referent but relates to a referent that is extraneous to it. Hence, if a meaning value were to be considered without its function with respect to a referent, it would not be a meaning value but merely cognitive contents expressed as an image, a word, or a collocation. In contrast, a belief is an independent cognitive unit that has its own referent, namely, the meaning value that serves as its grammatical subject. Second, beliefs can serve as meaning values but meaning values cannot figure as beliefs unless they first combine with their referent to form a new integrated unit.

From a dynamic point of view, the most important feature of beliefs is their potential orientativeness. Orientativeness is the meaning-derived power of a belief to indicate its relevance to a given domain. Thus, a belief may have orientativeness with regard to the legal system, the domain of moral postulates, the rules of grammar, and so on. These different types of orientativeness are not identical. A belief may be potentially orientative in one sense but not in another, yet any belief may be potentially orientative in different senses.

The CO theory is concerned with only one specific but highly important kind of potential orientativeness of beliefs—their potential orientativeness with regard to molar behavior. Orientativeness in regard to behavior is the meaning-derived power of a belief to indicate one or more courses of action in a more or less direct manner. A belief may suggest or point toward different actions; for example, ''It would be nice if we could let some air come in'' suggests opening a door or a window, or ''He should be told the truth'' indicates breaking some news to someone. Sometimes the belief points toward very few or even just one course of action, as when the belief is ''I want to eat a steak'' and the indicated action is obviously ''eating a steak.'' At other times a belief may indicate so many different courses of action that from an orientative viewpoint it may be seem to be neutral until brought into conjunction with one or more other beliefs. For example, the belief ''Today it is December 12'' appears neutral until combined with a belief such as ''On the twelfth of every month I have a faculty meeting.'' Again, a belief may sometimes seem to be devoid of any behavioral implications but acquires distinct orientativeness when conjoined or even just juxtaposed with another belief (e.g., "There is a sale of electric clocks in the big store in town" may seem neutral until combined with the belief, "Our electric clock is ruined beyond repair"). In the same vein, even a very explicit and narrow behavioral implication of a belief, such as "Now I want to eat steak tartar," may undergo radical changes through the evocation of another belief, such as "Here in Lima it may be dangerous to eat raw meat" or "I am supposed to be on a low-cholesterol diet." Accordingly, we regard single beliefs not as orientative but rather as potentially orientative. The potential becomes orientatively effective only through interaction with one or more concomitantly evoked beliefs. It is the common orientative impact of several beliefs that brings about the specification of a belief's orientative implication.

Moreover, since a belief may potentially have different behavioral implications, other beliefs with which it is conjoined may bring about the salience of specific behavioral implications rather than others. For example, the orientativeness of the belief about self, "I shiver," differs when conjoined with the belief, "I lowered the thermostat an hour ago," or "Yesterday I had high fever." In the former case, the behavioral orientativeness would consist of actions such as raising the thermostat or putting on some more clothes; in the latter case, it would consist of actions such as taking one's temperature, swallowing an aspirin, or going to bed. Hence, orientativeness of a belief depends on the content of the other beliefs with which it is conjoined.

On the basis of our empirical research and the work of others in the broad domain of beliefs or attitudes and their behavioral impact (Hintikka, 1969; Kluckhohn, 1951; Lazarus, 1966; Parson, Shils, & Olds, 1951; Schwartz, 1970), we distinguish between four types of belief.

1. *Beliefs about Goals (Go).* Formally the belief consists of the meaning value "I," as subject, linked to one or more meaning values by a meaning value that reflects the desired relation, which may be positive (wanted) or negative (rejected). The goal may be general (e.g., "I want to be rich"), particular (e.g., "I want to divorce Linda"), permanent (e.g., "I want to live"), or transient (e.g., "Now I want to sleep").

2. *Beliefs about Self (BS).* Formally the belief consists of the meaning value "I," as subject, linked to one or more meaning values by a meaning value that reflects a factual relation (i.e., is so, is not so). Beliefs of this type express information about one's self, such as one's habits, inclinations, actions, feelings, sensations, abilities, in the present, past, or future (e.g., "I am ambitious," "I do not take moral rules too seriously," "Next year I will still be living in this town").

3. *Beliefs about Norms and Rules (N).* Formally the belief consists of a non-I meaning value, serving as subject, linked to one or more meaning values by a meaning value that reflects a normative relation (should, ought, should not,

ought not). Beliefs of this type express ethical, aesthetical, social, and other rules and standards (e.g., "One should help one's neighbors," "People should not be too fat," "One should walk cautiously on frozen snow").

4. *General Beliefs (GB)*. Formally the belief consists of a non-I meaning value, serving as subject, linked to one or more meaning values by a meaning value that reflects any factual relation (i.e., is so, is not so). Beliefs of this type express information about people, objects, events, situations, or any aggregate or aspect of these in the past, present, or future (e.g., "People lie a lot," "Cheaters are frequently very successful").

Common to all four types of beliefs is their potential orientativeness. As noted, it is through interaction between concomitantly evoked beliefs that the orientative impact of single beliefs becomes highlighted and specific. The four belief types form a particular matrix for the elaboration of orientativeness toward molar acts of behavior.

C. Belief Evocation and Cognitive Orientation Clustering

The transition from meaning generation to belief evocation and the almost concomitant formation of CO clusters are monitored, as it were, by the specific questions that are implicitly posed by every input, namely, whether action is required, and if so, what to do. The transition is mediated not only by the shift from retrieval of meaning values to the retrieval of beliefs but also by greater emphasis on specific meaning dimensions, mainly Action and Potentialities for Action, Antecedents and Causes, and Consequences and Results. It seems plausible to assume that far more beliefs are activated or, rather, set in a state of suspension than are actually evoked. Again, far more beliefs are evoked than are actually used for the guidance of action in a specific case. Evidently some of the evoked beliefs are retrieved (see Section XII) and some are generated under the specific conditions of the particular action(s) considered, by interactions among beliefs. For example, two beliefs such as "Capriciousness means changing one's mind and preferences unaccountably" and "I often change my mind and preferences without good reason," may generate the new belief "I am capricious."

Beliefs have certain relations to each other. These relations can be characterized in terms of meaning (e.g., one belief expresses the causes for that which is stated in another belief), or in terms that are often identified as structural (e.g., beliefs are arranged in hierarchies, beliefs summate additively) or as formal–logical (e.g., beliefs contradict each other, are in consonance or balance). But whatever the principles guiding activation, evocation, and generation of beliefs, one principle figures as the most prominent in adult subjects: evocation of beliefs of the four belief types. The finding (Section XI) that 4- to 5-year-old children still use, at least in some domains of action, beliefs of fewer than four or three belief types indicates the role of experience and learning in the process of belief evocation. Goal beliefs and beliefs about self are most probably the types of belief that are integrated and become functionally viable earlier than the others. This developmental sequence is mirrored by the most frequent sequence in actual belief evocation. Though in principle a belief from any of the four types can arise first, it is usually a goal belief that appears before beliefs of the other types or at least very early in the sequence, and stands a better chance than the others to fulfill the task of a focal belief. In more general terms, the earliest evoked belief with the clearest behavioral implication serves as a focal belief. It is often a goal belief, but neither always nor necessarily so. The task of the focal belief consists in triggering and guiding the evocation of other beliefs that are meaning-related to its behavioral implications. In case none of the early evoked beliefs has a clear behavioral aspect, belief evocation may terminate even before reaching a clear decision that the input does not require or deserve any behavioral reaction. Again, a directly or indirectly indicated behavior is required for bringing to the fore other beliefs of the four types that relate to it positively, negatively, or sometimes even in an ambivalent or conflicting manner.

However, belief interaction is not that simple. Our empirical findings and statistical manipulations show that only beliefs of the same belief type form an ad hoc functional unit by matching and pooling their differential orientative aspects. The orientative aspects govern the process. The beliefs that support the indicated behavioral implication of the focal belief are pooled together, as are the beliefs that negate this behavioral implication and the beliefs that are neutral with regard to this behavioral implication or relevant with regard to another behavioral implication. The three groupings of beliefs—those that support, those that negate, and those that are neutral—are compared. The crucial comparison is between the supporting and negating beliefs. In case of a stalemate between the number of supporting and the number of negating beliefs, for example, six supporting and six negating norms, the norm beliefs will not exert an orientative impact. Otherwise, the grouping with the majority of beliefs in the particular belief type comes to represent the particular belief type in the context of the specific action. This indicates that, insofar as the support or negation of the focal belief is concerned, the majority is decisive, whereas the minority is overlooked for the time being in the sense that it is not acted upon.

Surprising though it may be, the extent of the majority proved to be irrelevant for the strength of the orientative impact, beyond a certain threshold that was taken as reflecting a minimum criterion (H. Kreitler & S. Kreitler, 1976, pp. 165–169; Section IV,A). Beyond this threshold, it appeared immaterial whether the majority was minimal, medium, or substantial. Hence, orientativeness of beliefs seems to function in accordance with two interwoven principles: the principle of exclusiveness, whereby only one course of action is supported and eventually acted upon, and the principle of all-or-nothing, whereby only strength beyond a certain threshold is considered regardless of degrees. It may not be accidental that the first principle is found to govern behavior in general (even when several courses of action are combined, at any one time only one action is carried out), whereas the second principle dominates some physiological events, such as the firing of a synapse, and cognitive phenomena, such as the occurrence of an idea or a solution to a problem that may be later discarded as inadequate but upon occurrence is as full-fledged as a valid or adequate solution.

This interaction between beliefs of the same type results in the formation of what we call the four CO components (e.g., the norm component and the goal components). The confrontation of the four CO components and their resulting interaction give rise to the CO cluster. Within the CO cluster, each of the four components functions like a single belief representing the componential majority. It either supports or does not support the focal behavior. Indeed, this additive effect of beliefs within and across CO components is so primitive that it could be accounted for without invoking any kind of interaction, were it not that any threat of stalemate is at once countered by refined meaning interaction, rearrangements, and adjustments both across and within the components.

If the focal belief is supported by all four or three CO components, a behavioral intent (BI) in line with the supported behavior will ensue. When the number of supporting CO components is only three, and there is concomitantly no support of all four CO components for another course of action, attempts may be made to modify or rearrange the beliefs in the nonsupporting CO component (e.g., in the goal component by retrieving secondary goals that support the indicated behavior, replacing the dominant goal belief by a goal lower in the hierarchy) with the purpose of turning it into a supporting component. If one or more of the CO components has no specific orientational impact in regard to a particular behavior, or the situation allows for only one behavior that corresponds to the behavior indicated by the focal belief, support of only one or two CO components may result in undertaking that action, but the probability for this is low and, hence, prediction unreliable.

Less frequent but not at all rare is the simplest kind of stalemate that may arise when two CO components support the hitherto focal behavior while the other two components oppose it. Methods are available for overcoming the difficulty in these and similar cases. The most common method is belief substitution guided by existing belief hierarchies and mediated by slight modification of belief meanings. The success depends on internal factors, such as rigidity of belief hierarchies, the availability of a sufficiently refined store of meaning values, or the ability to produce the meaning values required for small but effective meaning modifications.

A more dramatic development is the concomitant formation of two competing CO clusters. A great variety of constellations can yield such an outcome. Common to all is the emergence of two goal beliefs with two inconsistent behavioral implications, each of which is supported by beliefs of all CO components. The outcome of two competing CO clusters is two competing behavioral intents, a constellation that we call conflict (see Section III,D).

Sometimes the tendency to form four CO components cannot materialize simply because there may be no beliefs of one type or another that are pertinent to the input. The result is an incomplete CO cluster. A CO cluster is incomplete if one CO component is missing. A case in point is window-shopping. The input is, for example, an antique table; a BS, "I liked it in my grandparents' house"; an N belief, "One should possess such things"; a GB, "Recently many people have bought antique furniture"; no goal beliefs. Incomplete CO clusters are frequently induced in foreign countries. For example, the input is a waiter presenting the bill; the Go belief, "I want to tip him"; the BS, "I liked the meat he recommended"; the GB, "In some countries tips are forbidden"; no norm beliefs. Unoperational CO clusters are clusters induced by a focal belief that, as a result of meaning generation, does not pertain to real, overt, molar behavior but either to imaginative as-if performance (e.g., daydreaming) or merely to cognitive activities, such as problem solving, rethinking, speculating, and analyzing. Both types are of utmost importance but will not be discussed here, partly because the CO theory was developed for explaining, predicting, and modifying overt molar behavior, but mainly because the analysis of imagining and thinking presupposes more information about our theory of meaning than can be presented in the present context.

Not all CO clusters, probably only a minority, are ad hoc productions. CO clusters that have recurred frequently or that have guided successful performance may be stored in long-term memory and, hence, can be retrieved by the original focal belief or by a similar one. However, even if the retrieval of such CO clusters has turned into a kind of conditioned response (e.g., answering the question "What is the time?"), a single deviating belief (e.g., "The tone of the person who asked the question was not polite enough") may frustrate their orientative impact. When this is the case, the retrieved cluster is either reshaped or completely abandoned in favor of new belief evocation and CO clustering.

Some of the stored CO clusters do not relate to a particular course of action but serve as guidelines for the acquisition or production of beliefs as well as for the formation of more specific CO clusters. The following is an example of such a general CO cluster. The Go belief is: "I want to be successful"; the BS, "I am a bright and convincing fellow"; the N, "One should never antagonize society"; the GB, "Success is the ultimate justification." Due to their interaction with personality traits (Section III,E), these generalized CO clusters shape the behavioral manifestations of personality. Moreover, on closer scrutiny some of the more permanent traits turn out to be summarizing manifestations of one or another generalized CO cluster.

As mentioned previously, we regard the four-component CO cluster as determining the course of action and constituting the core material for predicting and modifying human molar behavior. Considering the importance of these functions, one may wonder why we designate it by such a vague and noncommital term as "cluster" instead of "CO unit" or "CO structure," thus emphasizing its wholistic qualities. The reason for this is methodological. Notwithstanding our conviction that it is a structure or gestalt that functions as a whole, we must stick to what we have been able to demonstrate so far. We have ample evidence that the combined value of the four CO components correlates highly and significantly with molar behavior (see Sections V through X). Moreover, it was demonstrated that experimentally induced modification of beliefs in one or more CO components results in behavior modification in line with the componential belief modification (see Section V,B). Hence, it is justifiable to regard the relation as causal. We have not yet been able to show that the four CO components form a unit, a structure that does more than can be attributed to the additive value of the CO components. We do not yet have sufficiently convincing proof of what gestalt psychologists would call the oversummative impact of the cluster. If, nonetheless, we uphold the term "CO cluster," hoping that eventually it could be superceded by the term "CO structure," we do it because of the following consideration. There is evidence that subjects try to change beliefs of one or more CO components in order to overcome a stalemate. Mutual adjustment is a common means for structuring and seems to be guided by the concept of a final structure. In terms of gestalt psychology, this rationale may be convincing but does not constitute a sufficient substitute for empirical evidence. Therefore, the term CO cluster is still adequate (for empirical studies concerning beliefs and CO components, see H. Kreitler & S. Kreitler, 1976, chap. 13).

D. BEHAVIORAL INTENT AND BEHAVIORAL PROGRAM

If three or all four components of a CO cluster support a particular course of action, the overriding behavioral direction is modified into a belief about self expressing the personal commitment to an action, for example, "I will do it now," "I will go there at such a time," or "I will call her later." The behavioral intent usually differs from the underlying focal belief, often a goal belief, in terms of meaning. Whereas meaning values of the meaning dimension Consequences and Results dominate the meaning of the focal belief, meaning values of the dimension Action and Potentialities for Action are more prominent in the meaning of the intent. However, one of the functions of the intent requires that it also carry meaning values pertaining to the expected or derived outcome. If CO clustering resulted in two orientatively inconsistent CO clusters, two behavioral intents arise and either constitute a conflict or relate to behaviors in two concomitantly foreseen situations. The latter may happen if a subject is required to answer in front of his classmates the question whether he would volunteer for the highly prestigious but dangerous marine corps of frogmen. The subject may form two behavioral intents: (a) to answer the question affirmatively and to sign the necessary papers; and (b) to find ways and means not to be accepted in this corps. This is one of the reasons why a behavioral intent, and in particular its public announcement by the subject, as used in some studies of attitudes or intention and behavior (e.g., Fishbein & Ajzen, 1975, chap. 8), should not be regarded as a reliable predictor of molar behavior. Another reason is that even very honest subjects are likely to mistake one of their goals for a behavioral intent. Finally, it is easy for the subject to fake a behavioral intent. But it is extremely difficult, if not outright impossible, for all subjects to fake their answers to a CO questionnaire of beliefs since they cannot know which behavior is indicated by the different beliefs that they endorse or reject (see Section IV).

Although the behavioral intent should not be used directly for predicting and modifying behavior, it plays an important role in the evocation of molar behavior. By virtue of its orientative meaning values, it guides selection, modification, or ad hoc construction of behavioral programs and serves as a frame of reference for supervision of current program execution, intermediate evaluation of the adequacy of the program's operational aspects, a first evaluation of the outcome, and activation of the stop mechanism.

Whereas prediction and modification of molar behavior do not require particular consideration of behavioral intents, the availability of adequate behavioral programs must be taken into account. Without a behavioral program the behavioral intent remains unoperational. Reviving the sequence of implicit answers to implicit questions, we can regard the CO cluster as stating what to do, the behavioral intent as summarizing what will be done, and the behavioral program as outlining how it can be done. Behavioral programs are detailed instructions for the sequential execution of overt motor behavior. However, since even minute phases of automatized motor actions retain some adjustability, most neurophysiologists from Head to Pribram assume an underlying schema. Therefore, we call the two aspects of the behavioral program Program Scheme and Operational Program. The first is more akin to a plan, a blueprint of the action, or an overall strategy; the latter is bound with physiological specifications. Together they constitute what we call Program.

Because of its emphasis on dynamic features the CO theory categorizes behavioral programs according to their origin. Summarizing the findings of many researchers concerned with behavior execution, we distinguish between four kinds of behavioral programs.

1. *Innate programs.* They guide the execution of reflex behavior as well as of classical conditioned reflexes. Thus, they underlie primarily the output on the submolar level, but are also involved in some parts of the performance of molar behavior.

2. *Programs that are partly innate and partly acquired.* They guide instinct

behavior in the sense of Tinbergen (1951) and Lorenz (1969) and daily actions such as walking and running. They are involved in some programs for conflict resolution, such as the basic defense mechanisms described by psychoanalysis, and are prominent in the phonetic part of language behavior. Most frequently the program scheme is innate while the operational program is acquired.

3. *Learned programs.* Examples include anything from programs for problem-solving strategies to habitual behaviors such as rigidity, functional fixedness, writing, typing, and looking at a watch.

4. *Ad hoc constructed programs.* Usually they make heavy use of already existing program schemes, including plans for plan construction (G. Miller, Galanter, & Pribram, 1960).

Again, the transition from behavioral intent to behavioral program is mediated by meaning processes. The meaning of the intent, mainly in terms of meaning values along the meaning dimensions Consequences and Results, Action and Potentialities for Action, Manner of Occurrence and Operation, and Locational Qualities and Temporary Qualities, guides the retrieval of meaning-related programs and the selection of the program with the best match or constitutes the guidelines for program construction.

Sometimes two behavioral programs seem equally adequate for implementing the behavioral intent. Thus, the CO theory allows for two kinds of conflicts: conflicts between behavioral intents and conflicts between behavioral programs. As mentioned previously (Section III,C), humans dispose of many and varied programs for conflict resolution. Indeed, a part of socialization consists in learning culturally approved programs for conflict resolution, such as, for example, sequential implementation of conflicting intents, flipping a coin, or carrying out one intent while rewarding oneself for foregoing the other. Of particular interest are programs for resolving a conflict in which at least one of the intents is unconscious in the Freudian sense. The most frequently applied programs for their temporary resolution are defense mechanisms, such as projection and rationalization (Sections V,A and VIII,B), but programs for dreaming and daydreaming may suffice. If a conflict between intents cannot be solved by means of a behavioral program, recourse is taken to renewed CO clustering.

In contrast, most program conflicts are perceived as situations requiring decision making and may be resolved by programs for decision making. But program conflicts are frequently only the manifestation of masked conflicts between intents. Hence, they require for their resolution more than can be provided by programs for decision making. A different point of view in regard to this issue was developed by Zakay (1976; Section X) in his experimentally founded model of decision making. Zakay assumed that decision making is triggered by a behavioral intent "to decide," likely to be formed under any one of five different conditions. One of these is, as stated previously, a conflict between programs, but another is a conflict between behavioral intents.

Like all the other processes described, the execution of molar behavior is cognitively controlled. The program scheme and the behavioral intent are the controlling agencies receiving feedback information. Purely automatic performance of molar behavior would not only increase the likelihood of failure but could endanger the whole organism, for example, if program execution proceeded despite danger signals from the environment. However, neither program scheme nor intent suffice for determining whether further execution of the ongoing program should be interrupted, delayed, or, if possible, combined with the new program. Renewed CO clustering and even further meaning generation may be required for coping with situations like these. The same is true if, after completion of program execution, a mismatch is discovered between expected and achieved results. In other words, feedback information may induce a new cycle of input elaboration. Therefore, we consider it likely that the processes delineated by the CO theory function almost permanently, even during the dream-promoting REM period of sleep.

The above description of the processes intervening between primary input elaboration and execution of output behavior, complex as it may appear, is less complex than what is shown in the flowchart (Fig. 1). This, in turn, constitutes a simplification of more detailed flowcharts in an earlier publication (H. Kreitler & S. Kreitler, 1976). In other words, many interesting aspects could not be mentioned here, as for instance, the specific pathogenic impact of malfunctioning and meaning distortion in each of the stages, CO processes that underlie emotions, or procedures for considering concomitantly several different CO clusters that may be necessary for successfully predicting specific behaviors, mostly more permanent ones that combine several orientative impacts (H. Kreitler & S. Kreitler, 1981). Nonetheless, we feel that skipping various aspects and recent developments is preferable to blurring the essentials through a profusion of details.

E. COGNITIVE ORIENTATION THEORY AND PERSONALITY RESEARCH

Every theory of human behavior that gives a coherent and causal description of the chain of events between input elaboration and execution of output behavior contains the essentials required for a theory of personality. In the case of the CO theory, we have the clear raw outlines of a personality theory, the major elements of which are perceivable external stimulation as well as internal signals stemming, for example, from need indicators or the limbic system acting as input to the cognitive system, which interprets them in terms of meaning and induces meaning-related belief evocation, retrieval of stored CO clusters, and ad hoc CO clustering for determining the course of action that is carried out according to a behavioral program, selected and controlled by the behavioral intent. However, our present concern is not to fill this skeleton with all the flesh, nerves, and organs required

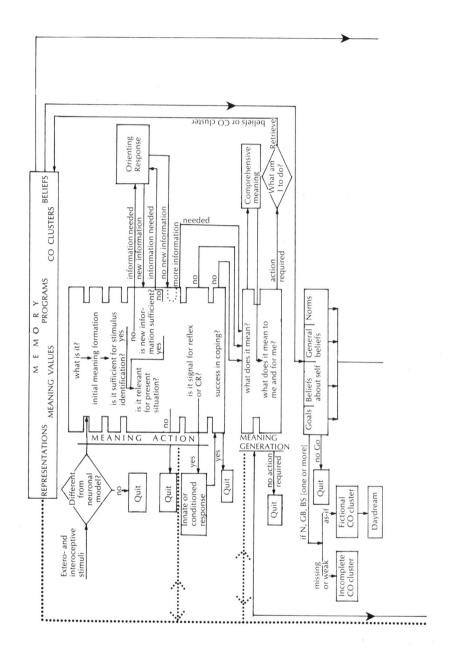

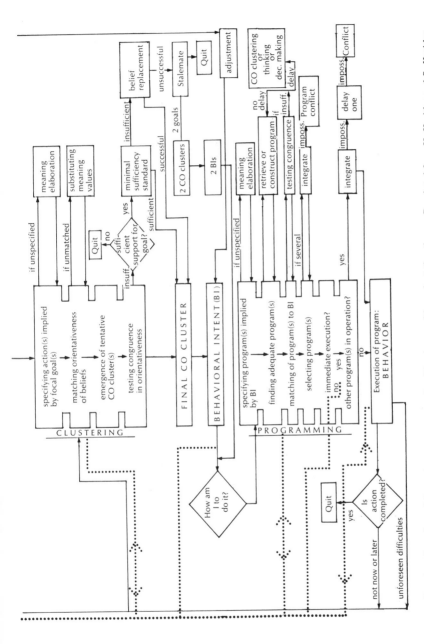

Fig. 1. Overview of the main processes postulated by the cognitive orientation theory. Reprinted from H. Kreitler and S. Kreitler, "Cognitive Orientation and Behavior," pp. 160–161. Copyright © 1976 by Springer Publishing Company, Inc., New York. Used by permission.

for applying and evaluating such a theory. Instead, we intend to give a highly condensed report of our recent attempts to solve three major problems in personality research by applying our theories of meaning and of cognitive orientation (S. Kreitler & H. Kreitler, 1982a).

1. Traits

Intrigued by the increasingly growing number of hypothesized traits and challenged by the absence of an ordering system or a unifying conceptualization, we administered to samples of subjects different commonly used personality measures and a questionnaire of meaning that enabled establishment of the subjects' meaning profiles (Section IV). This series of over 20 studies made possible comparisons and examination of interrelations between scores on personality variables and meaning profiles. The studies showed that each trait correlated significantly with a particular grouping of meaning variables and different referent–meaning value relations. These findings support the conclusion that traits such as introversion–extroversion, Cattell's 16 personality factors, Machiavellianism, and internal–external control can be considered as permanent or frequently recurrent constellations of meaning variables. Particular subtypes within the framework of the more encompassing traits may further be characterized in terms of specific meaning dimensions subservient (or secondary) to major meaning dimensions. More narrowly defined traits, like stinginess, may be characterized in addition in terms of specific meaning values. Findings of this kind show that our theory of meaning provides a conceptual framework that enables us to define, in terms of the same set of concepts, the different traits as well as other personality variables, notably cognitive styles, and tendencies within the spheres of emotion, imagery, and fantasy. Definition in terms of meaning facilitates comparison of traits, examination of their relations to each other, and prediction of their relations to other variables. Further, it is likely that studies of this kind could lead to the elimination of traits whose overall similarity has hitherto been masked by differences in conceptual background and terminologies; these studies could also make possible the detection of new traits on the basis of frequently recurring constellations of meaning variables.

Meaning variables indicate processes and contents used for the sake of meaning assignment. By applying the microgenetic method (S. Kreitler & H. Kreitler, 1977, 1982b, in preparation), it was possible to show that in the primary phase of input identification most subjects use similar meaning dimensions, whereas in a later stage of meaning assignment they apply, if possible, their preferred meaning variables. Thus, in terms of the CO theory, a trait would be manifested in the preferred use of particualr meaning variables, especially in the course of meaning generation. Accordingly, traits would affect belief evocation, namely, retrieval and generation of beliefs. Further, a number of studies showed that meaning variables are related to specific CO components and CO clusters (Section XII). The next logical step, which has not yet been taken, would be to test the assumption that particular traits correlate with specific permanently stored CO clusters. Confirmation of this assumption would reveal how meaning assignment tendencies and long-term motivational structures form the underlying dynamics of traditional personality variables.

2. Situations

Whereas so-called situationists (Bower, 1973) still cling to the naive physical realism of the nineteenth century, most other psychologists are aware of twentieth-century physics and its philosophical implications. They accept the notion that situations and their stimulating potentials cannot be properly evaluated without regard for the stimulated subject. However, they have no reliable means for determining prior to setting up an experiment whether or not a particular experimental situation will be the same for different subjects. Further, they have no measure for quantifying, or at least characterizing, the difference between two physically differing experimental situations. As a consequence, some of these psychologists escape into a kind of cognitive solipsism which is almost as unrealistic as Skinnerian naive realism.

The solution suggested by the CO theory is obvious. The system of meaning enables characterizing the meaning of situations objectively, from the viewpoint of subjects. The meaning of situations can be evaluated on the basis of the lexical meaning—in contrast to the personal meaning—that subjects are requested to assign to situations. This makes it possible to manipulate situational meaning. For example, on the basis of the meaning assigned by subjects to situations, an experimenter can select for the experiment a situation with the highest concordance of meaning for a particular sample, or two different situations with radically different meanings, and so on, as dictated by the hypotheses and design. Indeed, some progress was done in exploring the relations between the subject's meaning profile (Section IV) and the meanings assigned to situations (S. Kreitler & H. Kreitler, 1982a). These explorations showed that the latter are largely predictable from the former. Thus, it would be possible on the basis of the subjects' meaning profiles to select subjects who would assign specific predictable meanings to particular situations. It is evident that the major advantage in evaluating situational meanings objectively is the possibility for distinguishing unequivocally between so-called situational variables and personal variables. In operational terms, by assessing meaning prior to an experiment, it is possible to explore or determine the initial meaning (answering the question ''What is it?''), and the comprehensive meaning, resulting from meaning generation (answering the question ''What does it mean to me?''), while letting the experiment answer the question ''What am I to do?'' and/or ''How am I to do it?''

3. Consistency of Behavior

Whereas trait psychologists argue their case by invoking observed consistencies of behavior across situations, situationists cite the frequent inconsistencies of these behavior consistencies. According to the CO theory both arguments appear to be beside the point. Even a casual recollection of the previously described chain of events between input and output reveals that two different situations may evoke the same molar behavior while two identical situations could be coped with by two radically different behaviors. Examples for the first case can be frequently encountered in retarded children who, lacking adequate behavioral programs, tend to apply the same program for implementing different intents, for example, using a hammer for driving a nail into a board and knocking with a hammer against the head in order to bring in a piece of information that should be remembered. Less dramatic, though fairly obvious, is the tendency of some people to hit a malfunctioning machine as they would spank a disobedient child. The second case—different responses to apparently similar or identical situations—is probably due to new meaning values acquired for one of the situations, changes in the subject's belief hierarchies, or a shift in the meaning of the situation precisely because it is a recurrent situation encountered again after having once evoked a response. Indeed, that behavioral consistency could at all become an important issue is to our mind due to behavioristic education that brought about not only situationism but seems also to have exerted a lasting impact on the minds of many trait psychologists.

In sum, it is evident that so many processes intervene between so-called traits and molar behavior or between situations and molar behavior that no conclusion can be drawn from output behavior back to either one of them. However, when we trace the path from input to output we find that, apart from severe cases of psychopathology or neuropathology, many relevant features of situations are duly reflected in the products of meaning action, meaning generation, belief evocation, and, in particular, program selection and adjustment, that are often guided by meaning values carried over from initial meaning action. By the same token, preferred meaning constellations (i.e., traits), the more permanent CO clusters, as well as habitual programs, are effective behavior-shaping agents. However, there seems to be not one but several kinds of consistency on different levels, for example, consistency in input identification (meaning action), in meaning generation, in CO clusters, in behavioral intents, in programs, and in molar behaviors. On each level there may be different manifestations and causes of consistency or inconsistency. For example, consistency in meaning generation may depend primarily on traits, whereas consistency in programs may depend on the store of available programs and habitual modes of elaborating the meaning of the intents.

In more general terms, consistency is perhaps not an adequate term to describe behavior and human processes. Lawfulness or predictability would have been more appropriate, for in the final count what matters is not whether or not the indiviudal is consistent but rather whether the behavior is lawful and, hence, predictable. Thus, it seems likely that apart from its misconceived role in the trait–situation controversy, the quest for behavioral consistencies across situations may have been motivated by the hope to exploit these consistencies for predicting molar behavior. The CO theory demonstrates how this can be done in a conceptual framework and with empirical tools that do not capitalize on consistency.

IV. Some Elements of Technique

The CO questionnaire and the meaning questionnaire are basic tools used in the various studies to be mentioned or reported. In view of detailed presentations elsewhere (H. Kreitler & S. Kreitler, 1976, pp. 23–35, pp. 165–169; S. Kreitler & H. Kreitler, 1982a, 1983, in preparation), they will be described here only briefly.

A CO questionnaire is a questionnaire designed to provide scores for the four CO components concerning a specific behavior.[1] There are three major stages in constructing a standard CO questionnaire. The first stage consists in determining the major meaning aspects involved in the behavior to be predicted. For this purpose pretest subjects of the same population as the subjects of the study proper are asked to communicate the meaning of the behavior, the task, the situational context, and so on, according to standard instructions. Sometimes specific questions about the Action and Potentialities for Action, Consequences and Results, Causes and Antecedents, and so on, of the different referents are added. The responses of the subjects provide information about major aspects of meaning related to the examined behavior, namely, their contents and their orientative relation to the behavior. For example, the meaning exploration showed that striving for perfectionism and prevention of damage were major meaning themes of slowness (Section VIII,A) and that both were related positively to it.

The second stage consists in formulating the beliefs in the CO questionnaire. This is done by using the themes mentioned by a majority of the pretest subjects in the first stage as raw materials for formulating beliefs in terms of the four CO components, for example, when the theme is spontaneity (related negatively to the behavior of orderliness), a goal belief could be "I want to cultivate my spontaneity." The same themes occur in the four CO components, although in different forms. Positive and negative formulations are balanced. Each belief has a

---

[1]Copies of different CO questionnaires in English may be obtained upon request from the ETS Test Collection, Educational Testing Service, Princeton, New Jersey 08540.

predetermined orientational direction with regard to the examined behavior. The beliefs are checked by judges for clarity, nonsuggestibility, and plausibility.

The third stage consists in administering the questionnaire to pretest subjects. Their task usually consists in checking endorsement or rejection of each stated belief on a scale or in terms of presented response alternatives. The beliefs of each CO component are grouped together and presented separately with appropriate instructions. The instructions emphasize the requirement to respond in terms of the given CO component, for example, "In your answers, please consider only how things should or should not be rather than how they actually are" (instructions for the N component). The four subquestionnaires are presented together in random order. The subjects' responses are used for item selection according to standard psychometric criteria. Major among these are (a) a minimum of a .30 correlation of items within a CO component with other items in that component; (b) a minimum of .60 correlation between the items within a CO component with the total score of that component; (c) approximately equal distribution between responses in the categories of acceptance and rejection (i.e., above and below the neutral category); and (d) a low percentage of responses in the neutral midpoint category. If possible an attempt is made to select items that would minimize correlations between the four CO components.

The item analyses are used in order to select items for each CO component. Eventually the number of beliefs in each subquestionnaire may vary to some extent. It is evident that after item selection some themes are not represented to the same degree in all four subquestionnaires.

In most studies the separate scores of the four CO components are combined into an index called CO score. A CO score is determined by first assessing the individual's score on each CO component separately, then converting each of the four scores into 1 or 0 depending on whether it falls above or below the group's mean or median for the specific CO component, and finally summing up these converted scores. Thus, a CO score can range from a maximum of 4 (when all four CO components are above the group's mean) to a minimum of 0 (when none of the four CO components are above the group's mean). A CO 4 usually indicates that all four CO components support the specific behavior, whereas a CO 0 indicates that none of the four CO components supports it.

The above description refers to the standard procedure for constructing a CO questionnaire. Different variations exist and some are mentioned in the studies described later (Sections VIII,A and X,B). There are four basic features common to all CO questionnaires: (a) A CO questionnaire is behavior-specific in the sense that it refers to a particular concrete course of action; (b) a CO questionnaire includes items whose relation to the specific behavior has been established on the basis of meaning analysis; (c) a CO questionnaire is based on coding the subjects' responses in line with their orientativeness in regard to the specific behavior; and (d) a CO questionnaire provides four different scores, one for each CO component. The second and third features make it necessary to check each CO questionnaire before it is applied with a new sample.

Meaning assessment is used in the first stage of constructing a CO questionnaire. But it can be used also independently of a CO questionnaire (e.g., Section VIII,A). There exist standard instructions and stimuli for the assessment of an individual's meaning. The subjects' responses are analyzed in terms of the system of meaning (see Table I). The results of the analysis are in the form of a set of frequencies on each of the meaning variables. The frequencies are transformed into proportions out of the total. The transformed set of frequencies of responses on all meaning variables is called the subject's meaning profile. The focus of the analysis of meaning may be a situation. Parallel procedures provide for the set of data that could be called the meaning profile of a situation (Section III,E).

The regular methodology of studies in the framework of the CO theory is also marked by the following features. The CO questionnaire is administered to some subjects before the behavior is assessed and to others after it is assessed. The administration of the CO questionnaire is completely detached from the experimental situation in which the dependent variables are assessed. It usually takes place under different conditions, in a different location, and in the presence of experimenters different from those who are involved in obtaining the dependent measures. The time interval between the two kinds of sessions may be up to 3 months. There is almost no way for the subjects to relate the two parts of the experiment. After completion of the experiment the subjects are always debriefed.

V. Brief Review of Former Studies

A. PREDICTION STUDIES

The 12 following studies were published earlier and therefore will be described here only briefly. These studies deal with predicting behavior (or results of behavior) on the basis of CO scores (Section IV). Common to all the studies was the hypothesis that CO scores based on the subjects' responses to a CO questionnaire assessing orientation toward a particular behavior are related to the subjects' manifestations of that behavior. In all studies the availability of behavioral programs for executing the behaviors was checked or controlled.

The first study (H. Kreitler & S. Kreitler, 1976, pp. 169–181) dealt with achievement behavior assessed by performance on routine, well-practiced arithmetic tasks administered with achievement-oriented instructions under normal, postsuccess, and postfailure conditions. The dependent variables were the number of items solved, the number solved correctly, and an index based on these two criteria. The subjects were 50 high school students of both genders,

15-16 years old. The CO questionnaire included items designed to assess, for example, the subjects' readiness to make an effort, concern with excellence of performance, and standards for evaluating achievements. The findings showed that under all three conditions performance was highest in subjects with CO 4 on a CO questionnaire of achievement, lower in subjects with CO 3 or 2, and lowest in subjects with CO 1 or 0.

Another study (H. Kreitler & S. Kreitler, 1976, pp. 181–184) with 50 high school students showed that CO scores of accuracy were related significantly to an index variable of accuracy based on mean proportion of right items out of total items done in five routine tasks (arithmetic and crossing letters). Incidentally, CO scores of achievement were not related to accuracy.

Another study (H. Kreitler & S. Kreitler, 1976, pp. 184–190) with a group of 50 tenth- to twelfth-graders showed that CO scores for behavior postsuccess and CO scores for behavior postfailure predicted as expected increases, no change, and decreases in performance (assessed by an index based on the number of items solved and solved correctly) after success and after failure, respectively.

Another study (H. Kreitler & S. Kreitler, 1976, pp. 215–222) conducted in a naturalistic setting with 92 seventh-graders showed that CO scores for over- and underachievement differentiated significantly between overachievers and under-achievers defined in terms of the gap between actual GPA and the GPA expected on the basis of the student's IQ.

A separate study was conducted in regard to the GPA variable alone (H. Kreitler & S. Kreitler, 1976, pp. 212–215). It showed that the CO scores for postsuccess and for postfailure jointly differentiated between subjects with different GPA levels, whereas the CO scores for achievement were related in boys to mean of grades in natural sciences and in girls to mean of grades in the humanities, but in neither group to the total GPA.

A study (H. Kreitler & S. Kreitler, 1976, pp. 191–195) with 70 16- to 18-year-olds showed that CO scores for punctuality were related as expected to frequency of being late to school over a period of 3 months. The prediction was improved when CO scores keyed for orienting toward being on time were supplemented by CO scores keyed for orienting toward not being late.

A further study (Kreitler, Lobel, & Kreitler, in H. Kreitler & S. Kreitler, 1976, pp. 196–201) conducted with 112 undergraduates showed that CO scores for pain tolerance were related as expected to the threshold of pain tolerance and to an index based on the difference between the tolerance threshold and pain threshold but not, again in line with the expectation, to the sensitivity and pain thresholds or the subjective evaluation of pain.

An earlier study (H. Kreitler & S. Kreitler, 1969, 1972b) dealt with predicting the relative frequency of applying the three defense mechanisms, denial, rationalization, and projection, in different experimental situations after exposure to frustrating injustice. The CO questionnaire included beliefs about themes such as keeping calm, controlling action and emotions, noting minute details in the behavior of others, optimism, and the virtues of rationality. The rank-ordering of the three CO scores for the defense behaviors was related in 24 undergraduates to an index based on defensive description of the frustrating situation and partner, defensive response to portrayal of aggression in pictures, and responses to a Defense Mechanism Questionnaire.

A study with adult smokers (S. Kreitler, Shahar, & H. Kreitler, 1976) showed that CO scores for quitting smoking were related as expected to the amount of decrease in smoking that occurred following different kinds of behavior therapy for quitting smoking to which the subjects ($N = 57$) had voluntarily exposed themselves.

A study (S. Kreitler, H. Kreitler, & Zigler, 1970) conducted with 84 first-graders showed that CO scores of curiosity are related positively to 14 different measures of curiosity behavior that represent four of the five previously identified factors of curiosity (S. Kreitler, Zigler, & H. Kreitler, 1975), for example, number of exploratory manipulations performed with unfamiliar toys (saturated on manipulatory curiosity), number of times of switching glances between two presented stimuli (saturated on perceptual curiosity), number of complex stimuli preferred (saturated on curiosity about the complex), and number of choices of a hidden stimulus (saturated on reactive curiosity). Conceptual curiosity was the only factor whose variables were neither related to CO scores of curiosity nor expected to be since they do not involve molar behaviors.

In the context of probability learning (S. Kreitler, H. Kreitler, & Zigler, in H. Kreitler & S. Kreitler, 1976, pp. 228–234), the CO questionnaire of curiosity was related, as expected, positively to preoccupation with finding a pattern as evidence of hypothesis testing and negatively to response sequences manifesting preoccupation with reinforcement and withdrawal from the situation.

Finally, CO scores of intolerance of ambiguity were shown to be related in high school students, 17–18 years old, to different behaviors manifesting intolerance of ambiguity, for example, resistance to voluntary exposures to information contradicting one's opinions and speed of responding to ambiguous figures (Smock's series) (S. Kreitler, Maguen, & H. Kreitler, 1975).

These studies showed that CO scores representing beliefs orienting towards a particular behavior differentiate significantly between subjects who manifest the particular behavior in different degrees of intensity or frequency. The relation of CO scores to behavior was shown to be essentially linear. Two deviations from linearity were found (H. Kreitler & S. Kreitler, 1976, p. 224, var. 6; pp. 231–234), but at least one case seemed to point to the possibility of qualitatively different behaviors corresponding to the two involved CO scores. Linearity does not imply that the behavior differences corresponding to different CO scores form a ratio scale, that is, the difference between CO 4 and CO 3 may correspond to a larger or smaller behavioral difference than the difference between CO 2 and

CO 1. The relation of CO scores to behavior was shown to depend on the specific content and meaning of the belief in the underlying CO cluster. Thus, a specific CO score will not predict a behavior whose meaning is unrelated to the CO, regardless of how relevant it may seem to be (e.g., CO scores of achievement are not related to accuracy or overall GPA), but will predict a whole range of behaviors that may not even be correlated with each other provided that they have the relevant meaning (e.g., the CO score of curiosity predicted 14 different curiosity variables). This enables the use of CO scores for exploring motivational structures underlying different behaviors (e.g., H. Kreitler & S. Kreitler, 1976, pp. 184–191, 228–234).

Control analyses in the reported studies showed that the mere sum of the positively keyed beliefs, regardless of the differentiation into four CO components, was not related to behavior. Neither were combinations of fewer than the four components related to the studied behavior in a systematic and predictable way. In some studies one or another of the separate CO components was related significantly to one or another of the dependent variables but not in a consistent manner (H. Kreitler & S. Kreitler, 1976, pp. 386–390). The intercorrelations between the CO components do not seem to affect efficiency of prediction (H. Kreitler & S. Kreitler, 1976, pp. 374–378, 390). Administering the CO questionnaire prior to or following the behavior affected neither the behavior nor the relation of CO scores to the behavior. CO scores were related to behaviors of subjects regardless of age (the lowest in the studies was 6 years) and gender.

B. CHANGING BEHAVIOR STUDIES

Two studies confirmed the basic deduction from the theory that changing CO clusters brings about a change in the predicted direction implied by the CO cluster.

One study (with T. Boas, in H. Kreitler & S. Kreitler, 1976, pp. 238–253) focused on changing—for ethical reasons, only increasing—the curiosity behaviors of kindergarten children (4:10- to 5:11-year-olds) by changing beliefs affecting curiosity. The change procedures consisted in discussing with the children in group sessions various themes relevant to curiosity but none that related explicitly to the behaviors to be examined. In the experimental subjects, there were pronounced changes in all CO components and, as expected, significant changes in the different curiosity behaviors 1 week after termination of the group sessions and 2 months later.

Another study (with T. Lobel, in H. Kreitler & S. Kreitler, 1976, pp. 253–271) dealt with changing pain tolerance in adults. The method used for manipulating CO processes was role-playing of changed beliefs, behavioral intent, or behavioral program, geared to effect both increases and decreases in pain tolerance. Pain tolerance was assessed by responses to an actual pain stimulus produced through electric shocks increasing gradually in intensity. The change in pain tolerance was greatest when the subjects enacted changes in beliefs, less when they enacted changes in the BI, and least when they enacted changes in the program. But only the changes in pain tolerance due to changes in beliefs differed significantly from the changes in the control group.

The two studies showed that induced changes in COs result in predictable changes in behavior.

VI. Replications of Former Studies

A. PREDICTING PAIN TOLERANCE FROM COGNITIVE ORIENTATION COMPONENTS

Lobel (1981a) replicated the earlier study on pain tolerance (Section V,A) with a new sample of 44 undergraduate students at Tel Aviv University (22 females, 22 males in the age range 18–26 years). The same CO questionnaire was used as in the former study and the same procedure was applied. The pain stimuli were electric shocks administered in a series of increasing intensities, 5 μA per step. Each subject was examined individually. The subject's sensitivity threshold, pain threshold, and pain tolerance were recorded. The CO questionnaire was administered in small groups by experimenters different from those who administered the shocks. Half of the subjects received the CO questionnaire first, and half the experimental pain tolerance test. In the lab, half of the subjects of each gender were tested by experimenters of the same gender and half by experimenters of the opposite gender.

Each subject received five scores, four for the four CO components, and one for pain tolerance. The multiple correlation of the four CO components with pain tolerance was .48 ($p < .05$) and .50 when corrected for shrinkage (see Table II for the stepwise regression coefficients). Moreover, all four CO components were shown to be necessary for the prediction. These findings fully replicate those of the previous study (Section V,A) where the data were analyzed by analysis of variance. The correlations between the four CO components were all positive and significant (ranging from .43 to .68), again as in the earlier study (H. Kreitler & S. Kreitler, 1976, p. 377).

B. PREDICTING PUNCTUALITY FROM COGNITIVE ORIENTATION COMPONENTS

1. Study A

This study was not an exact replication of a previous study on this behavior (Section V,A). Lobel (1981b) constructed a different CO questionnaire which

TABLE II

MULTIPLE CORRELATIONS AND STEPWISE REGRESSION COEFFICIENTS OF COGNITIVE ORIENTATION COMPONENTS WITH DIFFERENT BEHAVIORS

Behavior	CO component	β	r	Multiple R	R (corrected for shrinkage)
Pain	GB	.34	.36	.36	
tolerance	BS	.15	.30	.40	
(based on	N	−.35	.10	.43	
Lobel, 1981a)	Go	.33	.32	.48*	.50*
Punctuality	BS	−.63	.55	.54	
(Study A)	Go	−.25	−.29	.55	
(based on	N	−.23	−.25	.58	
Lobel, 1981b)	GB	.10	−.24	.58**	.61**
Punctuality	BS	−.53	−.54	.54	
(Study B)	N	−.24	−.22	.58	
(based on	GB	.14	.01	.60	
Lobel, 1981b)	Go	−.04	−.16	.60***	.62***
Orderliness	N	−.41	−.41	.41	
(Study A)	BS	−.33	−.39	.47	
(based on	Go	.23	−.20	.50	
Lobel, 1981c)	GB	.02	−.25	.50**	.52**
Orderliness	N	−.32	−.40	.40	
(Study B)	BS	−.27	−.32	.45	
(based on	Go	.27	−.06	.49	
Lobel, 1981c)	GB	−.23	−.33	.53***	.55***
Assertiveness	GB	.55	.53	.53	
(Study A)	Go	−.02	.20	.53	
(based on	BS	−.02	.18	.53**	.55**
Lobel, 1981d)					
Assertiveness	BS	.56	.45	.45	
(Study B)	GB	−.07	.18	.46	
(based on	N	−.05	.33	.46	
Lobel, 1981d)	Go	−.03	.29	.46**	.47**
Conformity	GB	−.49	−.44	.45	
(based on	N	−.16	−.11	.50	
Lobel, 1981e)	BS	−.30	.29	.53	
	Go	−.28	−.00	.57**	.59**

*$p < .05$.
**$p < .01$.
***$p < .001$.

only partly overlapped with the earlier one, worked with undergraduates instead of high school students, and assessed punctuality in a direct manner and not on the basis of records in school files. The subjects were 44 undergraduates in the social sciences (22 males, 22 females) in the age range of 18–26 years. The CO questionnaire of punctuality was constructed according to the standard procedure (Section IV) and tested on a sample of 100 subjects from the same population as the subjects of the study. The questionnaire included 10 items in each of the Go, GB, and BS parts and 9 items in the N part. The α coefficients were .80, .64, .88, and .74 for the Go, GB, BS, and N parts, respectively. Some of the themes in the questionnaire were spontaneity and rigidity, respect for other human beings, and differences between business meetings and meetings with friends. The subject's task was to check acceptance or rejection of each belief on a five-point scale.

Every subject was requested to make five different appointments for participating in the different experiments at her or his convenience. The arrival times were recorded and compared with the appointment times. The score consisted of the number of times that the subject was late for an appointment, and ranged from a minimum of zero to a maximum of five. All the subjects were administered the CO questionnaire in small groups by experimenters who differed from those participating in other parts of the experiment. Half of the subjects received the CO questionnaire before their appointments, and half, after.

Each subject received five scores, four for the four CO components, and one for punctuality. The multiple correlation of the four CO components with punctuality was .58 ($p < .001$), or .61 when corrected for shrinkage (see Table II for the stepwise regression coefficients). This finding fully confirms those of the former study (Section V,A) the data of which were analyzed by an analysis of variance procedure.

The correlations between the four CO components were all positive and significant (ranging from .52 for GB–BS, GB–Go, and Go–BS to .68 for Go–N), again as in the earlier study (H. Kreitler & S. Kreitler, 1976, p. 376).

2. Study B

Lobel (1981b) replicated her previous study on punctuality (Section VI,B,1) on a different sample 3 years later. She used the same CO questionnaire and the same experimental procedure. The subjects were 59 psychology freshmen (16 males, 43 females), in the age range of 18–25 years. The multiple correlation of the four CO components with punctuality was .60 ($p < .001$), or .62 when corrected for shrinkage (see Table II for the stepwise regression coefficients). This finding fully confirms that of Study A (Section VI,B,1). The intercorrelations among the four CO components were in the range of .00 for BS–Go to .71 for Go–N and differed from those found in the previous study, particularly in the zero correlation of BS with the other components (in Section VI,B,1, the correlations were .52–.53).

C. PREDICTING ACHIEVEMENT BEHAVIOR FROM COGNITIVE ORIENTATION SCORES

This study (S. Kreitler & H. Kreitler, 1981) was essentially a replication of the earlier study on achievement behavior (Section V,A), but the CO questionnaire, the sample, and the dependent variable were different. The administered CO questionnaire was a version shortened after further item analyses of the CO questionnaire used in the original study. The sample was 42 fifth-graders (20 boys, 22 girls) in two classes of a school in the vicinity of Tel Aviv. As in the previous study, the task was of a routine kind, the performance of which required more motivation than skill. The task consisted of proofreading closely typed pages with different signs (slanted lines, dashes, boxes, circles, triangles, asterisks, and points). The proofreading consisted in comparing the material with a standard that was as closely typed, and crossing out the "mistakes." On each page there were 62 typed lines, and in each line 85 signs. Each subject was given a package of 20 pages. The mean number of randomly introduced "mistakes" was 7 per each 425 signs (five lines). The task was administered in group sessions and was introduced as "a test for duration of concentration." Special achievement-oriented instructions were given. The experimenter mentioned the importance of the task and the alleged interest of the teachers in the results. No time limit was set for the task ("work as long as you feel you can possibly do it") but it was emphasized that "the more one does, the better." The subjects were requested to mark the point at which they stopped. They were not allowed to continue after stopping and going over to the next task. In order to prevent effects of conformity with other group members, the subjects were seated apart and requested not to give back their work when finished but to go on immediately with a different task without doing anything to signal this transfer. The next task consisted in tracing the lines of a highly complex geometrical figure. Pretests showed this task not to be more enticing or interesting than the target task. Since the data showed the rate of overlooked "mistakes" to be extremely low, the dependent variable was simply the number of proofread lines.

Each subject received a CO score reflecting his or her relative standing on the four CO components (Section IV) and a score of proofread lines. The data showed that, on the average, subjects with CO 4 ($N = 8$) proofread 310.25 lines, subjects with CO 3 ($N = 14$) 302.11 lines, subjects with CO 2 ($N = 6$) 263.42 lines, subjects with CO 1 ($N = 10$) 64.80 lines, and subjects with CO 0 ($N = 4$) 59.02 lines. The linear trend is very clear, as is the sharp drop in performance between subjects with CO 2 and those with lower CO scores. A one-way analysis of variance showed that the differences between the groups are significant [F (4,

37) $= 8.69$, $p < .01$]. The following differences between means were significant by the Newman–Keuls method: the means of CO 4 and of CO 3 differed from those of CO 1 and CO 0 on the .01 level, and from CO 2 on the .05 level, whereas the mean of CO 2 differed from those of CO 1 and of CO 0 on the .05 level.

The intercorrelations between the four CO components were similar to those obtained in the former study (the range was .10–.40 as compared with −.09–.34; again we found N to be significantly correlated with BS ($r = .25$, $p < .05$) and Go ($r = .40$, $p < .01$).

VII. Predicting Behavior in Normals: New Studies

A. Predicting Behavioral Responses to Stress

Breier's (1980) study dealt with predicting on the basis of CO scores responses to stress that consist in coping primarily either with the external source of danger that is perceived as stressful or with the internal reactions of fear that constitute the stress. Following Leventhal's (1970) conceptualization in the domain of responses to fear communications, Breier called the former Danger Control (D.C.) and the latter, Fear Control (F.C.). Breier conceived of D.C. and F.C. as superordinate tendencies more basic and general than the relatively more specific responses such as affiliation (Sarnoff & Zimbardo, 1961; Schachter, 1959) and different coping or defensive reactions (Lazarus, 1966). Accordingly, he argued that any of the latter more specific responses may subserve one or the other tendency, for example, affiliation may subserve D.C. when undertaken for the sake of a concerted attack on the external threatening agent, but it may also subserve F.C. when indulged in for the sake of anxiety reduction through diversion, comfort, etc. Breier assumed that both D.C. and F.C. may coexist in the same individual though in different strengths. Since he assessed D.C. and F.C. in terms of verbal declarations (i.e., "speech acts"), Breier preferred to conceptualize these tendencies as behavioral intents.

Accordingly, Breier constructed a CO questionnaire for assessing the relative strength of the behavioral intents for D.C. and F.C. The questionnaire was constructed according to the standard procedures (Section IV). The questionnaire included statements to which the subject was requested to respond on a four-point scale ranging from "Almost Always" to "Almost Never" (in the BS, GB, and N parts) or from "Very True about Me" to "Not at all True about Me" (in the Go part). Each response was coded as orienting or not orienting toward F.C. The questionnaire was pretested on a sample of 80 subjects from the same population as the subjects of the study.

In its final form the questionnaire included 5 items in the BS part, 7 in the N part, 8 in the Go part, and 7 in the GB part. The α coefficients were .53, .85, .88, and .79 for the BS, N, Go, and GB parts, respectively. The intercorrelations among the four CO components ranged from $-.07$ (n.s.) for GB–N to .22 ($p < .05$) for Go–N.

The subjects of the study were 102 members of the Scouts youth movement (50 males, 52 females) with the mean age of 17 years. All subjects were students in regular or technical high schools, of a medium SES, and long-term members of the Scouts. All subjects were administered the CO questionnaire in group sessions in their regular meeting places in the framework of the Scouts. In addition, each subject was told that he or she would participate in the major phase of the experiment that was scheduled to take place "at the university" on a specific date. Before leaving collectively for the university in a truck that supposedly had to arrive in a few minutes, the experimental group subjects ($N = 62$; 34 females, 28 males) were told that the experiment in which they were to participate was conducted by the army and the university, was designed to examine the effect of physical stress on learning, and would involve getting painful though harmless electrical shocks in an increasing intensity until learning was complete. It was also explained that for technical reasons the subjects would have to wait for about 30 minutes in a location of their choice. Four types of locations were described differing in the possibilities for affiliation and for D.C. or F.C.

A location enabling affiliation was a large room in which the subject would wait in the company of other participants. A location enabling nonaffiliation was a smaller room in which the subject would wait alone. A location enabling F.C. was a room in which comfort and diversions were made available, for example, soft armchairs, music, refreshments, games, closed circuit T.V. set with movie strips, and comics. A location enabling D.C. was a room in which the subject could train on a model of the learning task and, thus, reduce the learning period during the experiment, and had the chance to be included in the group of those subjects out of which 10 would be randomly selected for the role of observers (who would receive no shocks) in the experiment. Each choice presented to the subjects was characterized by affiliation or nonaffiliation and by F.C. or D.C. The subjects of the control group ($N = 40$; 22 males, 18 females) got the same instructions but without reference to electric shocks. The control subjects were told that the experiment in which they were about to participate dealt with examining the effect of various kinds of background music on learning, and involved being strapped to different physiological devices without any pain.

When the explanation was over, a confederate entered the room and announced that the trucks had supposedly arrived. The experimenter then suggested that in order to avoid unnecessary confusion when they arrived "at the university" it would be best if the subjects stated their choices before leaving for the

TABLE III
ANALYSIS OF VARIANCE OF CHOICES OF LOCATIONS FOR WAITING[a]

Source of variation	df	MS	F
CO of F.C. vs D.C. (A)	1	2.83	5.78*
Stress of situation (experimental vs control group) (B)	1	2.04	4.16*
A × B	1	.00	1
Within	98	.49	

[a] Based on Breier (1980).
*$p < .05$.

trucks. They were then asked to check their first and second choices for waiting locations and to respond to the State Trait Anxiety Inventory (STAI) (Spielberger, Gorsuch, & Lushene, 1970[2]). The scores of State Anxiety confirmed the success of the manipulation.

Each subject got a CO score considered as orienting toward F.C. (when it was CO 4) or toward D.C. (when it was CO 3–CO 0), and a score reflecting his or her choices for waiting locations, considered as manifesting F.C. or D.C. only if *both* choices were F.C. or D.C., respectively.

Table III shows that the CO of F.C. and D.C. predicted significantly the choices of the subjects despite the harsh criteria applied in testing. Further, the absence of a significant interaction indicates that the prediction did not depend on the experimental situation of greater or lesser stress. Let us illustrate what this means. In view of the higher level of state anxiety in the experimental ($\bar{X} = 1.61$) than in the control group ($\bar{X} = 1.35$; $t = 2.66$, $p < .01$), it is not surprising that there were more subjects in the experimental group (40 out of 62, or 69.5%) than in the control group (14 out of 40, or 35%) who made consistently two F.C. or two D.C. waiting location choices ($z = 3.41$, $p < .001$). Nevertheless, in both groups there was a comparable proportion of subjects whose choices were predicted by their CO scores [in the experimental group 29 out of 40, or 72.5%, and in the control group 12 out of 14, or 85.71%; the difference between the proportions is not significant, $z (52) = .99$, or $\chi^2 (1) = .99$]. Also, in each group the difference between the number of subjects whose choices were predicted by CO scores versus the others was significant and comparable in both groups (29 vs 11, $z = 2.69$, $p < .01$ in the experimental group and 12 vs 2, $z = 2.41$, $p < .01$ in the control group). In sum, the findings

[2] The Hebrew version of the STAI was prepared and pretested by Dr. Yona Teichman, Department of Psychology, Tel Aviv University.

of this study clearly showed that CO scores predict behavioral intents basic for reactions to stress.

B. Predicting Orderliness from Cognitive Orientation Components

1. Study A

Lobel's (1981c) study dealt with orderliness conceived as a long-term behavior based on habits. The subjects were 77 undergraduates in the social sciences (22 males, 22 females) in the age range of 18–26 years. The CO of orderliness was constructed according to the standard procedure (Section IV) and pretested on a sample of 75 subject from the same population as that of the study. Each of the four parts of the questionnaire included 10 items. The α coefficients were .72, .68, .76, and .74 for the BS, GB, N, and Go parts, respectively. Some of the themes in the questionnaire were efficiency in work, reliability of people, rigidity, and closed-mindedness. The subject's task was to check degree of acceptance or rejection of each belief on a five-point scale.

Information about the orderliness of the subjects was obtained from ratings of their regular notebooks. Each subject was asked to hand in two notebooks, one in each of the two major domains of study, Introductory Psychology and Statistics. The subjects did not know that the notebooks would be rated for orderliness. The ratings—on a seven-point scale—were done independently by two judges who did not know to whom the notebooks belonged. Since the agreement between the judges was complete in 90% of the cases, the four judgments each subject obtained were pooled into one mean orderliness score. The CO questionnaire was administered to all subjects in small groups by experimenters different from the one who requested the notebooks. Half of the subjects received the CO questionnaire before handing in the notebooks, and half later.

Each subject received five scores, four for the four CO components and one for orderliness. The multiple correlation of the four CO components with orderliness was .50 ($p < .01$), or .52 when corrected for shrinkage (see Table II for the stepwise regression coefficients). This finding supports the major tenet of the CO theory that information about CO clusters enables the prediction of behaviors.

The correlations between the four CO components were all positive and significant (ranging from .53 for N–BS to .67 for GB–N).

2. Study B

Lobel replicated her previous study on orderliness (Section VII,B,1) on a different sample 3 years later. She used the same CO questionnaire and the same experimental procedure. The subjects were 59 psychology freshmen (16 males, 43 females) in the age range 18–25 years. The multiple correlation of the four CO components with orderliness was .53 ($p < .001$), or .55 when corrected for shrinkage (see Table II for the stepwise regression coefficients). This study fully confirms the findings of Study A (Section VII,B,1).

The intercorrelations among the four CO components were all positive and significant as in Study A, but lower (they ranged from .27 for BS–GB to .46 for BS–Go).

C. PREDICTING ASSERTIVENESS FROM COGNITIVE ORIENTATION COMPONENTS

1. Study A

Lobel's (1981d) study dealt with assertiveness conceived as standing up for one's rights in interpersonal situations. The subjects of the study were 77 undergraduates of both genders at Tel Aviv University. The CO questionnaire of assertiveness was constructed according to the standard procedure (Section IV) and pretested on a sample of 80 subjects from the same population as that of the study. In its final form the questionnaire included 9 items in the GB part, 9 in the N part, 10 in the BS part, and 7 in the Go part. The α coefficients were .62, .62, .78, and .72 for the GB, N, BS, and Go parts, respectively. Some of the themes in the questionnaire were reminding others to pay back their debts, asking someone who is noisy in the library to be quiet so as not to disturb, and backing off from arguments. The subject's task was to check degree of acceptance or rejection of each belief on a five-point scale.

Assertive behavior was assessed by ratings of assertiveness manifested in a role-playing situation. The situation was introduced together with other role playing items, after a proper warm-up. It consisted of letting the subject play the role of a student who, despite showing up for an experiment at the right time and place, is not accorded the credit for participation because the experimenter (stooge) happens to be too busy to work with him or her.

In this setup, assertiveness would be manifested in the subject's insistence on getting the credit due to him or her according to the department's regulations. The role of the experimenter, who also described the situation to the subject, was enacted by graduate students who did not know the subjects. Half of the subjects of each gender were tested by experimenters of the same gender, and half by experimenters of the opposite gender. Each subject's behavior was recorded and then rated independently by two judges on a five-point scale of assertiveness. Since the interjudge reliability was high ($r = .96$), the assertiveness score represented a mean of the two ratings. The CO questionnaire was administered to the subjects in small groups, to half before the role-playing enactment and to half after it.

Each subject was given five scores, four for the four CO components, and one for assertiveness. The multiple correlation of the four CO components with assertiveness was .53 ($p < .01$), or .55 when corrected for shrinkage (see Table II for the stepwise regression coefficients). The intercorrelations between the four CO components were all positive and significant (they ranged from .38 for BS–Go to .53 for N–Go).

To our mind, role-playing behavior does not differ from real-life behavior in essential characteristics if the role playing is of habitual behaviors and adequate techniques are used to ensure that the enactment is not slanted in the direction of one or another CO component (e.g., GB when the alleged expectations of the experimenter are enacted, or Go when one's ego ideal is enacted; H. Kreitler & S. Kreitler, 1976, pp. 259–261). Although role playing of experimental behavior may not compare well with the actual behavior displayed by subjects (McGuire, 1969; A. Miller, 1972), many studies show that role-playing of actual behaviors corresponds well to the actual behaviors (e.g., Borgatta, 1952; H. Kreitler & S. Kreitler, 1964, 1968; Raz, Kreitler, & Kreitler, 1976; Rotter & Wickens, 1948). In view of this rich evidence, we regard the prediction of assertiveness found by Lobel as confirming the basic tenet of the CO theory about the relation of CO clusters to behavior.

2. Study B

Lobel replicated her previous study on assertiveness (Section VII,C,1) on a different sample 3 years later. She used the same CO questionnaire and the same experimental procedure. The subjects were 59 psychology freshmen (16 males, 43 females) in the age range of 18–25 years. The multiple correlation of the four CO components with assertiveness was .46 ($p < .05$), or .47 when corrected for shrinkage (see Table II for the stepwise regression coefficients). This finding confirms the finding of Study A (Section VII,C,1).

The intercorrelations among the four CO components differed from those in the previous study; GB was unrelated to any of the other CO components while the other correlations were positive, in the range of .34 for Go–N to .51 for BS–N.

D. Predicting Conformity from Cognitive Orientation Components

Lobel's (1981e) study dealt with conformity defined in a way similar to Asch's original definition. The subjects were 44 undergraduates (22 males, 22 females) in the social sciences, in the age range of 18–26 years. The CO of conformity was constructed according to the standard procedure (Section IV) and pretested on a sample of 99 subjects from the same population as that of the subjects of the study. In its final form it included 6 items in each of the N and Go parts, and 7 items in each of the GB and BS parts. The α coefficients were .67, .78, .83, and .70 for the N, Go, GB, and BS subquestionnaires, respectively. Some of the themes in the questionnaire were the hazards of voicing one's opinion, familiarity with a certain domain, and being liked by others. The subject's task was to check degree of acceptance or rejection of each belief on a five-point scale.

Conformity was assessed in a situation introduced as a test of visual memory in which the experimenter projected 18 slides for 10 seconds each, and after each projection asked one or two questions. The slides presented simple scenes or objects, and the 22 questions asked about them were selected on the basis of pretests as those to which all 60 pretest subjects gave correct answers. One subject and three stooges participated in each session, the subject being seated in the next to last seat in a row of four. The questions were asked by the experimenter and each participant was requested to answer in his or her turn. There were 12 randomly chosen target questions, posed at predetermined positions in the series, to which the stooges were instructed to give clearly false answers. The conformity score was the number of times out of 12 that the subject responded to the questions in line with the false answers given earlier by two stooges.

The stooges were students like the subjects. Lobel found that a remarkably high percentage of subjects (92%) were not in the least suspicious of the procedure. She found no differences in the mean conformity scores of subjects who underwent the experiment in the presence of one or another of the three groups of stooges.

Each subject was given five scores, four for the four CO components, and one for conformity. The multiple correlation of the four CO components with conformity was .57 ($p < .01$), or .59 when corrected for shrinkage (see Table II for the stepwise regression coefficients). This finding supports the major tenet of the CO theory that information about CO clusters enables prediction of the behavior they imply.

The intercorrelations between the four CO components were partly nonsignificant (i.e., N–BS, N–Go), partly negative (BS–GB, $-.31$, $p < .05$; Go–GB $-.40$, $p < .01$), and partly positive (BS–Go, .78, $p < .01$; Go–N, .72, $p < .01$).

E. Predicting Graduation Grades in Cadets' School on the Basis of Cognitive Orientation Scores

This study focused on predicting by means of CO scores the graduation grades in a cadets' school of the Israeli army (Sheppes, 1977). This dependent variable is highly complex for a number of reasons. First, it represents the evaluation of performance and behavior over a period of many months and not at some strictly defined point in time. Second, it reflects evaluations of performance and behavior of different kinds (e.g., leadership, social cooperation, acceptable ethical behavior, discipline, as well as physical state and mastery of the studied subject matter) by different people (i.e., the superiors in the school) and not of some clearly defined and specific act of behavior. Third, it is based partly on considerations and information not all of which are explicit or specifiable, for the grades reflect essentially the judgment of the superiors about the suitability of the cadet to serve as an officer. Fourth, there persists a high degree of unclarity about the nature of leadership, the major determinant of the dependent variable. Fifth, cadets in the school are a highly select group which represents a narrow band of variation precisely in those characteristics that are basic for the dependent variable. Soldiers are admitted to the cadets' school if they pass certain criteria in IQ tests, years of schooling, tests of different traits, including leadership, and if they consent to serve as officers (which entails either serving longer in the army or embarking on a military career). In sum, graduation grades are a highly complex variable whose prediction may be expected to be attended by many difficulties.

Following the standard procedure (Section IV), Sheppes constructed a CO questionnaire for predicting graduation grades upon completion of the cadets' school. The questionnaire focused on different aspects of leadership and its manifestations, for example, helping subordinates in their personal problems, developing skills versus promoting interpersonal relations, reactions to stress, drawing attention in company, affiliation, risk taking, originality, the relation of means to ends, decision making. Leadership was chosen as the focus of the questionnaire because it is the major and basic theme common to different conceptions of leadership (Sheppes, 1977), and because grades in leadership correlate with the total graduation grades ($r = .94$, $p < .001$) more highly than any other single variable.

The questionnaire was first administered to a pretest sample of 81 male subjects, trainees in a cadets' school. In its final form the questionnaire included 23 items in each of its four parts. The subjects were requested to check their responses to each item on a seven-point scale ranging from "Fully Agree" to "Fully Disagree" in the N part, from "Completely True" to "Completely Untrue" in the BS and GB parts, and from "Very Much Want" to "Completely Reject" in the Go part. The α coefficients were .73, .76, .83, and .59 for the BS, N, Go, and GB parts.

The subjects of the study were 171 trainees in the cadets' school. All the subjects were male (the school then had no females), all had passed an earlier basic preparatory training for officers, and all had been in the army for at least 1 year (military service in Israel is obligatory). The CO questionnaire was administered in group sessions at the beginning of the training. The subjects were told that the questionnaire was administered purely for research purposes. The questionnaires were stored away so that none of the superiors in the school could have access to them. After termination of the course, the trainees' grades were extracted from the files. The scale of grades included six grades, ranging from 50 to 95 in nine-point intervals. An analysis of variance (Table IV) shows that the CO scores were related significantly to the graduation grades. The intercorrelations between the four CO components were all positive and significant, ranging from .46 ($p < .01$) for N–BS to .27 ($p < .01$) for Go–GB.

The finding about the relation of CO scores to graduation grades is of particu-

TABLE IV
ANALYSIS OF VARIANCE OF GRADUATION GRADES OF CADETS[a]

Graduation grades	CO 4	CO 3	CO 2	CO 1	CO 0
$\bar{X}$	68.25	77.77	72.35	72.36	70.75
SD	13.85	12.22	13.32	13.14	12.13
N	36	35	31	33	36
F	2.57*				
df	4, 166				

[a] Based on Sheppes (1977).
*$p < .05$.

lar interest for a number of reasons. First, some of the difficulties (mainly restricted range of the dependent variable, the unclarity of its determinants, and the selected nature of the group) greatly decrease the likelihood of demonstrating the relation. Second, the dependent variable is a kind of sum-total of different molar behaviors but neither a specific molar behavior nor a behavior for which there are specific, commonly accepted criteria, whereas the CO theory was designed for predicting specifically particular acts of behavior. Third, the data show that the mean grade of subjects with CO 4 tends to be lower than the mean of subjects with CO 3. Though the difference is not significant and this is the only deviation from linearity in these data, the tendency itself seems to us to be potentially interesting. A similar tendency was noted in another study (S. Kreitler, H. Kreitler, & Zigler, 1975, in H. Kreitler & S. Kreitler, 1976, pp. 228–234) that showed scores CO 4 of curiosity to be related with less systematic exploration than scores of CO 3. An examination of the data suggested the possibility that there exist two strategies of exploration, one more variable and less conventional, and one more systematic and conventional as was shown in a later study (S. Kreitler, Zigler, & H. Kreitler, 1982). It seems plausible that in regard to officers, too, there may be a qualitative difference between those with CO 4 and those with CO 3. Informal observations suggest that trainees with CO 4 may have leadership qualities different from those characteristic of trainees with CO 3, for example, they may be more charismatic and inspiring, but probably also less conventional, and may therefore seem to be less reliable from the viewpoint of their superiors.

F. PREDICTING SOCIAL WITHDRAWAL ON THE BASIS OF COGNITIVE ORIENTATION SCORES

This study examined the relation between CO scores and social withdrawal in elementary school children of the eighth grade. Adler (1980) constructed a CO questionnaire of social withdrawal following the standard procedure (Section IV). In its final form the questionnaire had 18 items in its BS part, 15 in its GB part, 12 in its N part, and 12 in its Go part. The responses were to be given by checking one out of six alternatives ranging from "Very True about Me" to "Completely Untrue about Me." Some of the themes in the questionnaire were self-confidence, sense of inferiority, and defensive tendencies. The α coefficients were .88, .81, .76, and .86 for the BS, GB, N, and Go parts, respectively.

The subjects of the study were 116 eighth-graders (61 males, 55 females) from three different schools. All the subjects were of medium to high SES. The CO questionnaire was administered to the subjects in a group session.

There were seven criteria for social withdrawal: (1) spending long periods of time alone when the company of other children is available; (2) not playing with other children during the recess periods at school; (3) not participating in group activities at school; (4) not participating in social discussions and conversations; (5) not going to parties; (6) having no friends; and (7) tending toward sadness and depression when in the vicinity of other children.

Information about the social withdrawal of the subjects was obtained from the teacher of the class who had known the children for at least 1 year. The teacher was asked to check on a five-part scale ranging from "Very Frequently" to "Practically Never" how often each subject manifested each of the following (which correspond to the seven criteria of social withdrawal, some formulated positively and some negatively): (1) withdraws alone; (2) is alone during the recess; (3) participates in social life; (4) participates in social conversation and discussions; (5) goes to parties; (6) has friends; and (7) is sad, depressed. Four checks were made on the validity of these ratings. First, the teacher was asked to rate the subjects again on the same items 1 month later. The correlations between the two sets of ratings were all high and significant beyond the .001 level (they were .83, .80, .83, .87, .83, .87, and .83 for the seven behaviors, respectively). These findings show that the ratings have a high test–retest reliability. Second, concerning a random sample of 19 subjects drawn from the total sample of 116, independent observations about the same social withdrawal behaviors were obtained from another teacher who had known the children for 1 month (while she replaced the regular teacher, who was sick). There was no communication between the two teachers concerning the questionnaire. The correlations between the replacing teacher's observations and the responses of the regular teacher were .74, .80, and .79 (all $p < .001$) with the first, second, and pooled observations of the regular teacher, respectively. Third, concerning a random sample of 26 subjects out of the total sample, ratings about social withdrawal were obtained from a clinical psychologist who worked in the school. Her ratings correlated .84, .89, and .87 (all $p < .001$) with the first, second, and pooled observations of the teacher, respectively. Fourth, concerning a random sample of 17 subjects out of the total sample, direct observations of the children's social behavior during five samples of 4 hours each (in the course of lessons and recess periods at school) extending over several days were made by an independent observer, an educational psychologist. Her observations correlated .77, .88, and .90 (all $p < .001$) with the first, second, and pooled observations of the teacher, respectively. These findings show that the teachers' ratings are a valid measure of the examined behavior.

Since there were significant differences between the distributions of the teachers' scores for social withdrawal in the three schools, the scores were subjected to a normal transformation (with a mean of 0 and an SD of 1).

Accordingly, each subject received two scores, one for the CO of social withdrawal and one a normalized score of social withdrawal in behavior, based on the teacher's observations. The findings show that subjects with higher scores of social withdrawal had higher incidence of social withdrawal behaviors than subjects with lower scores of social withdrawal (CO 0 + CO 1, $\bar{X} = -.28 \pm .81$, $N = 40$; CO 2 + CO 3 + CO 4, $\bar{X} = .15 \pm 1.03$, $N = 76$; $t = 2.30$, $p < .05$). These findings support the hypothesis that social withdrawal is predictable on the basis of CO scores.

VIII. Studies in Psychopathology

The first two studies to be reported in this section extend the range of predictions on the basis of CO to samples of abnormal subjects. In both cases the behaviors predicted were not specifically abnormal. The demonstration that CO scores predict behavior in mental patients is important for both practical and theoretical reasons. Practically it indicates that the prediction range of the CO theory is not limited by the subjects' mental health. Theoretically it indicates that the prediction made possible by CO scores does not depend on cognitive processes of the kind that may be impaired in mental patients. However, predicting behaviors in mental patients does not constitute a direct contribution to a CO theory of psychopathology, whose outlines were laid out in H. Kreitler and S. Kreitler (1976, chap. 10). A contribution along these lines is represented by Study C (Section VIII), which deals with the CO of children with behavior problems.

A. Predicting Slowness in Mental Patients

Two features characterize Ziv-Av's (1978) study about slowness in schizophrenics. The first is that, strictly speaking, slowness is not a specific behavior but a property that characterizes different behaviors. Thus, if slowness is assumed to depend on a CO cluster, that CO cluster can be considered as an "adjunct" cluster, accompanying other CO clusters that generate the major BI of the specific actions. Empirically, the problem may be bypassed by using simple tasks whose execution may involve no more than the BI to cooperate in the experiment. The second feature is that Ziv-Av's findings show that characteristics of the individual's meaning system and programming ability may interact with CO scores and account to some extent for individual differences within subgroups of subjects with the same CO clusters.

The subjects of the study were 30 hospitalized mental patients (mean duration of hospitalization 87.7 days)—mostly schizophrenics (the sample included only one manic depressive, one anxiety neurotic, and one psychopath)—in the age range of 18.5–47 years (mean age 27.16 years), 14 males and 16 females, with a mean of 12.2 years of schooling. They were administered a CO questionnaire, different performance tasks, the standard measure of meaning, and a test of programming efficiency.

In constructing the CO questionnaire, Ziv-Av applied a variation on the standard procedure (Section IV) that consists in a systematic use of the meaning system in devising belief statements. Thus, with regard to each theme found to be meaningfully related to slowness (e.g., concern with perfectionism, fear of causing damage or harm) she constructed within each CO component three primary questions (referring to whether the theme was at all related to slowness, the causes for it, and its consequences), and with regard to each of these four secondary questions (referring to specification in terms of the subjects of range of application, the objects of range of application, temporal and locational qualities). Interrelations between themes (in the range of $r = .45–1.00$), primary questions, and secondary questions (in the range $r = .48–.52$) within each CO component were examined in pretests with normals and hospitalized patients. They confirmed the assumption that the discrimination among the primary questions was higher than among the secondary ones. Thus, in the final form the questionnaire included in each CO component primary and secondary questions about each of eight themes. The questions of the four CO components were asked in proximity with regard to the same focal theme. The scoring reflected both whether the subject stated that the theme was related meaningfully to slowness, and the generality of this relation. The scoring range for each CO component was 0–36. CO scores were assigned according to the regular procedure. The intercorrelations between CO components in the sample of the study ranged from .30 (n.s.) for N–BS to .82 ($p < .001$) for N–Go.

There were five performance tasks chosen to represent a variety of motor and cognitive functions: a motor task that required circling a specific cipher on cards that included 55 0–9 ciphers in random order; a picture identification task that required identifying (or labeling) six pictures, one neutral and five representing intriguing (e.g., a bathroom device in the form of a hand) or unclear scenes (e.g., a hazy figure of a man in the background and a magnified telescope lens of a revolver in the foreground); a role-playing task that consisted of two scenes out of the Psychodramatic Role Test (H. Kreitler & S. Kreitler, 1964, 1968); a decision-making task that required the subject to decide on a response to the experimenter's invitation to have a cup of tea or coffee; and a classification task that consisted of the first part of Sharan's (1971) variation of Sigel's (1953) sorting task and required the classification of 15 familiar objects into groups according to any preferred criteria. The motor, role-playing, and classification tasks each provided two duration variables, one for the period ranging from presentation of the task to beginning of the performance, the other for the performance per se. The identification task provided data only for a performance variable, and the decision-making task only for the variable preceding action. Due to differences in the ranges of the raw data provided by the different tasks, the scores were standardized and pooled together into indices. Thus, each subject received three separate standardized index scores: one for the duration of time preceding performance (based on four separate variables, with standard scores in the range of 1–7 and $\bar{X} = 4$ for each task, and a total range from a minimum of 10 to a maximum of 70); one for the duration of time devoted to performance per se (based on three separate variables, with standard scores in the range of 1–7 and $\bar{X} = 4$ for each task and a total range of 3–21); and a combined index of durations preceding performance and of performance (representing a sum of the two former indices, in the range of 13–91).

In addition each subject was administered a meaning questionnaire, according to the standard procedure (Section IV; H. Kreitler & S. Kreitler, 1976, p. 24; S. Kreitler & H. Kreitler, 1982a), which provided a measure of the number of different meaning dimensions used by the subject in the meaning profile, and an exploratory task of programming (devised by Nehari, S. Kreitler, & H. Kreitler, 1975, and further developed by Ziv-Av, 1978) which provided a measure of the number of questions the subject asked of the experimenter prior to starting action. It was expected that the higher the number, the slower the subject gets into action.

All the tasks were administered to the patients in one or two individual sessions, in random order. The subjects were unaware that time was the major variable of the study and that their performance was timed. Instructions for the performance tasks included no reference to time limitations or any requirement to speed up.

Table V shows that subjects scoring high on CO of slowness are significantly slower than low-scoring subjects on all three indices of slowness. Further, the CO of slowness is related more closely to the variable of duration (the results are significant not only for the total index but also for the five separate tasks; see Table V) than to the variable of the time preceding performance, which is more akin to reaction time. These findings confirm the major hypothesis of the CO theory. Further, a series of two-factor analyses of variance yielded several interactions with meaning and programming variables indicating that these factors,

TABLE V

Mean Duration Preceding Action and during Performance of Schizophrenics High and
Low on Cognitive Orientation Scores of Slowness[a]

| Variable | CO scores | | |
	High (3–4) (N=13)	Low (0–2) (N=17)	t
Motor action (performance)	34.3	20.8	2.41**
Picture identification (performance)	25.5	23.5	2.22**
Role-playing (performance)	35.8	19.5	1.47*
Classification (preperformance)	12.5	6.1	1.67*
Classification (performance)	31.6	9.6	2.26**
Total index (preperformance)	42.2	38.9	2.24**
Total index (performance)	13.1	10.7	3.59***
Total index[b] (performance preperformance)	55.3	49.6	4.25****

[a] Based on Ziv-Av (1978).

[b] In subjects with high CO: when number of meaning dimensions is high, $\bar{X} = 56.4$; when number of meaning dimensions is low, $X = 52.3$. In subjects with low CO: when number of meaning dimensions is high, $\bar{X} = 50.2$; when number of meaning dimensions is low, $\bar{X} = 49.0$ [based on $F(1,26) = 18.63, p < .001$]. In subjects with high CO: when number of questions is high, $\bar{X} = 56.1$; when number of questions is low, $\bar{X} = 53.5$. In subjects with low CO: when number of questions is high, $\bar{X} = 51.7$; when number of questions is low, $\bar{X} = 48.5$ [based on $F(1,26) = 24.28, p < .001$].

*$p < .10$, one-tailed.
**$p < .025$, one-tailed.
***$p < .005$, one-tailed.
****$p < .0005$, one-tailed.

in particular the number of habitual meaning dimensions, may account for individual differences around the common mean, especially of subjects scoring high on CO of slowness (see footnote to Table V).

B. Predicting Responses to Conflict in Schizophrenics and Normals

Zemet (1976) dealt with predicting different responses of schizophrenics and of normals to conflict situations. The predicted responses were the defensive reactions rationalization, denial, and projection, and in addition behaviors of coping as well as of doing nothing about the problem. The same three defensive responses were also predicted on the basis of CO scores in a previous study (Section V,A; H. Kreitler & S. Kreitler, 1972b). However, the present study differs from the previous one in several crucial respects: a broader range of eliciting conflict situations was used, a greater variety of behavioral responses was examined, the dependent variables were assessed by a different method, and a sample of schizophrenics was added to the normal subjects.

Zemet performed her study with two different samples because of the special interest in studying modes of conflict resolution not only in normal but also in abnormal subjects. Accordingly, one sample consisted of 30 hospitalized schizophrenics (22 males, 8 females) in the age range of 18–60 years ($\bar{X}$ = 41.20), who had been hospitalized from 1 to 27 years. The other sample included 34 normal subjects (14 males, 20 females) in the age range of 18–40 years ($\bar{X}$ = 27.97), students in a Teachers Seminary and undergraduates in the Hebrew University, Jerusalem, with no known pathology in their background. Since the groups of schizophrenics and normals are not comparable in age and gender composition, the findings for each group are to be considered separately.

All subjects were administered a CO questionnaire of responses to conflicts. This was essentially an extended and elaborated version of the CO questionnaire of defense mechanisms constructed by H. Kreitler and S. Kreitler (1972b; Section V,A). It included items for the examining of orientation toward rationalization, denial, and projection and also toward two further behavioral reactions (i.e., "coping" and "doing nothing") that pretests showed to be common in conflictual situations. On the basis of further item analyses in new samples, the questionnaire was drastically shortened and included 28 questions, 7 in each of the four subparts BS, GB, N, and Go. The questionnaire was administered to all subjects individually in a separate session, to half of them prior to the experimental session and to half, after it.

The behavioral reactions to conflict were assessed by the role-playing of subjects in the context of a predetermined set of scenes. Zemet chose the role-playing method because it enabled her to study responses that would be hard or impossible to observe under natural field conditions. As noted earlier (Section VII,C), when habitual behavior is dealt with and proper precautions against biased enacting are undertaken, there is no reason to expect role-playing behavior to differ in essential characteristics from corresponding "real-life" behavior. Hence, it may be expected to be predictable on the basis of CO scores.

Zemet used 14 scenes structured and administered essentially as in the Psychodramatic Role Test (H. Kreitler & S. Kreitler, 1964, 1968). In each scene, the subjects were requested to enact both the role of themselves and of another person. The scenes were distinct and unrelated to one another. They differed in contents and setting, but each scene included some inconsistency or problem as its major theme, for example, a contradiction between a strong desire to hit someone who has snubbed one in public and the knowledge that this reaction would be harmful to one's self (i.e., a contradiction between Go and GB). The scenes represented a sample of major types of conflict, contradictions, inconsistencies, and dissonances, for example, conflicts between behavioral intents, between behavioral programs, postdecisional conflicts, contradiction between beliefs of the same CO components (e.g., two Go beliefs or two N beliefs), and contradictions between beliefs of two different CO components (e.g., an N belief and a Go belief). However, since the technique does not provide for controlling the manner in which the subject assigns meaning to the situation and elaborates on the presented inconsistency, Zemet used the various kinds of contradictions and conflicts only as a means of guaranteeing comprehensive and adequate sampling of situations. The scenes were essentially the same for schizophrenics and normals and differed only in minor details that related specifically to life inside or outside the hospital. All the scenes were pretested for adequacy in terms of ease of enactment, variety of evoked responses, and inconsistencies or conflict in contents. The scenes were administered after proper warm up. Each subject was asked to enact all scenes.

All the behavioral and verbal responses were recorded. The enacted responses were analyzed according to predetermined criteria identifying the different types of response (i.e., coping, denial, projection, rationalization, "doing nothing") in each scene. The criteria were established prior to collecting the data in line with judgments of clinicians and common clinical standards.

Each subject was given 10 scores—five CO scores (one for each of the behavioral responses, i.e., coping, denial, projection, rationalization, "doing nothing"), and five behavioral scores reflecting the frequencies with which he or she manifested behaviors indicating those behavioral responses.

By way of an indirect check on the validity of the role-playing method it should be noted that, as expected on the basis of given psychopathological theory, schizophrenics responded significantly more often than normals with denial and projection and less often than normals with coping, rationalization, and "doing nothing" (Zemet, 1976, p. 97).

The results presented in Table VI show that in both schizophrenics and normals CO scores are related to four out of the five behavioral responses significantly and in the expected direction. The one exception in the group of the normals concerns projection, where the difference between high and low CO scoring subjects is not significant, perhaps because of the very low frequency of such responses. The one exception in the schizophrenics group refers to coping and consists in a significant but reversed relation. One possibility for understanding the reasons for this reversal is based on examining the responses characteristic of schizophrenics scoring high or low in CO of coping. Zemet found that schizophrenics scoring high on the CO of coping responded with projection significantly more than low scoring schizophrenics ($\bar{X} = 1.33$ vs $\bar{X} = .27$, $p < .001$), and with "doing nothing" significantly less than low scoring schizo-

TABLE VI

COMPARISONS OF BEHAVIORAL RESPONSES OF SCHIZOPHRENICS AND NORMALS HIGH AND LOW IN
COGNITIVE ORIENTATION SCORES ORIENTING TOWARD THE EXAMINED RESPONSES[a]

| | Means of behavioral responses | | | |
| | Schizophrenics[b] | | Normals[b] | |
Responses	High CO	Low CO	High CO	Low CO
Coping	4.80	6.93*	12.23	2.35***
Denial	4.60	2.93*	3.99	1.24**
Projection	1.10	.50*	.16	.32
Rationalization	4.67	1.07**	4.98	2.96*
Doing nothing	4.60	.47**	4.94	.94**

[a] Based on Zemet (1976).
[b] High CO includes CO 4 and CO 3; low CO includes CO 2, CO 1, and CO 0.
  $*p < .05$.
  $**p < .01$.
  $***p < .001$.

phrenics ($\overline{X} = 1.27$ vs. $\overline{X} = 3.80$, $p < .001$). These findings suggest that for schizophrenics projection may be the behavioral program meaningfully bound with coping. However it may be, the reversal phenomenon will have to be further explored.

C. COGNITIVE ORIENTATION COMPONENTS IN COGNITIVE REPRESENTATIONS

Adler (1974) applied the system of four CO components to the exploration of cognitive representations bound with a meaningful theme, such as the mother image in psychopathological and normal subjects. Her subjects were three groups of boys 10–12 years old: 30 boys who were enrolled in regular schools but because of their behavioral and adjustment problems received a special group treatment 2–4 times each week; 30 boys who studied in schools for children with special adjustment problems; and 30 controls. On the standard adjustment scale (0–12) of students used by the Ministry of Education and Culture in Israel, the mean rating given by teachers to the students of the first group was 6.70, to the students of the second group, 11.15, and to the controls, 5.40. The differences are highly significant [$F(2, 84) = 26.83$, $p < .01$]. In each group, half of the children were of European origins, and half of Middle-Eastern origins. All boys were of normal intelligence (90–120 IQ) and lived at home with their natural mother during the study. The set of 48 questions about the mother was derived mostly from Schaefer's (1965) inventory, by carefully selecting on the basis of pretests and clinicians' judgments 24 items manifesting "the good mother" and 24 manifesting "the bad mother." All 48 items were administered to each child with regard to four different referents in random order: the child's actual mother, the desirable mother, the desired mother, and the child's drawing of a mother. The answers to the different referents may be interpreted as corresponding to different CO components: the first to BS, the second to N, the third to Go, and the fourth either to GB (an interpretation we prefer) or to a projective image, that is, a variation on BS (an interpretation Adler presented). The subject reacted to each item as "True," "So So," or "Untrue." Thus, the scoring ranged from 0 to 3 and could in principle be divided between two separate scores, the one for "the good mother" and another for "the bad mother." Since the two scores complement each other, it suffices to deal with only one of them. Adler concentrated on the score of "the good mother."

In a series of comparisons, some of which are summarized in Table VII, Adler showed that there were specific predictable differences in the four components in the different groups. In all groups the highest scores were obtained for the "desired" mother and the lowest for the GB or projected mother. The three

TABLE VII

THREE-FACTOR ANALYSIS OF VARIANCE OF SCORES OF THE "GOOD MOTHER"[a]

Source of variation	df	MS	F
Groups (A)	2	1746.56	3.63*
Cultural community (B)	1	17,710.70	36.81**
CO component (C)	3	8832.16	33.21**
A × B	2	2136.79	4.44**
A × C	6	415.99	1.56
B × C	3	522.29	1.96
A × B × C	6	1559.50	5.86**

Means of scores

Groups	CO components			
	BS	N	Go	GB or BS (projection)
Special treatment	96.93	102.97	107.43	79.37
Special school	101.70	100.20	107.60	82.37
Controls	102.09	101.73	108.71	85.44

[a] Based on Adler (1974).
*p < .05.
**p < .01.

groups of boys did not differ in their scores for the normative and for the desired mother, but they differed in their scores for the actual mother (BS) and for the common or projected mother (GB); in both of these components the scores were lowest for the special treatment group and highest for the normal controls, as would be expected if the scores reflected at least experienced reality. Another finding characteristic only of the special treatment group is the significant difference between the scores for BS and N, which do not differ in the other groups. Boys of the European community had mostly higher scores than boys of the Middle-Eastern community. Further, intercorrelations between the four scores were higher in the group of normals (mean $r = .53$) than in the two groups of disturbed subjects (mean $r = .26$; difference significant at $p < .005$). Correspondingly, the gap (in absolute terms) between the four scores was significantly larger in the groups of disturbed subjects than in normals [the sum of the score differences was 90.42 in the special treatment group, 77.19 in the special school group, and 70.17 in the normal group; $F(2, 87) = 7.91$, $p < .01$]. Again, the gap was larger in the disturbed boys of the European community ($\overline{X} = 102.06$) than in those of the Middle-Eastern community ($\overline{X} = 65.35$; $t = 9.58$, $p < .001$).

The presented findings illustrate how the CO components may contribute toward charting a psychopathologically significant domain of representations. They also show that, in constructing CO questionnaires and interpreting scores, attention should be paid to the psychopathological and cultural context of the respondents.

IX. Predicting Behavior when Meaning of Situations Is Explicitly Known

All situations have meaning, but their meanings typically vary across individuals. Without specifically assessing it, we can only guess approximately what the meaning could be, relying on projections and half-founded conjectures. But some situations have an explicit, publicly known meaning attached to them. For example, admission to the graduate school of a highly prestigious university carries the label of "being bright," imprisonment is a kind of declaration that the person is suspected of involvement in some criminal charges, and an examination in school signifies the dependence of one or another event on the results. Situations with an explicitly stated meaning are of particular theoretical and practical interest. From the viewpoint of the CO theory, they are important especially because they enable an independent assessment of the impact of the situation's meaning. Whereas in most prediction studies on the basis of the CO the meaning of the situation is included in the CO scores and does not figure as an independent factor, explicit statement of the situation's meaning abstracts this factor out of the total matrix of orientative cognitive contents guiding an action and allows for studying its effects. According to the CO theory, the meaning of the situation is a basic element that makes prediction possible. It is always taken into account but, due to the group design characteristic of most studies, only approximate meanings, meanings valid for the majority of subjects, can be considered. If, however, situation meanings are explicit, the range of individual variation in assigning meaning to situations is likely to be reduced and, consequently, prediction may be expected to be improved. Thus, theoretically it is important to demonstrate that this expectation, derived from the CO theory, is actually confirmed. If that is so, the practical importance of this demonstration is great. Whenever it is possible to specify the meaning(s) of the situation without compromising the whole sense of the experiment or action, meanings should be made explicit for the sake of improving predictions under laboratory and real-life conditions. For example, when economic deflationary measures are undertaken by a government, it may be advisable to specify the sense of each regulation and, thus, increase the likelihood of the public's behaving as would be predicted on the basis of the CO theory were it used by economists.

We shall present briefly the two studies that deal with this problem since they are described in detail in a forthcoming book (S. Kreitler & H. Kreitler, 1982a). Further data relevant to this problem are presented in Section X,B.

A. Specifying the Meaning of the Behavioral Alternatives Presented for Selection

S. Kreitler and H. Kreitler (1982a) examined the relations of CO scores and the meanings of behavioral alternatives to selections made by subjects. The subjects were 60 fourth- and fifth-graders of both genders to whom CO questionnaires of curiosity and of affiliation had been administered on a previous occasion. The subjects were selected from a larger sample so that 30 had a high CO score (3 or 4) on curiosity and a low CO score (1 or 0) on affiliation, whereas another 30 had a high CO score (3 or 4) on affiliation and a low CO score (1 or 0) on curiosity. The subjects were presented with a list of behavioral alternatives designed to serve as prizes for their participation in another larger experiment (eventually they got the prizes). The list included six alternatives, three of which were likely to satisfy curiosity and three affiliation according to pretest analyses of meaning. However, half of the subjects in each subgroup of CO scores were given the list without any comments, whereas the other half were given it with specified meanings which were, however, contrary to the commonly expected ones that figured in the pretests (e.g., going to a party was specified as likely to satisfy curiosity rather than affiliation). The subjects were asked to select the three most highly preferred alternatives out of the six presented ones.

The hypothesis was that the selection of behavioral alternatives would correspond to the CO scores and the meanings of the alternatives under all conditions, that is, when the meaning was unspecified and when it was specified, but the prediction was expected to be more accurate under the latter condition than under the former.

The results showed that, in the subgroups that received lists without specified meanings, 65.6% of the selections (59 out of the 90 choices) were in line with the predicted choices, whereas in the subgroups that received lists with specified meanings, 92.2% of the selections (83 out of 90 choices) corresponded to those predicted. Thus, as was hypothesized, under both conditions a significantly larger number of selections were in line with the hypothesis than counter to it, but when meanings were specified the number of selections in line with the prediction was significantly larger than under the condition when meanings were left unspecified, that is, assumed to be approximately as determined in the pretests.

B. Specifying the Meaning of the Task

S. Kreitler and H. Kreitler (1982a) studied the effects of specifying the meaning of the task as relevant or irrelevant for achievement when the predicted behavior was achievement. The subjects were 54 eighth-graders of both genders. They formed a part of a larger sample to whom the CO questionnaire of achievement (Section VI,C) had been administered. Half of the subjects ($N = 27$) had high CO scores of achievement (3 or 4), and half ($N = 27$) had low scores (0 or 1). The subgroups were each randomly split into three groups, each of which included nine high- and nine low-scoring subjects. All three groups were administered a task that consisted of two-cipher multiplication exercises. They were asked to solve as many of the items as they could within the unspecified available time. One of the three groups was told nothing further (this served as the control group with unspecified task meaning). Another group was told that the task was particularly relevant for achievement, and the third was told that the task was not particularly relevant for achievement. The expectation was that the differences between subjects scoring high and low on the CO of achievement would be larger when the task's meaning has been specified as relevant to achievement than when it was specified as irrelevant to achievement. A two-factor analysis of variance showed significant main effects for CO scores [$F(1, 48) = 9.56$, $p < .01$], for task meanings [$F(2, 48) = 12.41$, $p < .01$], and a significant interaction between these two factors [$F(2, 48) = 8.34$, $p < .01$]. The means of the number of solved items showed that, whereas the subjects with low CO scores hardly changed their performance across the three conditions (their total mean was 12.23 of solved items), the subjects with high CO scores had the lowest mean when the task's meaning was specified as irrelevant to achievement ($\overline{X} = 20.62$), and had their highest mean when the task's meaning was specified as relevant to achievement ($\overline{X} = 49.95$). The mean under the condition with unspecified task meaning was in between the extremes ($\overline{X} = 35.94$). Thus, as hypothesized, the subjects with high CO scores on achievement manifested more achievement in behavior than the low scorers, but the differences were larger and, hence, the prediction more accurate when the task's meaning was specified as relevant to the examined behavior than when it was specified as irrelevant or left unspecified. Further, the finding that only the high scorers were sensitive to the manipulations of the task's meaning shows that—as maintained by the CO theory—the task's meaning is not independent of CO scores.

X. "Decision by Meaning": A Model of Decision Making Embedded within the Cognitive Orientation Theory

A. THE DECISION BY MEANING

The decision by meaning (DBM) (Zakay, 1976)—presented here in a simplified version—describes a decision-making subroutine (i.e., a specific program controlled by a major behavioral program), triggered by a BI "to decide" or "to choose," which is likely to be formed under one of five conditions, for example, conflict between two BIs, conflict between two behavioral programs, the meaning of the input situation includes the need to choose between alternatives (e.g., "Will you have tea or coffee?").

The major process of the DBM is meaning assignment to the discerned behavioral alternatives. The products of the meaning assignment are formation of an ideal alternative, meaning representation of the alternatives (including the ideal), and a specification of the importance weights of the meaning values assigned to the alternatives. The subroutine provides for calculating the distances between the meanings of each alternative and the ideal one. The output of the subroutine includes the selected alternative, which is the one with the least distance, the mean distances between it and the other available alternatives, and the confidence in the decision (which is a function of the distances involved). These parameters are used in the reclustering process designed to form (or not to form) a BI for executing the selected alternative. Zakay showed that this model is more general than other decision-making models—which occur as special cases—and resolves major controversial issues in the decision-making domain.

B. EMPIRICAL PREDICTIONS OF CHOICES

In a series of studies, Zakay (1976) applied the DBM model for predicting choices of subjects in specific situations. For example, in one experiment Zakay (1976, pp. 159–164) focused on predicting choices in a real-life situation. The subjects were 40 undergraduates (15 male, 25 female) with the mean age of 20.7 years. There were two sessions, in one of which the independent variables were assessed and in the other the dependent variables of the choices proper. Their order was random. The choices were between alternative proposals of psychological experiments, each of which was described by three binary meaning values: high versus low chances to gain money in the experiment, confidence in other people needed or not needed for participating in the experiment, and large versus small degree of social interaction required in the experiment. Zakay constructed a specific CO questionnaire for each of the behavioral aspects involved. For each item he used five response alternatives, ranging from "Untrue" (assigned the score of 1), through "Unable to decide" (set aside; scored 3 points) to "Absolutely true" (scored 5 points). In constructing the questionnaire, he followed the standard procedure (Section IV; Zakay, 1976, pp. 155–158), but in view of the single subject design he used, Zakay devised a new rule for the assignment of CO scores that did not depend on means of beliefs across subjects. Instead, the average score across items was computed for each subject in each of the four CO components. This average could theoretically be in the range of 1–5. Since the score of "3" was designed as a theoretical midpoint, set aside as a response alternative whose use was minimized by instructions and later item analyses, it was considered as a theoretical midpoint for each subject. Accordingly, averages above this midpoint (i.e., 4 or 5) were scored as "1" and those below (i.e., 2 or 1) as 0. The sum of these scores across the four CO components was considered as the subject's CO score. In their final form, each of the three CO questionnaires included 20 items, five for each CO component. The α coefficients ranged from .75 (for norms of having confidence in other people) to .93 (for GB, of tendency for being involved in social interaction). The intercorrelations between the four CO components were all positive, in the range of .25–.37.

The CO scores were used for constructing for each subject the profile of what would be for him or her the "ideal experiment." The importance weights of the three meaning values were assessed by a graphic rating scale (Zakay, 1976, pp. 152–153).

The subjects were asked to make their choices of the experiment in which they wanted to participate without being aware that they actually participated in an experiment. Some subjects were presented with choices out of three alternatives, some out of four. The distances between the presented alternatives and the ideal one for each subject were computed according to the formulas, and the one with the least distance was predicted to be the preferred. For the subjects ($N = 10$) who chose out of three alternatives, there was a 100% fit between the predicted choices and those actually made. For those ($N = 30$) who chose out of four alternatives, the fit was perfect in 87% of the choices. In both cases the findings deviated significantly ($p < .000, \ldots, p < .005$, respectively) from chance.

In another experiment Zakay (1976, pp. 165–179) predicted vocational choices. The jobs were described in terms of three binary aspects: confidence in people, social interaction, and competitiveness. The importance weights of these meaning values for the subjects were measured by a graphic rating scale. As in the former study, CO scores toward the three aspects involved in the meaning of the jobs were used for constructing each subject's ideal job. Two of the CO questionnaires were the same as in the previous study, whereas the third (CO of competitiveness) was constructed especially for this study. Like the other questionnaires, it included 20 items, five for each CO component, its α coefficients ranged from .81 to .86, and the intercorrelations between its CO components were in the range of .31–.37. Each subject was seen individually in two sessions one of which, randomly determined, was devoted to assessing the independent parameters (weights and CO questionnaires) and the other to assessing the choices. The subjects of the study were 46 undergraduates (26 females, 20 males) of a mean age 22 years. For each choice situation, the parameters of each subject were computed and fed into a computer program that was constructed for predicting choices in line with the DBM model. The predicted choices were compared with the actual choices made by the subject. In all choice situations, the proportion of actual choices that were identical to those predicted by the model exceeded statistically significant criteria. The fit was perfect for 84.4–100% of the choices. In terms of confidence intervals, one may predict that in making job choices at least 77% of the subjects make choices in accordance with the DBM model at a 95% level of confidence. A further analysis of variance showed that when fewer than all the parameters specified by the model are considered, the accuracy of the prediction decreases (i.e., the .05 confidence intervals of the predictions were 71–92% when all three CO scores and weights were considered, decreased to 51–78% when fewer than the three CO scores were considered, and further decreased to 39–67% when the weights were overlooked).

A replication of these two studies was done using a ranking task (Zakay, 1976, pp. 184–188). The subjects were asked to rank in terms of preference eight alternatives describing psychological experiments in which the subjects were supposed to participate, and eight alternatives describing different jobs. As in the above reported studies, each alternative was described in terms of two meaning values. For each subject the ideal alternative in each content domain was set up on the basis of CO scores referring to the same aspects that described the alternatives. The subjects were 60 (31 females, 29 males) undergraduates (mean age 22.7 years). For each subject the distance of each alternative from the subject's ideal alternative was computed by using the simulated DBM program. Spearman rank–order correlations within each subject between the actual rank of the specific alternative and its predicted rank (as computed on the basis of its distance from the ideal alternative) were in the range of .77–.90, all significant.

Two features are common to the three Zakay experiments: CO scores are used for defining a standard (called "ideal alternative") against which actual or presented alternatives are evaluated; the meaning of the alternatives is explicitly and exhaustively stated. Both features present technical innovations that allow for new manipulations of variables within the CO theory.

Further, the three experiments extend the range of generalization of the conclusions stated in Section IX. They show that predictions of subjects' behavior—in this case, choices out of presented alternatives—are highly accurate when CO scores of subjects are considered *and* the meanings of the behavioral alternatives are clearly specified.

XI. Development of Clustering

Relatively little is known about the development of belief types that constitute the four CO components, and even less is known about the development of the processes underlying clustering and the formation of BI. Studies by Piaget (1960) and Luria (1961) clearly indicate that in the course of development behavior comes increasingly under the control of internal cognitions, but neither of these theories offer a workable model that specifies how this occurs (H. Kreitler & S. Kreitler, 1976, pp. 124-127). Marom's (1978) study of the development of clustering is a first attempt in this direction. She assumed that prior to clustering proper most clusters that children formed were merely quasi-clusters, dominated by beliefs of one or another CO component, mostly goals. Conflict or contradiction between goal beliefs and other beliefs, mostly norms, is the factor that causes goal beliefs to be increasingly subjected to clustering processes. Hence, conflict, or its cognitive representation in the form of contradiction between CO components, is a basic determinant for clustering. This conceptualization suggests that, in case there is an inconsistency between the two CO components Go and N so that Go orients toward a certain action and N away from it, older children are likely to consult the other available beliefs, that is, GB, or BS, or both, whereas younger children, in the preclustering stage, would not do so. Operationally, this implies that if in regard to some behavior there exists a nuclear clustering frame defined by Go+ and N−, in older children there would be a difference in behavior between those who score CO 3 and those who score CO 2. The reason for this is that due to clustering these subjects would also consider the orientational implications of the CO components GB and BS. If both support the Go component, the resulting CO score would be 3; if only one supports the Go component, the resulting CO score would be 2. In subjects who are able to cluster, the difference between CO 3 and CO 2 should be reflected in behavior. The two controls for this state of affairs are the occurrence of the same nuclear frame (i.e., Go+ and N−) in younger children, and the occurrence of the complementary frame (Go+ and N+) in older and younger children. In neither of these control states would clustering proper occur, in the former because of cognitive immaturity, in the latter because there is no necessity for it.

Marom studied 55 younger children (in the age range 4.5–5.5 years) and 77 older children (in the age range 7.8–8.3 years) of both genders. She examined the behavioral domain of curiosity. A CO questionnaire was constructed, with two items in each CO component. CO scores were assigned separately to the younger and older children. Curiosity was assessed by the duration of manipulation the child performed with an instrument that was used by S. Kreitler, Zigler, and H. Kreitler (1975) for the assessment of manipulatory curiosity. The instrument consisted of a wooden board provided with several screws, flaps, bars, etc. that could be manipulated in a variety of ways. Duration of manipulation was found to be saturated particularly on manipulatory curiosity, the dominant factor of curiosity in children. The results showed that in the case of Go+ and N−, the difference in behaviors by subjects with CO 3 and subjects with CO 2 is significant in the older subjects but not in the younger ones. Further, there is no parallel significant difference in the case of the complementary constellation defined by Go+ and N+ (Table VIII). These findings support the assumption that under the conditions of incongruity between goals and norms (i.e., Go+ and N−), older subjects engage in some form of clustering, whereas the younger ones hardly do so. Accordingly, it should not be surprising that the whole range of CO scores was found to be related to curiosity more closely and regularly in older subjects than in younger ones (Table IX).

XII. Formation and Retrieval of Beliefs

Formation and retrieval of beliefs is the least researched domain of the CO theory up to now. The studies reported in the original publication of the theory were oriented particularly to methodological issues. Thus, one study (H. Kreitler & S. Kreitler, 1976, pp. 365–374) showed that most subjects regard the statement of a belief in its brief nuclear form as sufficient in about half of the cases and in need of some minimal extension in the other half of the cases, particularly if the beliefs are accepted as true, but regardless of their judged importance and of the CO component to which they adhere. Thus, the findings indicate that the unit of belief consisting of two meaning values related through a third implied meaning value is experienced as meaningful and probably has psychological reality. Another study (with Zemet, 1976, pp. 292–298) showed that though statements of beliefs, such as goal beliefs, may be identical in normals and schizophrenics, the beliefs themselves may differ in their meanings for these two groups of subjects.

More recently, some headway was made in studying belief formation and retrieval. The studies will be summarized briefly (for a full presentation, see S. Kreitler & H. Kreitler, 1982a).

In one study the subjects—90 undergraduates in the social sciences—were

TABLE VIII
DIFFERENCES IN CURIOSITY BEHAVIOR OF SUBJECTS WITH DIFFERENT COGNITIVE ORIENTATION
SCORES IN TWO KINDS OF COGNITIVE ORIENTATION CONSTELLATIONS[a]

Cognitive orientation constellations	Younger subjects (4.5–5.5 years)			Older subjects (7.5–8.5 years)		
	N	$\bar{X}$	SD	N	$\bar{X}$	SD
Subjects with Go+ and N−						
CO 3	5	9.2	4.0	7	11.1	9.1
CO 2	5	6.2	6.9	5	3.6	2.0
t		.83			1.92*	
Subjects with Go+ and N+						
CO 4	15	7.2	12.3	27	7.6	6.5
CO 3	6	5.3	12.1	17	4.6	7.0
t		1.3			.6	

[a] Based on Marom (1978).
*$p < .05$.

presented with lists of six goals hierarchically ordered from the most to the least desired, and short descriptions of two real-life situations, one of which was presented as likely to promote one pair of goals with a given probability and the other, another pair. The combinations of goals and probabilities of attainment

TABLE IX
COGNITIVE ORIENTATION SCORES AND CURIOSITY IN YOUNGER AND OLDER SUBJECTS

Subjects	CO 4	CO 3	CO 2, 1, and 0	F
Younger (4.5– 5.5 years)				
$\bar{X}$	5.3	9.6	5.6	3.10*
SD	7.2	11.3	6.0	
N	15	16	24	
Older (7.5– 8.5 years)				
$\bar{X}$	7.6	6.8	3.6	3.23**
SD	4.6	7.4	2.6	
N	27	30	20	

[a] Based on Marom (1978).
*$p < .10$.
**$p < .05$.

produced a matrix. The subjects were asked to imagine that the goals were those of a described fictitious character that had to make a choice between the situations. The different possibilities of the total matrix were distributed across the subjects randomly so that each subject made only eight judgments. The regular pattern consists in preferring a situation that allows for satisfying a more highly desired goal to one that allows satisfying a less desired goal. Most of the choices (88.75%) conformed to this pattern. But those that did not followed another principle that is of interest in the present context: a somewhat less desired goal, rather than a more desired one, was selected if the probability of its attainment was higher. This tendency was manifested characteristically more often in regard to goals of medium desirability (i.e., ranks 3 and 4 on a scale of six) rather than of high or low desirability. A replication of this study in regard to personal goals confirmed the finding that a higher probability of attainment may compensate for a lower degree of goal desirability. Thus, the study suggests that the goals that make up the CO component of goals are selected at least partly by considering general beliefs and perhaps also beliefs of other components.

Another study dealt with the relations between the subjects' preferred meaning dimensions and major stored beliefs of the four components. The guiding assumption was that since the four CO components represent major and constantly recurrent types of issues that guide orientation, it is plausible to expect that the basic raw data in the four components would be shaped in line with one's dominant meaning dimensions. The subjects were 35 individuals in the age range of 18–22, partly serving in the army and partly students. They were administered a standard meaning questionnaire and a Belief Questionnaire that tapped beliefs in major domains of life, unbound to any specific actions or situations. The findings showed that an appreciable percentage of beliefs in the four CO components were in content domains that corresponded to the subject's preferred meaning dimensions (56% were in domains that corresponded to the dimensions above the median in the subject's meaning profile). Thus, it seems that preferred meaning dimensions affect the general type of beliefs that a subject tends to form and which contribute the raw data out of which beliefs are generated as needed in the course of clustering. The same study showed that subjects have preferred domains of contents for forming beliefs of norms and of goals that correspond to meaning dimensions he or she uses frequently in conjunction with the meaning dimensions Judgments and Evaluations and Feelings and Emotions. Again, it seems these meaning dimensions constitute guidelines for the formation or retrieval of beliefs in these particular CO components.

A third study showed that specific meaning variables are related to CO components and CO clusters. The content domain investigated was the CO of defense mechanisms (Section V,A). A sequel to this study showed that the meaning variables found to be correlated with the CO scores predicted the CO scores of defense mechanisms in subjects of another sample. Together these studies indicate that meaning variables may serve as guidelines and perhaps provide shortcut procedures aiding in the formation of CO clusters.

XIII. Concluding Remarks: Prediction and Determinism

Most people would like to know how other persons will behave, and a great many people are in need of this knowledge in order to fulfill their tasks as planners in one or another domain of life. On the other hand, the deterministic notion, so frequently associated with behavior prediction, is an anathema to the majority of people living in what is now called the western world. They cherish the idea of free will and, moreover, are afraid that an instrument enabling behavior prediction could be misused for controlling and manipulating their lives and, thus, curtailing their individual freedom. Usually this dissonance is dormant, because our hope to foresee the behavior of others and our fear that others could control us by successfully predicting our future behaviors are not brought into close conjunction. However, the predictive achievements of the CO theory and its potentials for further improvement may give rise to some embarrassing questions about merits and hazards of behavior prediction, as well as about its ultimate limits. Indeed, the answer given to the latter question is likely to determine whether the merits of future behavior prediction could be impaired by its eventual hazards. Therefore, let us first address ourselves to the question of limits.

Hitherto our method for reconstructing CO clusters to provide a basis for behavior prediction has been rather crude, but there is no doubt that it could be subjected to further refinement. Meaning manipulations, as mentioned in Sections IX and X, more intensive work with individual subjects, techniques borrowed from psychoanalysis, computer simulation, and application of other methods for studying blackbox processes are likely to result in considerable improvement of behavior predictions based on CO. For the sake of argument, we could venture to cross the border between science and science fiction and imagine future methods of brain scanning that would inform us about every meaning value and every belief in the cognitive system of our subjects, aided by a monster computer that calculates the most probable CO constellations. Nevertheless, even these behavior predictions would not be perfect, partly because one out of the myriads of involved meaning values or beliefs could pop up in the last instant and modify the predicted constellation, but mainly because of the same hurdle that has ultimately shattered the traditional determinism of classical physics, that is, the unavoidable interference of the observing system with the function of the system to be observed. However, we must not invoke the uncertainty principle of quantum physics to recognize the inherent limitations of all psychological behavior prediction and control of behavior. It suffices to recall that the very knowledge that enables us to predict and control behavior is readily accessible to our subjects who could use it for gaining greater awareness of their belief structures and for modifying their CO clusters. Indeed, this is what should eventually happen and, it is to be hoped, would actually happen. Finally, since there is no known limit to the human ability to produce and modify meanings, methods of behavior prediction and control cannot be perfect, nor can they become a dangerously effective tool for unwanted manipulation of human fate.

Again, human society is in need of reliable behavior predictions, as partly rendered and partly promised by CO theory. Yet cognitive orientation not only provides a suitable basis for predicting behavior but explains why people will always retain the ability to do the unforeseen, even the unpredictable.

References

Adler, E. *Differences in the perception of the mother image in different levels of personality in normal and disturbed boys.* Master's thesis, Department of Psychology, Tel Aviv University, 1974.

Adler, E. *Predicting social withdrawal on the basis of CO scores.* Unpublished manuscript, Tel Aviv University, 1980.

Anokhin, P. K. The role of the orienting-exploratory reaction in the formation of the conditioned reflex. In L. G. Voronin, A. N. Leontiev, A. R. Luria, E. N. Sokolov, & O. S. Vinogradova (Eds.), *Orienting reflex and exploratory behavior.* Moscow: Publishing House of the Academy of Pedagogical Sciences of RSFSR, 1958.

Bar-Hillel, Y. An examination of information theory. *Philosophical Science,* 1955, **22**, 86–105.

Berlyne, D. E. *Conflict, arousal, and curiosity.* New York: McGraw-Hill, 1960.

Berlyne, D. E. *Structure and direction in thinking.* New York: Wiley, 1965.

Borgatta, E. F. An analysis of three levels of response: An approach to some relationships among dimensions of personality. *Sociometry Monographs,* 1952, No. 26.

Bower, K. S. Situationism in psychology: An analysis and critique. *Psychological Review,* 1973, **80**, 307–336.

Breier, G. *Effects of cognitive orientation on behavior under threat.* Master's thesis, Department of Psychology, Tel Aviv University, 1980.

Broadbent, D. E. *Perception and communication.* Oxford: Pergamon, 1958.

Bykov, V. D. On the dynamics of the orienting-exploratory reaction during the formation of positive and inhibitory conditioned reflexes and their alterations. In L. G. Voronin, A. N. Leontiev, A. R. Luria, E. N. Sokolov, & O. S. Vinogradova (Eds.), *Orienting reflex and exploratory behavior.* Moscow: Publishing House of the Academy of Pedagogical Sciences of RSFSR, 1958.

Cherry, C. *On human communication.* New York: Wiley, 1957.

Deese, J. *The structure of associations in language and thought.* Baltimore, Maryland: Johns Hopkins Press, 1965.

Deutsch, J. A., & Deutsch, D. Attention: Some theoretical considerations. *Psychological Review,* 1963, **70**, 80–90.

Fishbein, M., & Ajzen, I. *Belief, attitude, intention and behavior: An introduction to theory and research.* Reading, Mass.: Addison-Wesley, 1975.

Graham, F. K., & Jackson, J. C. Arousal systems and infant heart rate responses. In H. W. Reese & L. P. Lipsitt (Eds.), *Advances in child development and behavior* (Vol. 5). New York: Academic Press, 1970.

Hintikka, J. *Models for modalities*. Dordrecht, The Netherlands: Reidel, 1969.

Jeffrey, W. E. The orienting reflex and attention in cognitive development. *Psychological Review,* 1968, **75**, 323-334.

Johnson, L. C. *State conditions and the OR*. Paper presented at the meeting of the APA, San Francisco, 1968.

Kluckhohn, C. Values and value-orientations in the theory of action: An exploration in definition and classification. In T. Parsons & E. A. Shils (Eds.), *Toward a general theory of action*. Cambridge, Mass.: Harvard Univ. Press, 1951.

Kreitler, H., & Kreitler, S. Modes of action in the psychodramatic role test. *International Journal of Sociometry and Sociatry,* 1964, **4**, 10-15.

Kreitler, H., & Kreitler, S. The validation of psychodramatic behavior against behavior in life. *British Journal of Medical Psychology,* 1968, **41**, 185-192.

Kreitler, H., & Kreitler, S. *Cognitive orientation and defense mechanisms*. Princeton, N.J.: Educational Testing Service, 1969.

Kreitler, H., & Kreitler, S. The cognitive antecedents of the orienting reflex. *Schweizerische Zeitschrift für Psychologie,* 1970, **29**, 94-105.

Kreitler, H., & Kreitler, S. The model of cognitive orientation: Towards a theory of human behavior. *British Journal of Psychology,* 1972, **63**, 9-30. (a)

Kreitler, H., & Kreitler, S. The cognitive determinants of defensive behavior. *British Journal of Social and Clinical Psychology,* 1972, **11**, 359-372. (b)

Kreitler, H., & Kreitler, S. *Cognitive orientation and behavior*. New York: Springer Publ., 1976.

Kreitler, H., & Kreitler, S. *Changing molar behaviors in children by changing cognitive orientations and related meanings*. Unpublished manuscript, Tel Aviv University, 1981.

Kreitler, S. *Symbolerfassung und Symbolschoepfung: Eine experimental-psychologische Studie*. Basel-Munich: Reinhardt, 1965.

Kreitler, S., & Kreitler, H. Dimensions of meaning and their measurement. *Psychological Reports,* 1968, **23**, 1307-1329.

Kreitler, S., & Kreitler, H. *Perception and meaning assignment*. Paper presented at the International Conference on Microgenesis, Mainz, Federal Republic of Germany, June 1977.

Kreitler, S., & Kreitler, H. *Combining different CO scores for predicting molar behaviors in children*. Unpublished manuscript, Tel Aviv University, 1981.

Kreitler, S., & Kreitler, H. *Meaning in personality*. New York: Academic Press, 1982 (in press). (a)

Kreitler, S., & Kreitler, H. Perception as a process of meaning assignment. In W. Froehlich & J. Draguns (Eds.), *Path analysis*. 1982, in preparation. (b)

Kreitler, S., & Kreitler, H. *Meaning in cognition*. 1983, in preparation.

Kreitler, S., Kreitler, H., & Zigler, E. Cognitive orientation and curiosity. *British Journal of Psychology,* 1974, **65**, 43-52.

Kreitler, S., Maguen, T., & Kreitler, H. The three faces of intolerance of ambiguity. *Archiv für Psychologie,* 1975, **127**, 238-250.

Kreitler, S., Shahar, A., & Kreitler, H. Cognitive orientation, type of smoker and behavior therapy of smoking. *British Journal of Medical Psychology,* 1976, **49**, 167-175.

Kreitler, S., Zigler, E., & Kreitler, H. The nature of curiosity in children. *Journal of School Psychology,* 1975, **13**, 185-200.

Kreitler, S., Zigler, E., & Kreitler, H. Curiosity and demographic factors as determinants of children's probability learning strategies. *Journal of General Psychology,* 1982, in press.

Lazarus, R. S. *Psychological stress and the coping process*. New York: McGraw-Hill, 1966.

Leventhal, H. Findings and theory in the study of fear communications. In L. Berkowitz (Ed.), *Advances in Experimental Social Psychology* (Vol. 5). New York: Academic Press, 1970.

Lobel, T. *Predicting pain tolerance from CO components*. Unpublished manuscript, Tel Aviv University, 1981. (a)

Lobel, T. *Predicting punctuality from CO components*. Unpublished manuscript, Tel Aviv University, 1981. (b)

Lobel, T. *Predicting orderliness from CO components*. Unpublished manuscript, Tel Aviv University, 1981. (c)

Lobel, T. *Predicting assertiveness from CO components*. Unpublished manuscript, Tel Aviv University, 1981. (d)

Lobel, T. *Predicting conformity from CO components*. Unpublished manuscript, Tel Aviv University, 1981. (e)

Lorenz, K. Innate bases of learning. In K. Pribram (Ed.), *On the biology of learning*. New York: Harcourt, 1969.

Luria, A. R. *The role of speech in the regulation of normal and abnormal behavior.*   Oxford: Pergamon, 1961.

Lynn, R. *Attention, arousal and the orientation reaction*. Oxford: Pergamon, 1966.

Mackworth, J. F. *Vigilance and habituation: A neuropsychological approach.* Harmondsworth, England: Penguin Books, 1969.

Marom, S. *Examination of CO clusters in children based on the theory of cognitive orientation*. Master's thesis, Department of Psychology, Tel Aviv University, 1978.

McGuire, W. J. Suspiciousness of experimenter's intent. In R. Rosenthal & R. L. Rosnow (Eds.), *Artifact in behavioral research*. New York: Academic Press, 1969.

Miller, A. G. Role playing: An alternative to deception? A review of the evidence. *American Psychologist,* 1972, **27**, 623–636.

Miller, G. A. What is information measurement. *American Psychologist,* 1953, **8**, 3–11.

Miller, G. A., Galanter, E., & Pribram, K. H. *Plans and the structure of behavior*. New York: Holt, 1960.

Miller, J. G. Living systems: basic concepts. *Behavioral Science,* 1965, **10**, 193–237.

Moray, N. *Attention: Selective processes in vision and hearing*. London: Hutchison Educational, 1969.

Nehari, M., Kreitler, S., & Kreitler, H. *A test for assessing programming*. Unpublished study, Tel Aviv University, 1975.

Norman, D. A. *Memory and attention: An introduction to human information processing*. New York: Wiley, 1969.

Osgood, C. E., Suci, J. G., & Tannenbaum, P. H. *Measurement of meaning*. Urbana, Ill.: Illinois Univ. Press, 1958.

Parsons, T., Shils, E. A., & Olds, J. Values, motives and systems of action. In T. Parsons & E. A. Shils (Eds.), *Toward a general theory of action*. Cambridge, Mass.: Harvard Univ. Press, 1951.

Pavlov, I. P. *Conditioned reflexes*. London and New York: Oxford Univ. Press (Clarendon), 1927.

Piaget, J. *The psychology of intelligence*. Paterson, N.J.: Littlefield, 1960.

Pribram, K. H. *Languages of the brain*. New York: Prentice-Hall, 1971.

Raz, A., Kreitler, S., & Kreitler, H. *Actual behavior, role playing behavior, and paper-and-pencil behavior*. Unpublished manuscript, Tel Aviv University, 1976.

Rotter, J. B., & Wickens, D. W. The consistency and generality of ratings of social aggressiveness made from observation of role playing situations. *Journal of Consulting Psychology,* 1948, **12**, 234–239.

Sarnoff, L., & Zimbardo, P. Anxiety, fear, and social affiliation. *Journal of Abnormal and Social Psychology,* 1961, **62**, 356–363.

Schachter, S. *The psychology of affiliation*. Stanford, Calif.: Stanford Univ. Press, 1959.

Schaefer, E. S. Children's reports of parental behavior: An inventory. *Child Development,* 1965, **36**, 417–424.

Schwartz, S. H. Moral decision making and behavior. In J. R. Macaulay & L. Berkowitz (Eds.), *Altruism and helping behavior*. New York: Academic Press, 1970.

Sharan, S. *Developing classification skills in underprivileged kindergarten children*. Jerusalem: Ministry of Education and Culture, 1971. [In Hebrew]

Sheppes, S. *Predicting military leadership through the theory of cognitive orientation*. Master's thesis, Department of Psychology, Tel Aviv University, 1977.

Sigel, J. E. Developmental trends in the abstraction ability of children. *Child Development*, 1953, **24**, 131–144.

Sokolov, E. N. *Perception and the conditioned reflex*. New York: Macmillan, 1963.

Spielberger, C. D., Gorsuch, R. L., & Lushene, R. E. *Manual for the state-trait anxiety inventory*. Palo Alto, Calif.: Consulting Psychologist Press, 1970.

Tinbergen, N. *The study of instinct*. London and New York: Oxford Univ. Press (Clarendon), 1951.

Treisman, A. Strategies and models of selective attention. *Psychological Review*, 1969, **76**, 282–299.

Zakay, D. *Decision by meaning: A decision making model based upon the cognitive orientation theory*. Unpublished doctoral thesis, Tel Aviv University, 1976. [In English]

Zemet, R. *Cognitive orientation theory and patterns of behavior in conflictual situations in schizophrenic and normal subjects*. Master's thesis, Department of Psychology, Tel Aviv University, 1976.

Ziv-Av, Y. *Slowness in different types of action as a function of cognitive structures and contents*. Master's thesis, Department of Psychology, Tel Aviv University, 1978.

VALIDITY OF CHILDREN'S SELF-REPORTS OF PSYCHOLOGICAL QUALITIES[1]

Jerome Kagan, Sydney Hans,[2] Alice Markowitz, and Diane Lopez

DEPARTMENT OF PSYCHOLOGY AND SOCIAL RELATIONS
HARVARD UNIVERSITY
CAMBRIDGE, MASSACHUSETTS

Heidi Sigal

FOUNDATION FOR CHILD DEVELOPMENT
NEW YORK, NEW YORK

I. Introduction: The Concept of Self

All scientific disciplines have a small set of favorite constructs, most of which are replaced following critical logical analysis and/or reliable data that reveal a

[1]This research was supported by a grant from the Foundation for Child Development as part of its efforts to advance research methods and knowledge in the field of social and affective development. The first study reported in the manuscript was part of S. Hans' doctoral dissertation. The authors wish to thank Robin Mount and Mark Szpak for help in collecting and analyzing the data and Leland Miller, Mary Blessington, Mary Murphy, Peggy Silverio, Roz O'Sullivan, Alice Wadden, and the Cambridge public schools for their cooperation.

[2]Present address: Department of Psychiatry, University of Chicago, Chicago, Illinois 60637.

flaw in the idea. A smaller number of inventions live for a longer time, either because their complexity or ambiguity prevents the empiricist from penetrating their camouflaged defense or, less frequently, because they turn out to be empirically sound and theoretically useful. The concept of self is one of the few psychological ideas that observers of children and adults continue to promote. It is still not clear, however, whether its persistence in our explanations of human behavior is due to the fact that it is theoretically potent or because it is consonant with our intuition. The fact that it has proven so difficult to operationalize has prevented us from resolving this dilemma.

Consciousness of one's ability to act and to feel and comparison of one's qualities with another's, although different functions, are such phenomenologically compelling experiences that it would take a remarkably coherent collection of scientific evidence to convince most thinking citizens that these are not real events entitled to a central place in a theory of human functioning. But intuitions are not always proper guides to validity. The intuitions that the world is flat and the sun travels around the earth are equally compelling, self-evident truths which educated persons have given up in order to maintain the more important belief in their rationality.

As Lewin (1951), Barker (1968), and Mischel (1977) have noted, the immediate social context is the first, and most important, determinant of behavior in a particular situation. In societies with well-articulated rules for action to which most persons conform there can be minimal variability in behavior in many contexts. Explanations of these normative behaviors do not require a "self-concept." But in communities in modern America and Europe, where there is an emphasis on individuality, a permissive attitude toward conformity to normative rules, a celebration of change through the life span, and the autonomous generation of a personal philosophy of action, there is far greater behavioral variation in all contexts (Brim & Kagan, 1980). The variety in behavior in an eighth-grade classroom in New York City, compared with a classroom in Peking, cannot be explained by appealing to the rules applicable to the situation; the investigator must look to other factors.

Traditionally, psychologists have explained the variation by appealing to constructs such as motivation, expectancy, hierarchy of acquired habits, and conflict. One of the major conceptual agreements reached during the last 20 years is that the expectation of gaining a goal is the vital link between a motive for a goal state and behavioral attempts to attain that goal. Children, like adults, create these expectancies from evaluations of their ability to obtain the desired goal without excessive stress or effort. One can translate that statement into a proposition about the child's conception of his or her liabilities and talents. The bases for these expectancies are assumed to be (a) past history of successes and failures in particular domains and (b) beliefs about the self's properties relevant to the attainment of particular goals (Bandura, 1977). Although history influences these beliefs, most scholars are persuaded, as are we, that the conceptualization of one's properties is not totally veridical with the history of successes and failures. Festinger's (1954) classic paper, "Theory of social comparison processes," postulated that all persons "have a drive" to compare their properties with those of others and to evaluate the results of that comparison. The consequences of the cognitive evaluation are not totally predictable by the prior history of successes and failures, for it is influenced by the particular others the person has chosen for comparison. If the assumption that behavior is guided by expectancy is correct, it is necessary to evaluate the person's conceptualization of his or her properties, which is equivalent to his or her self-concept.

DEFINITIONS OF SELF

The idea of self has at least three separate meanings. Ontogenetically, the first meaning refers to the emergence of an awareness that one can affect people and objects and a consciousness of one's feelings and competences, what Preyer (1889) called the "I-feeling." The first nonlinguistic signs of this competence, which typically appear by 18 months, are followed 6–10 months later by utterances which contain the child's name or the pronoun *I* together with a predicate of action (Kagan, 1981). All of this typically occurs before the third birthday. Lewis and his colleagues (Lewis & Brooks-Gunn, 1979) have gathered a persuasive set of data indicating that by the second year children are able to recognize themselves in a variety of contexts. These investigators regard the ability to recognize the self as related to "how the young child constructs a concept of self" (p. 198).

This first meaning was of central importance to nineteenth-century observers of children. The diaries of Preyer (1889) and Hogan (1898), and the influential texts of Stern (1930) and Baldwin (1895), were concerned, in a major way, with the time when the child was first able to act self-consciously. Preyer believed that the child's reflections on his or her sensations and actions gradually led to the information of the "*I*" feeling.

> Only by means of very frequent coincidences of unlike sense-impressions, in tasting-and-touching, seeing-and-feeling, seeing-and-hearing, seeing-and-smelling, tasting-and-smelling, hearing-and-touching, are the intercentral connecting fibers developed, and then first can the various representational centers, these "*I*"-makers, as it were, contribute, as in the case of the ordinary formation of concepts, to the formation of the corporate "*I,*" which is quite abstract. (Preyer, 1889, p. 205)

The persistent concern with the emergence of self-consciousness by nineteenth-century observers was understandable because they were preoccupied with the important human quality of morality. No attribute of childhood, not even keenness of reasoning, was as important as good character. Self-consciousness was the basis of an autonomous conscience, and the first signs of this function announced the child's potential capacity to select morally proper actions from alternatives.

The nineteenth-century observer was far less concerned than his twentieth-century counterpart with individual variation in the feeling of self, for the former believed that temperamental qualities, not a history of habits sculpted by social experience, were major sources of individual differences.

A second meaning of self-concept refers to a set of properties the child believes apply to him or her. Among the most obvious are intrinsic dimensions such as physical characteristics, family name, gender, and ethnic-group membership. But the concept of self also possesses a set of comparative qualities.

Although a dog is a mammal with four legs and fur, a dog is also less aggressive than a wolf, stronger than a canary, and less poisonous than a snake. The self-concept, too, has both intrinsic and comparative dimensions. Although a particular child is a female, Canadian, Catholic, with brown eyes, she is also prettier than her sister, smarter than her best friend, and more fearful of animals than her brother. Typically, the child believes the characteristics based on comparison are more amenable to change.

McGuire has suggested that the psychological salience of the qualities that comprise the self-concept is a function of their distinctiveness in the mind of the person (McGuire, 1978; McGuire & Padawer-Singer, 1976; McGuire, McGuire, Child, & Fujioka, 1978). Possession of dark hair in a community of blondes is more significant for the child's concept of self than the same property in a community of brunettes, as is inadequate reading skill in a child surrounded by exceptionally competent readers.

A third meaning of self-concept consists of the private evaluation of one's qualities. This definition, when applied to properties that are valued by the culture, has almost become synonymous with the notion of self-esteem; the evaluation of the self's properties as good (or bad) is the source of the person's self-esteem.

The idea of self-esteem was of little interest to nineteenth-century investigators. But when adjustment to society replaced character as the criterion for mature growth in the 1930s, emotional security and intellectual competence quickly occupied central places in the definition of adjustment. The child's confidence in his or her ability to demonstrate to self and to others that he or she was valued, attractive, and talented became as important as character. This confidence rested, in part, on a comparison of the self's properties with those of others.

The writings of Cooley (1902) and Mead (1934) were seminal in the development of the last two meanings of self. Cooley (1902) argued that the person's concept of self was created from interpretations of how others reacted to ego; hence, Cooley is given credit for the phrase, ''looking-glass self.'' Mead (1934) refined Cooley's views and suggested that a person's conception of self was determined largely by the experiences with others which permitted ego to understand how alter reacted to ego (i.e., to view the self as an object with properties as others did). [See Wells and Marwell (1976) for an excellent review of the history of the self-concept, and Smith (1979) for a more personal history.]

Measurement of Self-Concept

The part of self-concept based on a comparison of ego's qualities with others has attracted the greatest interest among American psychologists and has led to many attempts at measurement. The knowledge structure that defines self-concept is more private and less amenable to direct inquiry than the child's knowledge of the external world, and measurement procedures have generally been subject to criticism. When ego processes were made popular by psychoanalytic theory, projective methods were used to provide scientific indexes of this construct (Murray, 1938). It is fair to say that this mission failed, and empirical, but not theoretical, interest in self-concept waned for a while. But the indomitable, empirical spirit in American psychology, which is eager to get on with the work, denied what it knew and attacked the problem directly. Investigators asked subjects, using relatively undisguised procedures, to describe their psychological properties. Because the answers produced significant correlations with some other quantifiable property, the pragmatic spirit prevailed and doubts about the validity of the original data were put aside.

The interest in children's categorizations of their psychological attributes has been accompanied by a proliferation of self-report instruments (Wylie, 1961, 1974, 1979). Some investigators simply ask the child directly whether he agrees or disagrees with a particular statement (e.g., I feel useless at times). Coopersmith's (1967) self-esteem inventory asked subjects to indicate whether a particular sentence was or was not descriptive of their personality (e.g., I'm pretty sure of myself) (see also Piers & Harris, 1964). Other commonly used rating scales ask a subject to indicate the extent to which particular descriptors apply to him or her. M. Rosenberg (1979) had subjects indicate (on a four-point scale) whether they agreed or disagreed with a particular item. (On the whole I'm satisfied with myself; I feel that I have a number of good qualities; I certainly feel useless at times.) Other investigators have asked the subject to describe the self (Livesley & Bromley, 1973) or write answers to the question, ''Who are you?'' (Bugental & Zelen, 1950). Some investigators ask the subjects to compare the self with others, either by rating themselves with reference to some group norm or by rank-ordering themselves and members of the group in terms of particular characteristics [Wylie (1974, 1979) and Wells and Marwell (1976) contain a complete review of these scales].

Although most psychologists recognize that the validity of these self-report instruments is flawed because some children report favorable characterizations of themselves which they know are inaccurate, or are inconsistent with less conscious evaluations, most investigators continue to use these methods. As a result questionable conclusions are drawn. For example, M. Rosenberg (1979) found no relation between ethnicity and a child's conscious statements regarding his self-esteem. As a result Rosenberg suggested that race and ethnicity had no influence on the child's self-esteem. "There is no indication that the distribution of self-acceptance in a group is related to the social prestige of that group in American society" (M. Rosenberg, 1979, p. 151).

Shrauger and Schoeneman (1979), after reviewing research on the relation between self-perception and evaluation of others, concluded that the relation was weak. However, rather than question the validity of the self-perception index, they assumed that self-evaluations were not strongly influenced by the feedback received from others.

"That there is minimal agreement between individuals' judgments of others' perceptions of them and their actual perceptions suggests that the communication of feedback to others may often be infrequent or ambiguous" (Shrauger & Schoeneman, 1979, p. 565).

Additionally, Bachman and O'Malley (1977) suggested that because high-school students' answers to phrases such as, "I feel that I have a number of good qualities" and "I feel I do not have much to be proud of" did not have unique variance associated with later occupational attainment (following a path analysis), self-esteem made a minimal contribution to later educational and occupational status.

Despite regular pleas by Wylie (1961, 1974) that investigators should worry about the reliability and validity of these procedures and warnings that the methodological bases for current work were fragile, her pleas have gone largely ignored. In the revised edition of her self-concept review, Wylie (1974) concludes:

> Consideration of all of the materials in this volume leads inevitably to the conclusion that the present state of affairs leaves much to be desired, differing all too little from the situation described in the 1961 edition of this book. . . . There are only two defensible alternatives: Abandon theorizing and research involving self-referent constructs or make whatever theoretical and methodological improvements are necessary in order to put such work on a more respectable scientific base. (p. 315) . . . On the whole, however, methodology and self-concept research has not shown the improvements in the last decade which one might, with reasonable optimism, have hoped for. Even the most prestigious laboratories and journals are occasionally publishing studies based on completely unvalidated instruments and flawed research designs. Accordingly, the contributions of substantive self-concept studies cannot add up to as much as their total numbers might imply. (pp. 317, 318)

Recent research has attempted to enhance the validity of self-report measures. For example, Harter (1979) has developed a new question format designed to reduce socially desirable responding with an instrument called "Perceived Competence Scale for Children.'' Harter has found support for the separateness of domains of self-reported competence. But it is still necessary to evaluate the validity of self-report measurements and to begin work on more sensitive procedures which might be used to provide supplementary information. The data in this article summarize studies whose aim was to address some methodological issues surrounding the assessment of the self-concept through direct interrogation.

II. Study 1: Rationale

The first study to be summarized reports a preliminary attempt to explore the validity of one self-report method—the ranking of self in comparison with same-sex peers in the child's classroom. Although this method is used less frequently than procedures in which the child indicates which or to what extent certain descriptive statements apply to him- or herself, the ranking of self in comparison with peers has the advantage of specifying a particular reference group and, therefore, permits a comparison of a child's self-evaluation with the evaluation made by the reference group of peers. We are assuming explicitly that among nonpsychotic children of adequate intelligence who are capable of comparing self with others, peer consensus regarding a particular child's possession of selected qualities that are public and salient—dominance and popularity are two examples—is a moderately valid index of that child's behavioral profile. More important, we assume that for this small set of salient qualities the child is, to some degree, aware of his or her psychological profile but that answers to direct questions about the profile are not necessary valid indexes of the child's private beliefs.

The main purposes of this study were (1) to assess the short-term reliability of self-evaluations given by preadolescents on five psychological attributes; (2) to assess the relation of the self-evaluations to evaluations given by peers and teachers; and (3) to determine whether a child's profile of responses on a triad sorting task, after being subjected to multidimensional scaling, added any important information to the self-evaluations obtained in the ranking procedure. In the method of triads the child's repeated sorts of trios of same-sex peers and self generate a similarities matrix which can be scaled in several dimensions and analyzed in relation to the psychological dimensions used by the child in the ranking procedures.

If children who were regarded by their peers as possessing undesirable qualities gave a positive evaluation on the self-ranking procedure, but sorted self in the triads with peers whom they regarded as not possessing desirable attributes, the triad method would be useful in separating valid from less valid self-ranks.

A. METHOD

1. Subjects

The 70 children (35 girls, 35 boys) in the study belonged to one of eight different same-sex groups from four classrooms in two public schools in Cambridge, Massachusetts. The eight groups ranged in size from 6 to 10 children. One school was located in a middle-class neighborhood; the other school in a working-class neighborhood. The 36 children from the middle-class school (17 girls, 19 boys) were third-graders ranging in age from 8 to 9 years. Eighty percent of the children had at least one parent with a college degree; 34 were caucasians and 2 were black. Three children spoke languages other than English in their home but all were fluent in English. The 34 children from the working-class school (18 girls, 16 boys) were mainly third-graders but included five fourth-graders who were members of the same classrooms. Their ages ranged from 8 to 10 years. This group contained 12 caucasians and 11 blacks who spoke English at home, and 11 Hispanic or Portuguese children who did not speak English at home but were fluent in the language. Typically the level of parental education was 8 to 12 years of formal schooling.

2. Procedures

Each child was tested individually in the school on several occasions by a female examiner. Testing began in the late fall to insure that the children had become acquainted with each other. The children were familiar with the examiner before any testing began.

a. Ranking of Self and Peers

Each child was asked to rank him- or herself and all the same-sex members of his or her classroom on five psychological attributes of concern to preadolescent children: academic skill, popularity, physical attractiveness, dominance with peers, and athletic ability. To ensure that all children were responding in terms of a common definition, the examiner defined the dimension in simple, concrete, behavioral terms. The phrases used to describe the positive and negative poles of the five dimensions were (1) someone who is good at reading—someone who is not good at reading; (2) someone the children like a lot—someone the children don't like; (3) someone who is good-looking—someone who is not good-looking; (4) someone who never gets pushed around—someone who gets pushed around a lot; and (5) someone who is good at sports—someone who is not good at sports.

The ranking was performed with the aid of a gameboard that had 15 squares, each a different shade of blue, arranged in a linear sequence from very light to dark blue. The children were first trained on the gameboard to make scaled judgments of animals. Each child was given small cardboard squares with the names of animals written on them and asked to arrange the squares on the board in accord with the size of the animal. After completing this ranking task they were asked to rank the same animals in accord with their dangerousness. No child experienced any difficulty in ranking the animals on these two qualities, indicating the children understood how to rank entities on both a physical and psychological dimension.

Each child was then given cards with the names of the self and the same-sex peers in his or her classroom written on them. (The examiner confirmed the subject could read the names of his peers.) The child ranked the self and all the same-sex peers on one attribute at a time. The dark blue end of the board represented the positive pole of the scale for all dimensions. Initially, the examiner familiarized the child with the meaning of the attribute by asking several questions. For reading the examiner might say, "Do you know who the good readers are in your class? Have you heard most of the kids in your class read?" When the examiner was assured that the child understood the attribute, the child was asked to place the cards representing the names of the same-sex peers, as well as him- or herself on appropriate squares. For reading, for example, the child was told that the very best reader in the classroom belonged on the dark blue square and the child who was poorest in reading belonged on the lightest square. There were always more squares than there were children and the subjects were discouraged from placing two cards on the same square. After ranking for one dimension was completed, the examiner asked the child to look carefully at the board to make certain he had placed the cards correctly. Whenever the experimenter felt the child was answering too quickly or without sufficient reflection, she asked direct questions about all adjacent children in the ranks, such as, "Is child A better at reading than child B; is child B better at reading than child C?"

The reliability of the rankings was assessed by having each child rank peers and self on one-half of the attributes 1 week later. The attributes selected for the reliability assessment were chosen at random. In addition, each of the classroom teachers was asked to rank the children within same-sex groups on each of the five attributes at the time the study began.

b. Triad Sorting of Self and Peers

We wished to generate a matrix summarizing the similarity between every pair of children in a same-sex group in a particular classroom. The most direct way of generating such a matrix is to ask subjects to rate the similarity of all possible pairs of children. However, the method of triads, an alternative procedure for generating a similarities matrix, is less demanding on children's time and cognitive abilities and, therefore, is a more appropriate technique with children. In the method of triads the child repeatedly sorts groups of three children into the pair that is the most alike, leaving the one who is most different from the other two. Most children were presented with all possible triads of the same-sex peers in his classroom (including him- or herself in some triads) and asked to decide which two people acted most similarly and which one acted differently. For the same-sex groups of 9 or 10 children, the number of triads in a complete set was too numerous (84 and 120 triads, respectively); hence, a representative sample of the possible triads was used, a procedure suggested by Burton and Nerlove (1976). In these cases the children made 60 triad judgments. No specific behavioral quality was mentioned, but children were told explicitly not to answer on the basis of a child's physical appearance. The names of the children were written on small pieces of cardboard which the child could sort physically. The number of times a particular pair of children was grouped together was the index of similarity for that pair of children.

Separate similarity matrices were generated for each child, and separate matrices for the boys and girls in each classroom were formed by summing the boys' or girls' matrices from a particular class, omitting all judgments which contained the child's own name. During a later session, after the sorting data had been analyzed and scaled, each child was shown the two-dimensional scaling solution generated from his or her data. The children were then told that the solution was a picture of the children in their class and they were asked to try to explain what the different arrangements of children might mean.

B. RESULTS

Because the eight same-sex peer groups varied in size it was necessary to standardize the ranks. Each child's ranks were converted to deciles. A score of 1.0 always signified the first rank (i.e., the best in reading); a score of 10.0 signified the last rank; and a score of 5.5 the mean rank, regardless of the group size. The distribution of each set of ranks was rectangular. All statistical manipulations of the rank data to be discussed in this article were performed on these standardized scores.

1. Characteristics of the Self-Evaluations

The mean ranks assigned to the self for each of the five attributes were significantly lower than 5.5 ($p < .001$), indicating that most children ranked themselves above average. The mean self-ranks were 3.8 for reading [$t(69) = 5.16$], 3.9 for popularity [$t(69) = 5.21$], 3.7 for attractiveness [$t(69) = 5.70$], 3.8 for dominance [$t(69) = 5.16$], and 3.5 for sports [$t(69) = 6.67$]. There were no significant differences in mean score among the five attributes. The proportion of children who ranked themselves above the mean was 70.0% for reading, 71.4 for popularity, 75.7 for attractiveness, 74.2 for dominance, and 81.4 for sports. Two-way analyses of variance performed on each attribute with sex and social class as independent factors revealed no significant main effects or interactions for four of the five attributes. Reading was the exception; there was a significant sex-by-social class interaction for reading [$F(1,66) = 4.85, p < .05$]. In middle-class rooms, boys ranked themselves as better readers than girls; in working-class rooms, girls ranked themselves as better readers than boys. The mean self-ranks for reading were 4.9 for middle-class girls, 3.1 for middle-class boys, 3.4 for working-class girls, and 4.3 for working-class boys. The mean difference between each child's lowest and highest self-rank was 4.1 for the entire sample of 70 children.

In order to compare the children's self-evaluation across the five attributes, product–moment correlations were computed between all possible pairs of attributes for all children (see Table I). For the whole sample there were statistically significant correlations between all pairs of variables, with the exception of reading and dominance, but the magnitudes of the correlations were not large (correlations ranged from .08 to .58 for the whole sample). Thus, a child's self-evaluation on one attribute was only moderately related to his or her self-

TABLE I
INTERCORRELATIONS AMONG STANDARDIZED SELF-RANKS ON THE FIVE ATTRIBUTES

Attributes	Middle-class ($N=36$)	Working-class ($N=34$)	Boys ($N=35$)	Girls ($N=35$)	Entire sample ($N=70$)
Reading/ popularity	.38**	.24	.05	.62***	.33**
Reading/ attractiveness	.45**	.45**	.40**	.49***	.45***
Reading/ dominance	.31*	−.14	−.10	.30*	.08
Reading/ sports	.41**	.06	−.01	.48**	.27*
Popularity/ attractiveness	.39**	.49**	.32*	.50***	.41***
Popularity/ dominance	.66***	.35*	.34*	.68***	.50***
Popularity/ sports	.57***	.57***	.68***	.52***	.58***
Attractiveness/ dominance	.33*	.12	.17	.29*	.22*
Attractiveness/ sports	.41**	.26	−.03	.62***	.33**
Dominance/ sports	.41**	.57***	.54***	.45**	.48***

*$p < .05$.
**$p < .01$.
***$p < .001$.

evaluation on other attributes. The highest intercorrelations occurred among popularity, dominance, and sports—the three attributes that involved observable social behavior. Table I also contains the interattribute correlations by sex and social class.

All interattribute correlations were significant for middle-class children and for girls. Among the working-class and the boys, however, the self-ranks for reading were not significantly related to those for popularity, dominance, or athletic ability. Similarly, the ranks for attractiveness were minimally related to the ranks for dominance and athletic ability in these groups. This split between academic ability and attractiveness, on the one hand, and dimensions of social behavior, on the other, did not occur among the middle-class children or among the girls.

2. Peer Evaluations

In order to determine the degree of agreement among the children in their ranking of their peers, Kendall coefficients of concordance (W) were computed for each attribute (see Table II).

There was considerable consensus among the children within each of the groups for all attributes. Thirty-six of the 40 coefficients were statistically significant; working-class boys showed the least agreement. A series of Kruskall–Wallis one-way analyses of variance by ranks performed on the coefficients in Table II revealed a significant effect for social class [$H(1) = 6.53$, $p < .05$]. The middle-class children showed greater concordance than the working-class children, but there was no significant effect of sex.

3. The Relation between Self- and Peer Evaluations

Correlations were computed between the self-ranks and the ranks given by peers for each attribute. Table III summarizes the correlations between self- and peer ranks by sex and social class. (The peer ranks were also standardized scores.) For the total sample, the self-evaluations were only moderately related to the peer evaluations for four of the attributes and unrelated for physical attractiveness (the correlations were reading $r = .38$, $p < .001$; popularity $r = .39$, $p < .001$; attractiveness $r = .08$, nonsignificant; dominance $r = .24$, $p < .05$; sports $r = .38$, $p < .001$). In general the same pattern was evident across all groups. Peers and subjects disagreed most on physical attractiveness; they agreed most on popularity, reading, and sports.

The reason for the low correlations between self- and peer ranks is that more than half of the children who were ranked below the mean on a particular quality by their peers ranked themselves above the mean—59% for reading, 61% for popularity, 65% for attractiveness, 68% for athletic skill, and 71% for dominance. By contrast, of the children ranked above the mean by peers, a much smaller proportion placed themselves below the mean—from 2 to 18% for the five qualities.

TABLE II

INTERSUBJECT AGREEMENT FOR PEER RANKS (COEFFICIENT OF CONCORDANCE)

	Peer groups							
Attribute	Middle-class girls I ($N=8$)	Middle-class boys I ($N=9$)	Middle-class girls II ($N=9$)	Middle-class boys II ($N=10$)	Working-class girls I ($N=8$)	Working-class boys I ($N=10$)	Working-class girls II ($N=10$)	Working-class boys II ($N=6$)
Reading	.47***	.65***	.70***	.72***	.68***	.38***	.22*	.40*
Popularity	.73***	.50***	.84***	.74***	.52***	.22*	.41***	.34
Attractiveness	.44***	.43**	.63***	.21	.45***	.23*	.44***	.34
Dominance	.50***	.30*	.62***	.61***	.11	.53***	.56***	.46
Sports	.45***	.41**	.83***	.75***	.66***	.48***	.49***	.54**

*$p < .05$.
**$p < .01$.
***$p < .001$.

The self-evaluations were also moderately related to the ranks awarded by the teachers for all the attributes, except physical attractiveness (reading $r = .50$, $p < .001$; popularity $r = .51$, $p < .001$; attractiveness $r = .11$, nonsignificant; dominance $r = .43$, $p < .001$; sports $r = .42$, $p < .001$).

In sum, there was only moderate agreement between self-ranks, on the one hand, and peer and teacher evaluations, on the other, for most of the attributes. Although the lack of a strong relation between self- and other ranks does not invalidate the self-rankings, clearly it leads one to question whether the self-ranks are a sensitive index of the child's beliefs.

TABLE III

RELATIONSHIP BETWEEN SELF- AND PEER RANKS BY SEX AND SOCIAL CLASS

Attribute	Middle-class ($N=36$)	Working-class ($N=34$)	Boys ($N=35$)	Girls ($N=35$)	Entire sample ($N=70$)
Reading	.50***	.52***	.35*	.53***	.38***
Popularity	.67***	.45**	.47**	.54***	.39***
Attractiveness	.10	.30*	.04	.23	.08
Dominance	.32*	.39**	.35*	.25	.24*
Sports	.63***	.51***	.29*	.49**	.38***

*$p < .05$.
**$p < .01$.
***$p < .001$.

4. The Reliability of Peer and Self-Evaluations

Correlations were computed between each child's rankings for self and peers for each attribute over the two assessments administered 1 week apart. The median correlations for peer and self-rankings appear in Table IV.

The reliabilities for peer ranks were relatively high, with correlations for the total sample ranging from .81 to .87. There were no consistent class or sex differences in the reliabilities.

The reliabilities of the self-ranks were lower than the comparable coefficients for peer ranks, ranging from .50 to .81 for the entire sample with popularity the most stable attribute for all children. The reliability coefficients were equally high for both middle- and working-class children for popularity and dominance. But the coefficients were higher for the middle-class children for reading (.79 vs .21), attractiveness (.69 vs .40), and athletic ability (.84 vs .62). Girls' self-ranks were more stable over the 1-week period than those of boys for reading and attractiveness, but less stable for dominance. The low reliabilities for reading and attractiveness among working-class children were due primarily to the responses of boys rather than girls. But because the working-class boys and girls had high reliabilities for popularity we assume that the subjects understood the instruction and were responding with the proper mental set. It may be that the working-class boys were less aware of their reading competence in comparison with their peers

TABLE IV
TEST–RETEST RELIABILITY ACROSS 1 WEEK

Attribute	Middle-class ($N=36$)	Working-class ($N=34$)	Boys ($N=35$)	Girls ($N=35$)	Entire sample ($N=70$)
A. Peer Ranks					
Reading	.92***	.77***	.81***	.88***	.84***
Popularity	.94***	.76***	.82***	.85***	.85***
Attractiveness	.83***	.77***	.73***	.89***	.81***
Dominance	.76***	.92***	.89***	.78***	.84***
Sports	.90***	.89***	.92***	.87***	.87***
B. Self-ranks					
Reading	.79***	.21	.39*	.63**	.50***
Popularity	.81***	.88***	.77***	.85***	.81***
Attractiveness	.69***	.40*	.25	.66***	.53***
Dominance	.65***	.62**	.80***	.41*	.64***
Sports	.84***	.62**	.77***	.78***	.76***

*$p < .05$.
**$p < .05$.
***$p < .001$.

or that they cared less about their standing on reading and attractiveness than on popularity, dominance, and sports.

5. Scaling of Triad Sorting Data

Data from each subject's responses to the triad sorting procedure were converted into a similarity matrix in which the cell values were the number of times a subject sorted particular pairs of children together. Matrices were also generated from the group data; cell values represented the number of times all children in the same-sex groups sorted particular pairs of children together, after eliminating triads in which the child who was sorting was also a member of the triad.

Nonmetric multidimensional scaling (MDS) solutions were derived from the group and individual matrices using POLYCON (Young, 1974). A Euclidian distance metric was employed. Multidimensional scaling plots points (in this case, children) in space in such a way that the distances between pairs of points are related monotonically to the degree of similarity between them (in this case, similarity was determined by triad sorting). [See Shepard, Romney, and Nerlove (1972) for a more complete discussion of multidimensional scaling.]

MDS solutions can be obtained in any number of geometric dimensions. The goodness of fit of a solution increases as the dimensionality of the solution increases. "Stress" is a statistical index which is inversely correlated with the goodness of fit. Stress values can range from 0 to 1.0, where 0 indicates a perfect monotonic fit. In the present study, stress values for two-dimensional group solutions ranged from .023 to .313, with a median value of .20. Stress values for two-dimensional individual solutions ranged from .0 to .459, with a median value of .05. According to the criteria suggested by Rabinowitz (1975), these group solutions ranged from excellent to fair; most fell in the good category. The individual solutions ranged from perfect to poor; most fell in the excellent category. Even though some of the stress values could have been lowered by increasing the dimensionality of the solutions, it was decided to use two-dimensional solutions because of the greater ease with which they can be interpreted visually.

6. Relation between Group MDS Solutions and Peer Ranks

It will be recalled that when sorting the triads, subjects were instructed to sort the names on the basis of each child's general behavior, rather than any specific quality or physical attribute. The children could use private dimensions as a basis for responding. The MDS scaling solutions should reflect whatever dimension or dimensions the children actually used. For example, if ethnic group membership were used by most children, one should find distinct clusters of white, black, and Hispanic children in the MDS plot. If an evaluative factor were being used, one would find children at one side of the plot who had a particular desirable quality in excess, while children at the opposite side would be deficient in that quality.

One question of interest was whether the children used any of our five ranking attributes in their triad sorts, even though the sorting instructions were maximally permissive. As we shall see, they did. It is possible to determine statistically the relation between a unidimensional scale (such as peer ranks on reading) and a multidimensional configuration through multiple regression techniques (Cliff & Young, 1968; Funk, Horowitz, Lipshitz, & Young, 1976; S. Rosenberg & Jones, 1972). In the present study the unidimensional scales were the mean rank values given each child by his or her peers on the separate attributes. A series of linear multiple regressions were calculated for each group and each attribute. The independent variables were each child's cartesian coordinate values on the two-dimensional MDS configuration; the dependent variable was the mean of the peer ranks for each child on the particular attribute being analyzed. The ratio of the regression weights (b) obtained from the multiple regression determines the slope of the line that is the best linear fit of the ranked attribute to the MDS configuration. The square of the multiple correlation coefficient based on the regression solution reflects the proportion of variance in the ranked attribute accounted for by the dimensions of the MDS configuration.

The squares of the multiple correlations for each of the five attributes (for each of the eight groups) appear in Table V. The MDS solution accounted for a moderate amount of variation in the peer ranks, suggesting that the children were using all five attributes in their triad sorts. But the eight groups varied considerably in the degree to which they emphasized each of the five attributes. That is, the groups differed in the degree to which the ranked qualities were reflected as independent dimensions in the MDS configurations. The MDS configuration for one of the eight groups is displayed in Fig. 1*A*. Vectors showing the results of the regression analyses described above have been plotted on the configurations. The vectors have the same slope as the line of best fit and are oriented so that the arrows point toward the positive, or desirable, end of the dimension. The length of each vector is proportional to the square of its multiple regression coefficient (i.e., the degree to which the peer-rank attribute is represented in the MDS configuration). All configurations have been rotated so that the high-dominance vector is horizontal and points to the right. (The dominance attribute was chosen as referent because it had the largest multiple correlation across the groups.) In the group of middle-class boys illustrated in Fig. 1*A*, the attribute vectors all pointed in the same direction (within a range of 45°). The configuration revealed a cluster of four boys (Bh, Kf, Mr, Mt) who are competent at reading and athletics and attractive, dominant, and popular. Children on the opposite side of the configuration (Ro, To) were ranked negatively on all five attributes.

Seven of the eight groups produced similar configurations to the one illustrated in Fig. 1*A*. There was typically a small group of children at the positive end of the dimension, a group of two or three at the opposite pole, and two or three children in intermediate positions. For example, the boys in the other middle-

TABLE V

SQUARE OF THE MULTIPLE CORRELATION VALUES FOR REGRESSION OF TWO-DIMENSIONAL
MDS SOLUTIONS ON MEAN PEER RANKS

	Reading	Popularity	Attractiveness	Dominance	Sports
Middle-class girls I (N=8)	.48	.61	.77*	.71*	.55
Middle-class boys I (N=9)	.53	.92***	.90**	.94***	.84**
Middle-class girls II (N=9)	.25	.70*	.40	.85**	.86**
Middle-class boys II (N=10)	.61*	.86**	.66*	.73*	.62*
Working-class girls I (N=8)	.77*	.51	.77*	.60	.68*
Working-class boys I (N=10)	.61*	.15	.04	.66*	.71*
Working-class girls II (N=10)	.64*	.75**	.87***	.85**	.88***
Working-class boys II (N=6)	.86	.48	.63	.84	.85

*$p < .05$.
**$p < .01$.
***$p < .001$.

class room produced a solution with five boys at the positive pole on all five dimensions and two boys clearly at the negative pole. The one exception to this generalization occurred for one group of working-class boys where some of the vectors formed a 180° angle with other attributes (the attributes were negatively correlated; see Fig. 1B).

The academically talented boys (Ni and Pl) were regarded as incompetent at sports and minimally dominant. The dominant, athletic boys were regarded as less talented in reading (Vc, Da, and Hu). This particular classroom had a great deal of social turbulence. Physical fights and verbal intimidation, which were frequent, made dominance an important personal characteristic. Although the group was composed of three different racial ethnic groups, ethnicity was not reflected in the MDS configuration (Da and Wi were black; Hu, Ad, Ag, and Cs

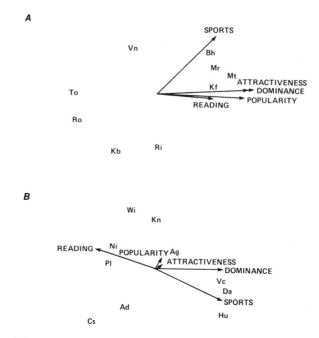

FIG. 1.   *A,* Group configuration for boys in middle-class room; *B,* group configuration for boys in working-class room.

were Hispanic; and Vc, Pl, Ni, and Kn were caucasian). It is important to note, therefore, that a child's behavior, not his ethnic-group membership, was more significant in guiding the children's triads sorting. This was true for all eight groups. These data suggest that the triads procedure with a multidimensional scaling analysis may be a useful technique to reveal the psychological dimensions children might be using in judging psychological similarities among peers.

7. Relation of Self-Ranks to Individual MDS Solutions

We now consider the data that relate to the major purpose of this research—the validity of the self-rankings—and ask a simple question. What is the correspondence between the child's self-ranks, on the one hand, and the individual multidimensional scaling solution of that child's triad responses? It will be recalled that the children who were ranked by peers as having desirable qualities acknowledged their privileged status on their self-ranks. But a proportion of the children who were ranked low by their peers (i.e., indicating possession of undesirable characteristics) assigned themselves high ranks. There are several reasons why a child who was regarded by others as unpopular or incompetent at reading might rank him- or herself as possessing these desirable properties. The most likely is that the child did not wish to acknowledge to the examiner his undesirable status. Second, we acknowledge that some children may have been unaware of their status and some might be using defensive denial. But because these qualities are so public and the child regularly receives information on his or her position, we shall assume that most of the children were aware of their positions on these dimensions. If the positive self-ranks for these children were a conscious distortion, some children might reveal their more private beliefs on the more disguised triads procedure. In categorizing the children's self-ranks, we have adopted the following designations. Children who rank themselves in accord with the perceptions of others were called "acknowledgers," while children who ranked themselves markedly different from the views of others were classified as "deniers." Our use of these terms is not intended to be synonymous with their definitions in dynamic theories of defense and motivation. Children whose self-rankings fell in between the two extremes were called "ambiguous."

8. Children Ranked as Undesirable

We examined the data for all 70 children and selected those whose mean standardized peer ranks were equal to or greater than 8.0 for four or all five of the attributes. This extreme group of 12 children included 5 middle-class boys, 1 working-class boy, 3 middle-class girls, and 3 working-class girls (17% of the group). The uniformity of peer rankings for these 12 children suggests that their position on most of the five attributes was less desirable. Only one child (N), a middle-class girl, acknowledged her uniformly low status. She ranked herself 8 to 10 on four attributes and below the median on the fifth attribute, dominance. The remaining 11 children gave themselves ranks higher than those given to them by their peers on one or more dimensions (see Table VI). In order to evaluate the degree of distortion we decided that if a child awarded the self a standardized rank of 1, 2, or 3 on any attribute in which his mean peer rank was 8, 9, or 10, he was seriously denying his position on that psychological quality. If a child ranked the self 7-10 we regarded that child as acknowledging his low position. Three children (Ro, Pt, and Su) showed an extreme degree of denial on all five attributes; four children showed this amount of denial on two or three attributes, and four denied on one attribute. Thus over 90% of the children ranked themselves on one or more dimensions in a way that was a serious distortion of the peer evaluations. We now examine how these children placed themselves in their individual scaling solutions. We regard these solutions as heuristic for they cannot be evaluated statistically. We consider first the three children who denied the self-ranks for all five attributes—Ro, Su, and Pt, noting teacher comments and the impressions of the female examiner.

a. Subject Ro, Boy, Middle-Class School: Denier

Ro is the son of professional parents who, despite an average IQ score, was not performing well in school. He often disrupted the classroom by screaming,

TABLE VI

Relation between Self-Ranks and Individual Scaling Solution for 11 Children Negatively Evaluated by Peers on Four or More Qualities but Denying on One or More Attributes

Subjects	Reading (self/peer)	Popularity (self/peer)	Attractiveness (self/peer)	Dominance (self/peer)	Sports (self/peer)	Child's self-ranks	Triads/scaling re traits denied on ranks
Ro	1.6/10.0	1.6/8.8	1.6/10.0	1.6/8.8	1.6/8.8	Deny[a] on all five attributes	Deny
To	1.0/8.9	10.0/10.0	2.1/8.9	6.6/10.0	6.6/7.8	Deny on reading and attractiveness	Deny
Gl	2.0/9.0	8.0/9.0	5.0/9.0	8.0/9.0	8.0/9.0	Deny on reading	Ambiguous
Je	6.0/8.0	5.0/8.0	2.0/7.5	2.0/8.0	5.0/8.0	Deny on attractiveness and dominance	Ambiguous
Sh	3.0/10.0	9.0/10.0	1.5/10.0	3.0/10.0	9.0/10.0	Deny on reading, attractiveness, and dominance	Acknowledge
Sv	6.4/10.0	2.8/10.0	1.0/10.0	1.0/2.8	4.6/10.0	Deny on popularity and attractiveness	Ambiguous
J	6.1/9.4	3.6/8.7	8.7/8.7	1.0/10.0	10.0/10.0	Deny on dominance	Ambiguous
Bu	6.6/10.0	10.0/10.0	1.0/10.0	10.0/10.0	5.5/10.0	Deny on attractiveness	Acknowledge
C	2.3/8.7	3.6/8.7	4.9/10.0	3.6/8.7	6.1/8.7	Deny on reading	Deny
Pt	3.0/10.0	3.0/10.0	2.0/10.0	1.0/10.0	2.0/10.0	Deny on all five attributes	Deny
Su	2.0/9.0	1.0/9.0	2.0/8.5	2.0/9.0	1.0/9.0	Deny on all five attributes	Acknowledge

[a]Deny means subject ranked self 1, 2, or 3.

challenged the other children competitively, and was hostile to the examiner. Ro placed himself spatially close to the boys whom the peers regarded as having positive attributes and maximally distant from To, who was the only other boy ranked negatively on all five attributes. Thus Ro did not acknowledge his low status on either the self-ranks or the triad procedure (see Fig. 2A).

b. Subject Su, Girl, Working-Class School: Acknowledger

Su, who was labile of mood and often expressed her anger, also denied her status on all five attributes. But as seen in Fig. 2B, Su placed herself closer to the other children with low status, especially Pt, who had very low status with the peers. Thus, unlike Ro, Su acknowledged her low status on the triads but not on the ranks.

c. Subject Pt, Girl, Working-Class School: Denier

Pt, who whined a great deal, often sought attention, and was physically unattractive, placed herself closer to W, F, and T, who were rated as desirable children, than to Su who, with Pt, was the least desirable. Thus we classify Pt's solution as denial. (See Fig. 2C.)

d. Subject To, Boy, Middle-Class School: Denier

To, who was being seen by a psychologist for behavior problems, often sought attention from peers and teacher by disrupting the class, but was the best artist in the class. To denied his low status on reading and attractiveness on the self-ranks but acknowledged it on the other three attributes. To placed himself spatially close to Ri and Mt, who were ranked above the median on most traits, and close to Mr, who was given a rank of 1 or 2 on all traits. By contrast, To placed himself relatively distant from Ro, who had uniformly low status. Thus To denied his status on reading and attractiveness on both procedures. (See Fig. 2D.)

e. Subject Gl, Boy, Middle-Class School: Ambiguous

Gl was moderately well behaved, motorically clumsy, and regarded by his peers as a nice boy with problems. On the self-ranks Gl denied his low status on reading and acknowledged it on popularity, dominance, and athletic ability. Gl placed himself distant from all other children, especially Bw and Dy who were the best readers in the class and relatively close to Sh who was the poorest reader. Thus although Gl ranked himself high on reading his individual solution reflected a self-conception more in accord with peer evaluation. (See Fig. 3A.)

f. Subject Je, Boy, Middle-Class School: Ambiguous

Although Je was a friendly boy, he was unpopular. On the self-ranks Je denied his status on attractiveness and dominance and did not acknowledge his low

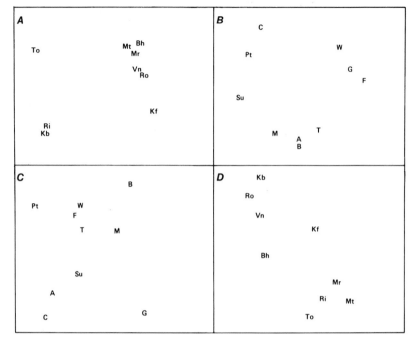

FIG. 2. *A*, Individual configuration for child Ro; *B*, individual configuration for child Su; *C*, individual configuration for child Pt; *D*, individual configuration for child To.

status on any dimension. Je placed himself distant both from Dy and Bw, who were the two most attractive and dominant boys, as well as from Sh and Gl, who were the least attractive and least dominant. Thus Je's triad data implied a less desirable self-evaluation than did his self-ranks. (See Fig. 3*B*.)

g. Subject Sh, Boy, Middle-Class School: Acknowledger

Sh lived with his mother and the mother's younger companion, the father having deserted the family when Sh was young. Sh wore only one set of dirty clothes, which resembled a military uniform, and was often unkempt. The peers disliked Sh but regarded him as an unfortunate child. On the self-ranks Sh denied his status on reading, dominance, and attractiveness and acknowledged his low status on popularity and sports. Sh placed himself closest to Ca, Mi, and Gl, none of whom was ranked in the top two positions on any quality. Sh did not place himself close to either Bw or Dy, the two boys who were the best readers and judged most attractive and dominant by the class. Thus Sh revealed a less positive assessment on the triads than he did on the self-ranks. (See Fig. 3*C*.)

h. Subject Sv, Boy, Working-Class School: Ambiguous

Although Sv tried to play the role of the tough boy in class he was neither feared nor respected by the other boys. Sv denied his unpopularity and lack of attractiveness and acknowledged his low status on none of the attributes. Sv placed himself distant from both Al, who was very popular, and R, who was unpopular. Thus Sv's solution is ambiguous, implying a less secure belief in the denial of his unpopularity and attractiveness (see Fig. 3*D*).

i. Subject J, Girl, Middle-Class School: Ambiguous

J was a quiet, timid girl who was concerned with her appearance, partly because of a bulge on her chest resulting from cardiac surgery. J denied her undesirable status on dominance and acknowledged it for attractiveness and

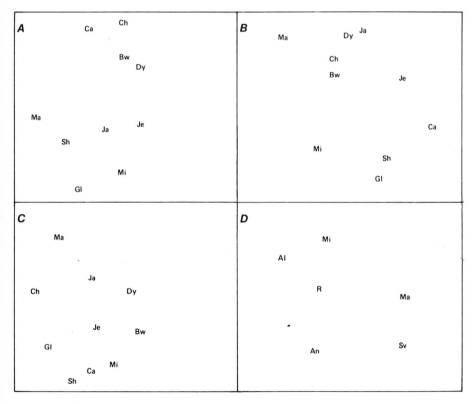

FIG. 3.   *A*, Individual configuration for child Gl; *B*, individual configuration for child Je; *C*, individual configuration for child Sh; *D*, individual configuration for child Sv.

athletic skill. J placed herself closer to A and K, who were of average dominance, than to H or C, the two most dominant girls, or to N, who was very low in
dominance. It appears that J's solution is ambiguous. (See Fig. 4*A*.)

j. Subject Bu, Girl, Middle-Class School: Acknowledger

Bu was a whining, demanding child who frequently sought approval from
adults and admitted to the examiner that she was disliked by the other children.
Bu denied her low status for attractiveness but acknowledged it for popularity
and dominance. Bu placed herself closer to In and Ai, who were ranked average
and low on attractiveness, and distant from Em and La, who were regarded as
most attractive. Thus Bu acknowledged her undesirable status in her configuration. (See Fig. 4*B*.)

k. Subject C, Girl, Working-Class School: Denier

C was an acquiescent girl who rarely participated in activities with the other
children. She denied the peer evaluation on reading and acknowledged none of
the peer ranks (most of her self-ranks were between 3 and 7). Figure 4*C* reveals
that C placed herself close to G, who was ranked the highest in reading, and far
from Th, who was ranked the lowest in reading. Thus C denied her low status in
reading.

Of the eleven extreme children who denied their low status on self-ranks for
one or more dimensions, four children continued to deny their status for these
specific traits on the triads procedure (Ro, To, Pt, and C). But the remaining
seven children did not place themselves close to the desirable children in their
configurations, suggesting that perhaps their positive self-ranks were a conscious
distortion of their private beliefs. Three children actually placed themselves close
to children whom the peers regarded negatively (Sh, Bu, and Su) for properties
they had denied on the self-ranks, and four children placed themselves in isolated
or ambiguous positions, close to neither positively nor negatively evaluated
children. These data suggest that the triads added information for about two-
thirds of the children whom the peers regarded as extremely negative on the
attributes studied. If the investigators who use self-ranks had also used a triads
procedure, the likelihood of correctly deciding whether this class of child had a
positive or negative self-concept for particular attributes would be improved
considerably.

9. Children Ranked as Desirable

We performed a similar analysis for the children who were given the top two
ranks (ranks 1 or 2) on three or more of the five qualities and received no rank
less than 6 on any attribute. Nine children fit these criteria. If any of these

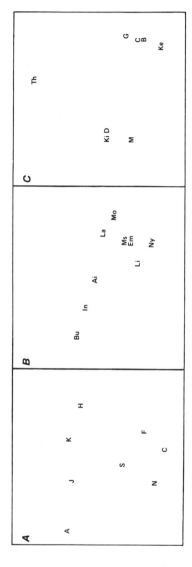

FIG. 4. *A*, Individual configuration for child J; *B*, individual configuration for child Bu; *C*, individual configuration for child C.

high-ranked children gave themselves a rank equal to or greater than 7.0, they were called deniers. If they gave themselves a rank of 1 or 2 on any attribute, they were called acknowledgers. Of the nine children who fit our criteria, three acknowledged their status on all five attributes, one on four attributes, one on three attributes, three on two attributes, and one child did so on one attribute. More important, there was only one instance of denial. One girl ranked herself low on dominance, although her peers ranked her high. Thus, unlike the children ranked negatively by their peers, those ranked positively did not deny their positive status. The individual scaling solutions for eight of the nine children revealed that these children placed themselves close to other children who had positive attributes. Only one of the nine children (a working-class girl) placed herself close to two girls who were rated by peers as low on the relevant attributes. Thus, children who were rated positively by their peers were likely to agree in their self-evaluations or individual scaling solutions.

C. DISCUSSION OF STUDY 1

The results imply that although a child's self-conscious evaluations of salient psychological qualities have some degree of validity, they should never be used as the *sole* index of the child's beliefs about the self. The correlation between self-ratings, on the one hand, and peer and teacher ratings, on the other, were only moderately positive. More important, there was an asymmetry in the validity of the data. The ranks of children who evaluated themselves positively and were similarly viewed by peers appear to be much more valid than the high positive self-ranks of children who were evaluated negatively by their peers. This fact should come as no surprise. The contribution of this study is to demonstrate that use of another technique (in this case multidimensional scaling of triad sorts) added important information for the two-thirds of the children who ranked themselves higher than the evaluation given them by their peers, but in their individual scaling solutions revealed that they did not regard themselves as positively as their self-ranks implied. It is suggested that investigators studying self-concept, as well as clinicians who wish to evaluate a child's perception of his position in a closed group, consider using the triads procedure.

Second, the data argue for a conceptualization of self in terms of specific psychological qualities and argue against the notion of global self-esteem (see also Harter, 1979). Most of the children ranked themselves and were ranked by others as high on some attributes, moderate on others, and low on others. Few children were very high or low on all five attributes. The children's evaluations across the five domains were positively correlated, but certainly not high enough to support the notion of a general quality of either high or low self-esteem or reputation.

III. Study 2: Rationale

The results of the first study suggested that the use of the triads procedure in combination with self-reports added some sensitivity to assessment of the child's self-concept when the child ranked himself positively but the peers ranked him negatively. The purpose of the next two studies was to explore the utility of a second procedure involving empathic identification with a model. If the child's pattern of empathy were in accord with his self-conscious evaluations, investigators could feel more confident about their classification of a child. But if there were a serious inconsistency between the two sources of data one might question the validity of the self-report information.

The rationale for the procedure is simple, and, additionally, has some degree of phenomenological validity. Every adult has had the experience of responding empathically to a person to whom he or she feels psychologically similar. The idea that children and adults detect psychological and physical similarities between self and others and react affectively to people who share qualities with the self is neither original nor of recent origin. It appears in the world's literature, as well as in the first psychological essays on self-consciousness. Additionally, identification with ethnic, religious, and racial groups is a common phenomenon (Kagan, 1958; Stotland & Dunn, 1963). If this experience could be captured in a laboratory, psychologists would have a useful tool for evaluating the person's private beliefs about the self, for empathic behavior is under less conscious control than evaluations given to an interviewer or answers to a questionnaire. There is some evidence that this process can be brought into the laboratory. Five-year-olds showed greater empathic involvement with their parent than with an adult of the same sex (Kagan & Phillips, 1964), and Maccoby and Wilson (1957) found that preadolescent children were more likely to identify with a child in a film who was of their own sex and similar social-class aspirations. Moreover, the children remembered more of the actions and words of the character with whom they identified in the film. In our studies we sought to determine if a child would show empathic identification with a film model who was described as possessing a salient attribute of the child. We wished to explore, as with the triads procedure, whether the child who denied an undesirable attribute on direct questioning might, nonetheless, show empathic involvement with a model who possessed that attribute.

A. METHOD

1. Subjects

The sample was composed of 25 preadolescent caucasian, middle-class boys who had been diagnosed as having severe reading disability, and 11 control boys, each of whom was matched with one reading-disabled subject on age, social class, and ethnicity. The control boys were reading at grade level or above. This group of 36 boys was participating in an extensive research project on reading disability at the time this particular set of procedures was initiated and we used the availability of the sample to pretest the technique. The median age of the group was 10 years with a range of 8–13 years; only two children were 8 years and three were 13 years.

The 25 reading-disabled boys were reading 2 or more years below their appropriate grade level, despite average or above average IQ scores. The diagnosis of reading disability was based on both standardized tests of reading skill administered by the research staff and test scores obtained from the schools. Each of the reading-disabled boys knew he had been classified by teachers as reading disabled.

2. Procedures

Each boy came to a laboratory in William James Hall with a female examiner. This group of boys was accustomed to the laboratory environment as a result of several prior visits to the same building over the course of 1 year. After some conversation, each boy was shown a 12-minute experimental film in color made on Super-8 film.

The experimental film depicted a competitive contest between two caucasian boys who were of similar physical appearance and age of our subjects. The contest was conducted by a woman. Each boy in the film was shown a drawing composed of a few lines and had to guess what the two objects in the picture might be if the drawing were completed. The film was edited so that each of the film models appeared alone on the screen for an equivalent length of time. The woman in the film would turn to one of the boy models as she administered a test item and that boy appeared on the screen alone both while he was working at the solution of the problem and immediately after being told the validity of his answer. The woman in the film rewarded each boy when he successfully identified the drawing and told him he was wrong when his answer was incorrect. The two boys in the film took turns in the contest (eight test items per film model) and the film was constructed so that each model was correct on four occasions and incorrect on four occasions. At the end of the film the woman declared a tie score and rewarded both boys.

The subject was told that he was going to see a film of a contest that involved two boys at a public school like his own. The examiner said that adults had judged the fairness of the contest but she wanted the child's judgment regarding its fairness. The examiner first showed the subject each of the incomplete and complete drawings that would appear in the film so that he would not be distracted from the film models' efforts by trying to solve the perceptual problem himself. Any of the child's questions were clarified at this time.

The examiner then added that the subject might want to know something about the two boys in the film named Sam and Joe. It was at this time that the female examiner assigned a psychological trait appropriate to the experimental subject to one of the film models, and the opposite trait to the other film model. For the 25 boys with reading disability the examiner described one of the film models as having a serious difficulty mastering reading; the other film model was described as being a good reader. The control subjects were given information about the birthdays and number of siblings of the two film models, neither of which was characteristic of the subject. The children were asked to repeat the communication given by the experimenter (i.e., to say what traits were assigned to each film model) in order to guarantee that each boy had assimilated the description of qualities assigned to the models.

For half the experimental subjects the boy that was called Sam was assigned the attributes appropriate to the subject; for the other half, the boy that was called Joe was described as having the traits that matched those of the subject. After the instructions and the child's repetition of the qualities ascribed to each model, the experimental film was shown. During the film each boy's behavior was recorded on audiovisual tape by a concealed camera of which the subject was unaware. After the film each subject was asked about his perceived similarity to each of the film models.

Coding of Film Data

The decision regarding the final coding of empathic involvement involved several steps. Initially we studied the records of a random set of the children to determine the range of behavior and the modal responses to the film. Most of the time the children sat quietly looking at the film, making no special behavioral response. There was a moderate amount of restless behavior—scratching of the face, movement of the fingers, adjustment of the trunk, and individual variation in these behaviors. However, it is not obvious whether these acts of restlessness represent boredom or tension that was the product of an empathic involvement with one of the models. Additionally, it was difficult to code these behaviors reliably for it is difficult to decide when a particular movement of the hand should be regarded as a change from baseline. We scored all the film records for restless movement but did not find sufficiently high intercoder reliabilities to have faith in this variable. On the other hand, some children on some occasions showed unambiguous signs of empathic involvement. They would openly cheer for and encourage one of the models or disparage or mock the other model. A second, slightly more ambiguous behavioral sign of empathic involvement was the occurrence of smiling following the success of his model or the failure of the alternate model, or smiling while his model was working on the problem. There were two slightly more ambiguous categories of behavior which could be regarded as indexes of affect. One was leaning forward to the screen when one of the models was present. This behavior might be regarded as an indication of interest. The other variable was an obvious change in facial expression— furrowing of the brow, grimacing, twisting of the mouth. Although it was not possible to name an emotion for these changes in facial expression (excluding smiling), these responses were clear and could be reliably coded. Because the face is regarded by many (Izard, 1971; Ekman, Friesen, & Ellsworth, 1972) as a muscle surface that is sensitive to changes in internal affective tone, we chose this variable as indicative of empathy. Finally, we used differential occurrence of talking as an index of emotional involvement.

As might be expected, children differed in the response modes they used to reveal affective involvement with one of the models. Some used the less ambiguous responses of cheering and encouraging. Others used differential smiling; still others only showed changed facial expressions. Because these response indexes differed in their ambiguity regarding identification with one of the models, we adopted the following strategy in scoring the film protocols for empathic involvement. If a child cheered for or encouraged one model and/or sneered and openly mocked the other (the most obvious signs of involvement), and no other behavior occurred which was inconsistent with those responses, we classified that child as involved with the model he cheered or encouraged or the one he did not disparage.

There was no case in which a child encouraged or cheered one model but showed, in other behaviors, greater involvement with the other model. If the child did not display these unambiguous signs of differential involvement, we used the pattern of appropriate smiling to classify the child's empathy. If a child smiled following one model's success or following the other model's failure, or smiled more while one model was working on the problem and no other behavior was inconsistent with the meaning of those responses, we classified the child as identified with the model to whom he showed the most frequent, appropriate smiling. Finally, if neither of the above behaviors occurred differentially, we used frequency of changes in facial expression, leaning forward toward the screen, and talking as indexes of involvement. We classified the child as identified more with one model than another if there was a difference in facial expression, talking, and leaning forward between one model and another. The reliability of the coding was assessed by having an independent coder view the films for 12 subjects. The median agreement across all variables was 95%.

B. Results

Of the 25 reading-disabled boys, 13 were assigned Joe as the model who had a reading handicap and 12 were assigned Sam. The boys' statements of perceived similarity given at the end of the film revealed that 13 children said they resembled the model who had the reading problem; that is, they acknowledged their reading disability. Only 4 children denied this attribute, saying that they were more similar to the film model who was a competent reader and 8 boys said they were not sure which model they more closely resembled. Among the 11 control boys, who were not given any basis for believing in differential similarity to one of the film models, only 4 stated they were similar to one of the models.

The analysis of the film data revealed that 16 of the 25 reading-disabled boys (64%) showed greater empathy with the model described as having a serious reading problem, and none showed greater empathy with the model described as a competent reader. By contrast, only 2 of the 11 controls showed differential empathic behavior with one of the models ($\chi^2 = 4.70$, $p < .05$). Thus it appears that when the child has a distinctive trait, even if it is undesirable, empathic behavior with one of the models does occur. The value of the empathic measure is evident when one compares the empathic classification with the children's statements (given at the end of the film) as to whom they resembled. Of the 12 reading-disabled boys who did not admit to the examiner that they were similar to the film model with reading disability, 7 showed greater empathic involvement with the model described as having that handicap. These data are moderately supportive of the hypothesis that measures of differential empathy might be of value in studying the child's private beliefs about his psychological qualities.

IV. Study 3: Rationale

The purpose of the third and final study was to replicate the implications of the first two investigations. The fact that almost two-thirds of the reading disabled boys were likely to display empathy with the model, together with the fact that the data of Study 1 implied that denial of the self's attributes was frequent among children with undesirable qualities, led us to select a group of boys who, according to peers and teacher, were at the extreme of unpopularity and poor reading ability in their classroom. We wished to determine if the triads and empathy measures would add important information to the more conscious self-evaluations for children who were regarded by others as having undesirable psychological properties.

A. METHOD

1. Sample

The original sample consisted of 75 fourth-grade boys from 16 classrooms in 10 public schools located in working-class neighborhoods in and around Boston, Massachusetts. Six schools were located in Cambridge, one in Watertown, and three in Boston. The boys were 9–10 years of age; 36 were caucasian, 13 were black, 9 were of Hispanic origin, and 17 from other ethnic groups. All children were fluent in English and all procedures were conducted in English. The group consisted of 42 boys who were extremely unpopular in their classrooms, severely retarded in reading ability, or both. A group of 33 control children was chosen to be matched to the experimentals on ethnicity, language spoken in the home, and classroom or neighborhood. However, the control children were not in the bottom quartile of their class on reading ability or popularity. That is, the control subjects did not possess the undesirable qualities for which their matched experimental subject was selected. It was not possible to find a control child for every experimental child. Moreover, due to moving during the school year, we lost three of the experimental subjects and one control subject, leaving a final sample of 39 experimental and 32 controls.

The experimental group included 11 boys who, according to consensual peer evaluation, were extremely unpopular—they were ranked as the two least popular boys in their class by their peers. There were also 16 boys who were the poorest in their class in reading; these boys were placed in the bottom two ranks in reading ability by their teacher. They also had reading scores below grade level based on standard achievement tests. Finally, there were 12 boys who were both unpopular and retarded in reading skill based on the same criteria previously described. The control children included 11 controls matched with the 11 unpopular children, 12 controls matched with the 16 children who had reading problems, and 9 controls matched with the 12 children who were both unpopular and poor in reading. Twenty experimental–control pairs came from the same classroom, seven from the same school, two from the same neighborhood, and 12 from different neighborhoods.

2. Procedures

Each of the 71 children was administered three procedures in the same order. They were (1) ranking of self and same-sex peers on popularity and reading ability, (2) a triad procedure, and (3) administration of the film.

a. Ranking

Each experimental and control child was asked to rank all the boys in this classroom, including himself, on popularity and reading ability. The procedure used was identical to the one described for Study 1.

b. Triads

Unlike Study 1, we were not interested in determining the dimensions the children might use to organize their peers but wanted to see whether a child who was given a specific psychological dimension to use in the triads would place himself with children who did or did not possess the desirable attribute. The subjects who were in the unpopular or poor reading groups were administered the triads procedure only once. They were asked to make their grouping either on popularity or on reading. The subjects who were both unpopular and retarded in reading were asked to do the triads twice, once for each characteristic. The child was given trios of boys in his classroom and asked to say which two were most similar and which one different on either popularity or reading ability. Each child received 36 triads for each quality. When the classrooms had adequate size, the subjects received 24 triads in which they were included and 12 triads in which they were not. However, when the classrooms were small this was not possible. Thus there were three different patterns of triads. *Pattern 1*, which was given to the majority of subjects, included the following triads with six items for each combination: SHH, SMH, SLH, SLM, HHL, and LLH. S refers to the subject, H refers to a child in the subject's class in the top third as determined by peer or teacher ranks, M refers to a child in the subject's class in the middle third as determined by peer or teacher ranks, and L refers to a child in the subject's class in the lowest third determined by peer or teacher ranks. *Pattern 2:* SMH (six items), SLM (seven items), HHL (seven items), SLH (eight items), and SHH (eight items). *Pattern 3:* SHM (12 items), SLM (12 items), and SHL (12 items).

The assignment of children to the category high, medium, or low was based on the mean rank assigned to a particular child by his peers for popularity or by the teacher for reading.

c. Film

The film was the same one described in Study 2 but two important changes were made in the procedure. First, despite the empathic identification with both Sam and Joe by the reading-disabled subjects, the data from Study 2 suggested that Sam was physically the more attractive model. More control children said they liked Sam on a postfilm interview and many subjects were less restless and more attentive when Sam was on the screen than when Joe was on camera. For this reason we made Joe the experimental model for all the subjects in order to avoid ambiguity over whether greater empathy with Sam was due to his attractiveness as a model. Second, in Study 2 the control children were given no basis for believing in any similarity between the model and themselves. In this study the control children were given the same basis as the experimentals. Thus the control child for the popularity group was told that Joe was popular and Sam was not. The control child for the reading group was told that Joe was a good reader and Sam was not. The control child for the experimental boys with both undesirable qualities was told that Joe was popular and good in reading while Sam had the opposite traits. By contrast, the experimental children were told the reverse. They were told that Joe was unpopular and that Sam was popular; Joe was a poor reader and Sam a good reader; or Joe was both unpopular and a poor reader while Sam had the opposite attributes. This strategy was based on the a priori expectation that the experimental subjects would be more likely to empathize with the undesirable model; the control subjects with the desirable model. Because Sam was inherently more attractive than Joe we would have "helped" our prediction by making Joe undesirable for the control subjects.

The coding of the film data was exactly as described for Study 2. That is, if a child cheered or encouraged one model and/or sneered or mocked at another, that child was classified as showing greater empathic identification with the former model. If these behaviors did not occur, a child who showed more appropriate smiling to one model than to the other was classified as being identified with that model. If neither of these two behaviors occurred, but if the child showed more changes in facial expression, talking, and leaning forward to one model than to the other, he was classified as identified with that model. The reliability of the coding was 90%.

B. RESULTS

The first question to be asked of the data is the degree of agreement among the child's responses to each of the three procedures—self-ranks, triads, and film— and the more objective evaluations of popularity and reading provided by peers and teachers. In order to answer this question it is first necessary to state explicit criteria for the judgment of agreement for each of the three measures. For all three procedures, we used three classification categories—acknowledgment of one's attributes, denial, or ambiguous.

1. Rankings

For the experimental subjects the child was classified as acknowledging his attributes on the self-ranking if he placed himself in the bottom quartile of his peer group (e.g., he gave himself a rank of 13 through 16 in a class of 16 subjects). A child who placed himself ninth in a class of 11 would be classified as acknowledging his low status. The classification of *denial* was used if the experimental subject ranked himself above the median on his self-rankings for popularity or reading ability. The child was classified as ambiguous if he ranked himself in the third quartile of his group.

Among the 27 experimental children ranked as either unpopular or poor readers by their peers and teachers, 13 acknowledged their low status by placing themselves in the bottom quartile for the relevant quality. Ten children denied their status and four were classified as ambiguous. Among the 12 experimental subjects who were low on both properties, 9 denied their status on one or both traits (4 denied on one trait, 5 denied on both traits). Only one subject acknowledged his low status on both characteristics. Two subjects acknowledged on one trait and were ambiguous in their self-ranking on the other trait. In sum, 19 of the 39 experimental subjects (49%) denied their low status on one or both qualities.

Among the control subjects, the great majority of the children ranked themselves in the same or adjacent quartile as that given to them by their peers and teachers. These control children were classified as acknowledgers and ambiguous, respectively. For the 23 control subjects in the single trait groups, 11 were acknowledgers and 10 were classified as ambiguous. Among the 9 control subjects in the combined-trait group, 4 acknowledged on both traits and 4 acknowledged on one trait and were ambiguous with regard to the other. Overall, only three of the 32 control children (9%) had a difference as large as two quartiles between the self-rank and the other ranks. These children were classified as deniers. By contrast, 49% of the experimental group placed themselves two or three quartiles higher than the rank given them by their peers or teachers on one or both traits. The difference between 49% deniers in the experimental group and 9% in the control group yielded $\chi^2 = 11.0$ ($p < .01$). It appears that significantly more experimental than control subjects gave themselves ranks which differed substantially from the ranks given them by others.

2. Triads

It will be recalled that each child was administered 36 triads. For children in the large classrooms, 67% of those triads included the self; for subjects in the smaller classrooms, either 81 or 100% of the triads included the self. The informative data involved the number of triads in which the child placed himself with boys the peers had ranked as high (the top third) in contrast to the number of times the child placed himself with peers who were ranked medium (middle third) or low (bottom third).

An experimental child was classified as an acknowledger if he filled either of two criteria: Child places self with a child who is in the bottom third five or more times and never places himself with a child who is in the top third, or the frequency of placement of self with a low child was three times the frequency of placement with a high child. The judgment of denial was symmetrical. A child was classified as a denier if he placed himself with a high child five or more times and never with a low child, or he placed himself with a high child three times more often than he did with a low child. If the child fitted neither of these criteria he was classified as ambiguous.

The criteria for the control children were comparable but because the distribution of ranks differed for the controls we parsed the distribution into quartiles rather than thirds. If a child was ranked by his peers for popularity or the teacher (for reading) in the first quartile, an acknowledger was one who placed himself with high-rank children five or more times and never with low-rank children, or he placed himself with a high-ranked child three times as frequently as he placed himself with a low-ranked child. For a child who was ranked in the first quartile to be called a denier, he had to place himself with a low-ranked child five or more times and never with a high-ranked child, or place himself with a low-ranked child three times more often as he did with a high-ranked child.

For control children who were ranked in the second or third quartiles, a child was called an acknowledger if he placed himself with a medium-ranked child five or more times, or placed himself with a medium-ranked child three times more often as he did with a low- or higher ranked child. In order to be classified as a denier, the child had to place himself with a medium child fewer than five times and more often with either a low- or high-ranked child than with a medium child, or place himself with either a low- or high-ranked child three times more often as he did with the medium-ranked child. All others were classified as ambiguous. There were no control children who were ranked in the fourth quartile. Although all the experimental children were in the fourth quartile, they had more triad sorts in which the self was placed with a high-ranked child than with a medium-ranked child and least often with a low-ranked child. The controls also produced more triad sorts in which they placed the self with a high- than with a medium- or low-ranked child. But the subjects in quartiles two and three placed the self with a medium child more times than the experimentals did with a low-ranked child. That is, for reading, control subjects ranked in quartiles two and three had a mean of 9.0 sorts in which they placed themselves with a medium child, versus 5.1 sorts of experimentals with low-ranked children. For popularity, the comparable means were 5.1 versus 3.8. For children with both handicaps, the means were 7.2 versus 4.5 for reading and 6.6 versus 2.3 for popularity. Although the controls also enhanced their status, they did so less seriously than the experimentals.

3. Film Data

The experimental subjects showed a greater tendency to identify with one of the models than the control children. Of the 39 experimental boys, 21 identified with one of the models, while among the 32 controls only 3 showed differential empathy with one of the models (two acknowledgers and one denier) ($\chi^2 = 13.1$, $p < .01$).

We believe this is because over half the control group were not at the extremes on the attributes of popularity or reading ability. Because most of the control children were of average ability or popularity, the qualities ascribed to the two models were not uniquely characteristic of them and, hence, there was no strong basis for affective involvement with one of the models. Among the experimental subjects, 16 acknowledged their attributes by showing more empathy toward Joe than toward Sam, while 5 denied by showing more empathic involvement with Sam than with Joe.

Despite similarities in age, social class, sex, and ethnic profile, the subjects who were extremely unpopular and/or poor in reading ability were more likely than the controls to identify with one of the models and the majority (76% of this group) showed greater affective involvement with the model who had the undesirable characteristics. The fact that more children identified with Joe when he was poor at reading than when he was described as unpopular (nine versus three children) suggests that conscious processes may be operating in the empathy procedure. We believe it is more threatening to this group of working-class children to be unpopular than to be deficient at school work.

4. Comparisons across Procedures

A significant proportion of the experimental children failed to acknowledge their poor reading ability or unpopularity on the self-ranking procedures. Among the 11 boys ranked as extremely unpopular by peers, 4 (36%) denied this characteristic; of the 16 boys judged by their teachers to be very poor readers, 6 (38%) denied this quality. Among the 12 boys considered to be both unpopular and poor readers, 9 denied on one or both traits (75%); 5 denied both traits and 4 denied one of the traits. Indeed only 14 of the 39 experimental boys (35%) acknowledged their low status on the self-ranks.

To what extent did the triads and film procedures add information which would lead one to doubt the positive self-evaluations given by so many of these children whom peers regarded negatively? The triads procedure in Study 3 did not prove quite as useful as it had in Study 1 for only 26% of the experimental subjects acknowledged an undesirable characteristic on the triads. And of those who did, the majority had already done so in their self-ranks. Only 3 subjects who had denied an undesirable characteristic on ranks acknowledged that characteristic on triads. But among controls 81% acknowledged their qualities on triads, in contrast to 26% of the experimentals ($\chi^2 = 22.6$, $p < .001$). Additionally, 41% of all the controls acknowledged on both ranks and triads, in comparison with 15% of the experimental subjects ($\chi^2 = 5.6$, $p < .05$).

The utility of the triads procedure is enhanced somewhat when one examines the number of experimental subjects who ranked themselves as possessing desirable qualities but whose triad scores were classified as ambiguous. Three boys who denied poor reading ability on their self-ranks had ambiguous triads and four boys who were both poor readers and unpopular produced ambiguous triads for at least one of their traits. Thus, although these subjects did not acknowledge their low status in the triads procedure, these seven subjects did indicate on the triads a self-evaluation more in accord with the judgment of others than they did on their self-ranks. A total of 9 of the 19 children (47%) who denied one or both undesirable qualities in the ranking procedure did not place themselves with the competent children in the triads procedure, implying some awareness of their undesirable characteristics.

The empathy measure also seemed to be of some value. Of the 19 experimental boys who had denied their undesirable qualities on the ranks, about one-third (6) showed greater empathy toward Joe, the model who shared their undesirable qualities.

The advantage of the film measure is revealed in the fact that 6 of the 11 children in the reading group (55%) who denied their inadequate reading ability on ranks or triads showed greater affective involvement with Joe, the model who was poor in reading. By contrast, no child who acknowledged his poor reading on self-ranks or triads showed greater empathy with Sam.

Additionally, there were more frequent signs of obvious emotional involvement among the experimental than among the control children. More experimentals encouraged one of the models or beat their fists into their hands if the model failed the question. These affective responses were less likely among the control children. The largest difference occurred for smiling; 41% of the control children smiled one or more times during the film versus 67% of the experimentals ($\chi^2 = 4.97$, $p < .05$). Not only did more experimental children smile, but they smiled more frequently. No control child smiled more than four times, while 10 experimentals smiled that often. But there was no difference in the frequency of changes in facial expression between the experimentals and controls.

There are at least two interpretations of the fact that the experimental children were emotionally more reactive than the controls. One is that the experimental children are temperamentally more excitable and therefore more likely to become affective than the controls in many circumstances. A second interpretation, and the one we prefer, is that the likelihood of empathic identification covaries with the distinctiveness of the traits of the model and the subject. To be extremely unpopular or deficient in reading comprises a distinctive psychological attribute. The child with one or both of these distinctive qualities is more likely to become empathic with a person he believes also possesses these attributes than a child of average popularity or reading ability.

V. General Discussion

A. IMPLICATIONS

The results of these studies have two implications. First, as indicated in the first study, children's responses to direct questions about their psychological qualities appear to be relatively valid indexes of the child's belief (if peer and teacher evaluations are used as criteria) when the self-ranks admit to the undesirable attributes. But positive evaluations are suspect, for at least one-third of all children who did not possess the positive attributes in the perception of peers evaluated themselves positively nonetheless. More important is the fact that some of these children were inconsistent in their positive evaluations across different procedures. Some denied an undesirable quality on the ranking procedures but acknowledged it on the triads or film. It should not be surprising that positive evaluations are ambiguous in meaning; what is surprising is that some investigators have refused to acknowledge that fact. These data, when added to the wealth of information gathered by others, lead us to suggest that investigators should stop using such instruments in their research when they are the only measures of the child's beliefs about the self. Wylie has made this claim many times, but it continues to go unheeded.

B. INTERPRETATIONS

There are at least three possible interpretations of the fact that a sizeable group of preadolescent children either consciously falsifies or denies some salient attribute of the self, especially if the quality is undesirable. The simplest interpretation is that the child simply does not know or is not aware of his or her psychological status. This may be a possibility for many properties. But in the case of academic failure and unpopularity, where objective feedback is so regular and unambiguous, it is likely that the average child does know, at some level, that he or she is not competent or well liked.

The second interpretation is that all children are aware of their undesirable qualities but willfully refuse to admit them. This interpretation is reasonable for the self-rankings but slightly less persuasive as an explanation for the film procedures where the intention is more disguised.

The third interpretation engages the psychological defenses of denial or repression. Here we assume that some children do have some knowledge of their attributes but defend against a clearly articulated recognition of those qualities. The strength of the defense is viewed as a continuous process with some children showing it to a moderate degree and others to an extreme. It is possible, even likely, that some of the children with undesirable qualities utilized this defense and consciously believed they were academically competent or popular. It is likely that all three types of children are represented in our samples. But informal conversation with the children before and after the experimental procedures lead us to suggest that the majority of children were aware of their undesirable status but did not want to reveal it to the examiner. That is why we suggest the utility of the triads and film procedures. The data reveal that a combination of self-ranks, triads, and film is more sensitive than either method alone in diagnosing a child's self-concept. It is likely that other methods may prove to be even more valid. Of the 19 children in Study 3 who ranked themselves high on reading or popularity (all of whom were ranked low by their peers), 7 acknowledged their low status on either the triads or the film. In this case the use of these two more disguised procedures increased the accuracy of classification of the child's private beliefs by more than one-third—a nontrivial gain in accuracy. Detection of complex psychological qualities requires complex procedures. Nature does not yield a child's private beliefs readily. Psychologists who are convinced that a child's conception of his or her attributes is an important determinant of behavior, as we do, should be prepared to invest as much effort in discovering those beliefs as was invested by the child in their establishment.

References

Bachman, J. G., & O'Malley, P. M. Self-esteem in young men. *Journal of Personality and Social Psychology,* 1977, **35**, 365–380.

Baldwin, J. M. *Mental development in the child and the race.* New York: Macmillan, 1895.

Bandura, A. Self efficacy: Toward a unifying theory of behavioral change. *Psychological Review,* 1977, **84**, 191–215.

Barker, R. G. *Ecological psychology.* Stanford, California: Stanford Univ. Press, 1968.

Brim, O. G., & Kagan, J. *Constancy and change in human development.* Cambridge, Massachusetts: Harvard Univ. Press, 1980.

Bugental, J. F. T., & Zelen, S. L. Investigations into the "self-concept." I. The W-A-Y technique. *Journal of Personality,* 1950, **18**, 483–498.

Burton, M. L., & Nerlove, S. B. Balanced designs for triad tests: Two examples from English. *Social Science Research,* 1976, **5**, 247–267.

Cliff, N., & Young, F. W. On the relation between unidimensional judgments and multidimensional scaling. *Organizational Behavior and Human Performance,* 1968, **3**, 269–285.

Cooley, C. H. *Human nature and the social order.* New York: Scribner's, 1902.

Coopersmith, S. *The antecedents of self-esteem.* San Francisco, California: Freeman, 1967.

Ekman, P., Friesen, W. V., & Ellsworth, P. *Emotion in the human face.* Oxford: Pergamon, 1972.

Festinger, L. A theory of social comparison processes. *Human Relations,* 1954, **7**, 117–140.

Funk, S. G., Horowitz, A. D., Lipshitz, R., & Young, F. W. The perceived structure of American ethnic groups: The use of multidimensional scaling in stereotype research. *Sociometry,* 1976, **39**, 116–130.

Harter, S. *Perceived competence scale for children.* Denver, Colorado: Univ. of Denver, 1979.

Hogan, L. E. *A study of a child.* New York: Harper, 1898.

Izard, C. E. *The face of emotion.* New York: Appleton, 1971.

Kagan, J. The concept of identification. *Psychological Review,* 1958, **65**, 296–305.

Kagan, J. *The second year.* Cambridge, Massachusetts: Harvard Univ. Press, 1981.

Kagan, J., & Phillips, W. Measurement of identification. *Journal of Abnormal and Social Psychology,* 1964, **69**, 442–444.

Lewin, K. *Field theory and social science: Selected theoretical papers.* New York: Harper, 1951.

Lewis, M., & Brooks-Gunn, J. *Social cognition and the acquisition of self.* New York: Plenum, 1979.

Livesley, W. J., & Bromley, D. B. *Person perception in childhood and adolescence.* New York: Wiley, 1973.

Maccoby, E. E., & Wilson, W. C. Identification and observational learning from films. *Journal of Abnormal and Social Psychology,* 1957, **55**, 76–87.

McGuire, W. J. *The spontaneous self-concept as affected by personal distinctiveness.* Presented at Self-Concept Symposium, Boston, Massachusetts, August 1978.

McGuire, W. J., McGuire, C. V., Child, P., & Fujioka, T. Salience of ethnicity in the spontaneous self-concept as a function of one's ethnic distinctiveness in a social environment. *Journal of Personality and Social Psychology,* 1978, **36**, 511–520.

McGuire, W. J., & Padawer-Singer, A. Trait salience in a spontaneous self-concept. *Journal of Personality and Social Psychology,* 1976, **33**, 743–754.

Mead, G. H. *Mind, self and society.* Chicago, Illinois: Univ. of Chicago Press, 1934.

Mischel, W. On the future of personality measurement. *American Psychologist,* 1977, **32**, 246–254.

Murray, H. A. *Explorations in personality.* London and New York: Oxford Univ. Press, 1938.

Piers, E. V., & Harris, D. B. Age and other correlates of self-concept in children. *Journal of Educational Psychology,* 1964, **55,** 91-95.

Preyer, W. *The mind of a child. Part II.* New York: Appleton, 1889.

Rabinowitz, G. B. An introduction to nonmetric multidimensional scaling. *American Journal of Political Science,* 1975, **19,** 343-390.

Rosenberg, M. *Conceiving the self.* New York: Basic Books, 1979.

Rosenberg, S., & Jones, R. A method for investigating and representing a person's implicit theory of personality: Theodore Dreiser's view of people. *Journal of Personality and Social Psychology,* 1972, **22,** 372-386.

Shepard, R. N., Romney, A. K., & Nerlove, S. B. (Eds.) *Multidimensional scaling: Theory.* New York: Seminar Press, 1972.

Shrauger, J. S., & Schoeneman, S. Symbolic interactionist view of self-concept: Through the looking-glass darkly. *Psychological Bulletin,* 1979, **86,** 549-573.

Smith, M. B. Attitudes, values and selfhood. In W. J. Arnold & D. Levine (Eds.), *Nebraska Symposium on Motivation* (Vol. 27). Lincoln: Univ. of Nebraska Press, 1979.

Stern, W. *Psychology of early childhood up to the 6th year of life* (6th ed.). New York: Holt, 1930.

Stotland, E., & Dunn, R. E. Empathy, self-esteem, and birth order. *Journal of Abnormal and Social Psychology,* 1963, **66,** 532-540.

Wells, L. E., & Marwell, G. *Self-esteem: Its conceptualization and measurement.* Beverly Hills: Sage Publications, 1976.

Wylie, R. *The self-concept.* Lincoln: Univ. of Nebraska Press, 1961.

Wylie, R. C. *The self-concept: A review of methodological considerations and measuring instruments* (Vol. 1). Lincoln: Univ. of Nebraska Press, 1974.

Wylie, R. *The self-concept* (Vol. 2, rev. ed.). Lincoln: Univ. of Nebraska Press, 1979.

Young, F. W. *Conjoint scaling.* Chapel Hill: Univ. of North Carolina, 1974.

NATIONAL DIFFERENCES IN ANXIETY AND EXTROVERSION

Richard Lynn

DEPARTMENT OF PSYCHOLOGY
NEW UNIVERSITY OF ULSTER
COLERAINE, NORTHERN IRELAND

This article is concerned with attempts to measure national differences in anxiety and extroversion and with the causes of such differences between the populations of different nations. Measurements of these national differences have been made both from demographic indices, such as national rates of alcoholism and suicide, and from questionnaire data from samples of national populations. The article begins with a summary of the author's work on the measurement of national differences in anxiety and extroversion from demographic data and considers criticisms which have been made of this research. It passes subsequently to questionnaire results on national differences in anxiety and extrover-

213

sion, compares these results with the demographic method, and considers what further inferences can be drawn from this additional set of data. Finally, some discussion is given of possible causes of national differences in anxiety and extroversion.

I. Measurement of National Differences in Anxiety and Extroversion from Demographic Data

National differences in the prevalence of suicide, alcoholism, accidents, mental illness, and similar demographic phenomena have perplexed students of the social sciences since they were originally documented and discussed by Durkheim (1897). During the 1970s this writer advanced the thesis that a substantial proportion of the variance in a number of these demographic phenomena can be explained in terms of national differences in the populations' levels of anxiety and extroversion. The general theoretical interest of the theory lies in its reductionist explanation of a wide range of social phenomena in terms of psychological constructs drawn from personality trait theory as formulated by Cattell, Eysenck, and others. The present theory attempts to accomplish this by regarding social phenomena as aggregates of individual behavior and treating differences in the prevalence of various social phenomena among different populations as following from mean differences in these two personality traits. In this respect it endeavors to achieve an integration between psychology and the social sciences which, though theoretically desirable, has rarely been attempted (Lynn, 1971, 1973; Lynn & Hampson, 1975, 1977).

This author's first attempt at the measurement of national differences in anxiety and extroversion from demographic data was published in *Personality and National Character* (Lynn, 1971). Subsequently, the theory was refined and extended in Lynn and Hampson (1975, 1977). The theory starts with the assumption that a number of demographic phenomena may be manifestations of the underlying personality traits of anxiety or extroversion in the populations. An example of such a phenomenon is national per capita alcohol consumption. There are substantial differences between nations in the consumption of alcohol. For instance, the per capita consumption of alcohol in France is approximately four times as great as that in Great Britain or the United States. What could be the explanation of these differences? Since alcohol is a well-known anxiety reducer, and many alcoholics are anxious people seeking anxiety reduction through alcohol, it seemed a possible hypothesis that the mean level of anxiety might be higher in France than in Great Britain or the United States. No doubt there could be other explanations as well, such as lower pricing policies in France or a stronger cultural tradition of alcohol consumption. However, a phenomenon such as national alcohol consumption is almost certainly determined by a number of factors and the postulation of additional explanations are not particularly damaging to the anxiety hypothesis.

What the hypothesis requires, of course, is strengthening. The theory is built on three lines of evidence. First, there are a number of social phenomena which are intercorrelated among nations and among which factorial analysis reveals the existence of two substantial factors interpretable as anxiety and extroversion. Second, it is shown that the national "anxiety" factor scores rose significantly in nations which suffered military defeat and occupation in World War II, such as Germany, Japan, and France, as compared with the nations which escaped military defeat. With the restoration of peace in the 1950s, the "anxiety" levels of the defeated nations subsided (Lynn & Hampson, 1977). In this respect the factor behaves as if it were anxiety and some predictive validity is provided for the interpretation of the factor.

Third, data collected with questionnaires from samples of the populations from a number of different countries can be used to validate the interpretation of the putative factors of anxiety and extroversion obtained from demographic data. Such questionnaire data have become available through the work of Hofstede (1976) and from numerous investigations using the Eysenck questionnaires. The results will be reviewed in the last section of this article.

These three lines of evidence for the theory will now be presented in greater detail.

II. Factor Structure of Demographic
Phenomena among Nations

Twelve demographic variables were used as possible indices of anxiety and extroversion among nations. These variables were the national prevalence rates of suicide, alcoholism, chronic psychosis, coronary heart disease, accidents, crime, murder, illegitimacy, and divorce, and the per capita consumption of calories, caffeine, and cigarettes. These 12 variables were used because their relationships with anxiety and extroversion are reasonably well established on both theoretical and empirical grounds. These relationships among individuals can therefore be used to set up a predictive model embodying a similar set of relationships among nations.

This model is shown in Fig. 1. The model summarizes the data on the relationship of the demographic variables of alcoholism, suicide, etc. to the personality traits of anxiety and extroversion. The empirical studies on which the model is based are described in the next section. We turn first to the testing of the model among nations. The object here is to obtain the data for a group of nations, intercorrelate and factor-analyze it, and see whether we obtain a factor structure which matches the model.

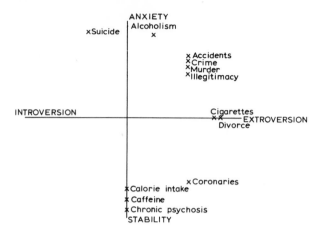

Fig. 1.   Model of the relation of demographic phenomena to anxiety and extroversion.

The data were obtained for the 18 economically advanced Western nations of northern Europe, North America, and Australasia shown in Table I. Strictly, the nations are all those with a per capita income above U.S. $450 in 1961, a population over 1 million, and for which data for at least 11 of the 12 variables were available. These are considered to be the universe of advanced Western nations fulfilling the specified criteria. Hence, it can be argued that the usual requirements of tests of statistical significance between the variables were not appropriate.

The data were collected for the year 1960. The values of these variables do not change greatly from one year to another and so it makes little difference which year is taken for analysis. The factor structure among the variables has been found to be stable over several decades, as shown in Section VI.

The data are shown in Table I and a description of the data and their sources is given below.

1. Cigarette consumption: number consumed per capita aged 15 and over, per annum. Source: Tobacco Research Council, London.

2. Crime: the number of prisoners per 10,000 population. Source: government statistical offices of the individual nations. Missing data: Switzerland does not record this information.

3. Divorce: number per 10,000 population. Source: United Nations Demographic Yearbooks. Missing data: Ireland and Italy do not permit divorce.

4. Illegitimacy: percentage of live births that are illegitimate. Source: United Nations Demographic Yearbooks.

5. Accidents: number of deaths from all types of accidents per 100,000 population. Source: United Nations Demographic Yearbooks.

TABLE I

THE DEMOGRAPHIC AND EPIDEMIOLOGICAL DATA

Country	Chronic psychosis	Calorie intake	Caffeine consumption	Coronary heart disease	Alcoholism	Suicide	Murder	Crime	Divorce	Cigarette consumption	Illegitimacy	Accidents
Australia	3.3	3140	6.6	256.2	4.8	10.6	1.5	6.6	6.5	2440	4.8	52.6
Austria	1.8	2970	1.9	242.8	23.3	23.1	1.2	11.5	11.3	1720	13.0	70.4
Belgium	3.0	3060	7.4	142.3	9.5	14.6	.7	6.3	5.0	1570	2.1	54.6
Canada	2.9	3020	5.5	237.0	6.1	7.5	1.4	9.6	3.9	2910	4.3	52.5
Denmark	2.2	3260	9.7	246.6	8.4	20.3	.5	3.1	14.6	1470	7.8	44.8
Finland	3.6	3110	7.9	221.5	3.3	20.5	2.9	15.4	8.2	2100	4.0	51.5
France	2.4	3190	4.6	78.4	29.3	15.8	1.7	5.9	6.6	1320	6.1	58.9
West Germany	1.7	2990	3.8	199.2	19.0	19.5	1.0	8.6	8.8	1630	6.3	56.2
Ireland	7.2	3480	6.9	313.5	2.0	3.0	.2	1.3	—	2560	1.6	32.5
Italy	2.2	2730	2.1	188.4	17.3	6.3	1.5	7.8	—	1300	2.4	40.7
Japan	.8	2330	1.6	50.1	9.7	21.6	1.9	7.7	7.4	1880	1.2	41.8
Netherlands	2.3	3160	6.4	168.2	3.5	6.6	.3	3.4	4.9	1700	1.3	36.7
New Zealand	4.3	3490	6.1	243.7	2.3	9.7	1.1	7.7	6.9	1930	5.3	46.0
Norway	2.0	2930	8.3	210.0	4.2	6.5	.4	4.4	6.6	550	3.7	43.8
Sweden	4.6	2990	10.1	281.5	5.1	17.4	.6	6.4	12.0	1160	11.3	46.4
Switzerland	3.5	3210	6.0	229.7	11.8	19.0	.6	—	8.7	2380	3.8	60.2
United Kingdom	3.4	3270	9.6	314.6	2.9	10.6	.6	5.8	4.8	2760	5.2	39.3
United States	3.4	3120	7.9	306.3	11.3	10.6	4.7	11.8	21.8	3810	5.3	52.1

6. Coronary heart disease: deaths from coronary heart disease and atherosclerosis per 100,000 population. Source: United Nations Demographic Yearbooks.

7. Suicide: number of deaths per 100,000 population. Source: United Nations Demographic Yearbooks.

8. Caffeine consumption: kilograms of coffee and tea imports retained for home consumption per annum, per capita; the index of caffeine consumption was derived by weighting tea consumption twice that of coffee because tea has approximately twice the caffeine content of coffee per unit weight. Source: Pan American Coffee Bureau, New York, and International Tea Committee, London.

9. Alcoholism: number of deaths from liver cirrhosis per 100,000 population. Source: United Nations Demographic Yearbooks.

10. Calorie intake: daily intake of calories per capita. Source: United Nations Statistical Yearbooks.

11. Chronic psychosis: number of psychiatric patients per 1000 population (because of the relatively rapid turnover of acute psychiatric patients, the number of patients in mental hospitals at any one time is heavily weighted in favor of chronic cases). Source: World Health Statistics Annual and government publications from the individual nations.

12. Murder: number of deaths from murder per 100,000 population. Source: United Nations Demographic Yearbooks.

The data shown in Table I were intercorrelated and factored by principal components analysis with unities in the main diagonal. The correlation matrix is shown in Table II and the results of the principal components analysis in Table III. There are three factors with eigenvalues above unity. The first factor is considered to be anxiety, with high loadings on suicide, alcoholism, and accidents and, negatively, on calorie intake, caffeine consumption, and chronic psychosis. The second factor is apparently extroversion, with high loadings on crime, murder, illegitimacy, coronary heart disease, accidents, and cigarette consumption. Crime, murder, illegitimacy, and accidents have approximately equal loadings on both anxiety and extroversion and coronary heart disease on extroversion and emotional stability (i.e., the negative pole of anxiety). The third factor has its highest loading on illegitimacy and will not be considered further.

The first two factors were rotated by varimax and promax. The varimax solution was closely similar to the principal components, as was the promax solution which is shown in Table IV. The correlation between the two factors in the promax rotation was $\pm.01$, which indicates, of course, that the two factors are virtually independent.

It is now possible to judge the success of our attempt to find a factor structure of demographic variables among nations similar to that present among individuals. This can be done most simply by comparing the model shown in Fig. 1 with

TABLE II

THE CORRELATION MATRIX (PRODUCT–MOMENT CORRELATIONS; DECIMAL POINTS OMITTED)[a]

	1	2	3	4	5	6	7	8	9	10	11	12
1. Chronic psychosis	(1.0)	—	—	—	—	—	—	—	—	—	—	—
2. Calorie intake	68	(1.0)	—	—	—	—	—	—	—	—	—	—
3. Caffeine consumption	47	55	(1.0)	—	—	—	—	—	—	—	—	—
4. Coronary heart disease	63	58	56	(1.0)	—	—	—	—	—	—	—	—
5. Alcoholism	-48	-27	-61	-45	(1.0)	—	—	—	—	—	—	—
6. Suicide	-43	-31	-18	-30	42	(1.0)	—	—	—	—	—	—
7. Murder	-12	-21	-12	00	19	14	(1.0)	—	—	—	—	—
8. Crime	-23	-26	-26	01	22	43	73	(1.0)	—	—	—	—
9. Divorce	07	03	17	37	18	25	57	25	(1.0)	—	—	—
10. Cigarette consumption	35	28	11	47	-22	-18	54	32	29	(1.0)	—	—
11. Illegitimacy	-06	10	10	33	35	51	00	25	41	-15	(1.0)	—
12. Accidents	-32	-06	-30	-13	64	61	26	57	16	-02	55	(1.0)

[a] From Lynn and Hampson (1975).

TABLE III
THE PRINCIPAL COMPONENTS ANALYSIS

Variables	Factor loadings		
	I	II	III
1. Chronic psychosis	76	33	07
2. Calorie intake	65	35	34
3. Caffeine consumption	67	31	28
4. Coronary heart disease	61	65	18
5. Suicide	−78	01	20
6. Alcoholism	−70	22	35
7. Murder	−36	62	−61
8. Crime	−56	57	32
9. Divorce	−14	72	01
10. Cigarette consumption	24	63	−54
11. Illegitimacy	−32	51	71
12. Accidents	−69	40	30
Eigenvalues	4.03	2.85	1.75
Variance (%)	33.56	23.73	14.62

the empirical results shown in Fig. 2. The largest discrepant variable is suicide which, it was thought, would lie in the anxiety–introversion quadrant, but which appeared in the results in the anxiety–extroversion quadrant. However, with the exception of this partially discrepant result, the factor structure obtained from the

TABLE IV
THE PROMAX SOLUTION

	Factor loadings	
	Factor 1 (anxiety)	Factor 2 (extroversion)
1. Chronic psychosis	79	26
2. Calorie intake	68	29
3. Caffeine consumption	69	25
4. Coronary heart disease	66	60
5. Suicide	−78	08
6. Alcoholism	−68	28
7. Murder	−31	65
8. Crime	−51	61
9. Divorce	−08	73
10. Cigarette consumption	29	61
11. Illegitimacy	−28	53
12. Accidents	−66	45

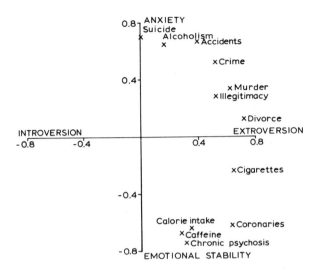

Fig. 2.   Principal components analysis showing loadings of demographic phenomena on anxiety and extroversion.

analysis fits the model shown in Fig. 1 reasonably closely, as may be seen from comparison of the two figures. It is suggested that the fit between the model and the results is sufficiently good to justify the theoretical extension of the personality traits of anxiety and extroversion into the field of national differences in demographic phenomena, where the theory is able to predict and explain a number of hitherto unknown relationships.

III. Interpretation of the Two Demographic Factors

As in any factor analysis, the interpretation of the factors must be justified from examination of the loadings of the variables on the factors. It is to this matter of interpretation that we now turn. The task here is to show that the correlations of the variables with anxiety and extroversion among individuals are of the same kind as those found with the demographic data among nations. In making a summary of the evidence, reliance has had to be placed in a number of cases on studies using one of Eysenck's questionnaires measuring neuroticism rather than anxiety. The two constructs are similar and highly correlated, as is well known, and it is considered that for present purposes the two may be considered as identical. Some of the principal strands of evidence relating the twelve variables to anxiety and extroversion will now be discussed.

A. Cigarette Consumption

The most extensive study of the relationship of cigarette consumption to extroversion and neuroticism appears to be that of H. J. Eysenck (1965) on a sample of 2400 subjects in Great Britain. This investigation showed a significant tendency for extroverts to smoke cigarettes more heavily. Several other investigators have confirmed this result. These include Schubert (1965) in a study of 1270 students in New England, Estabrook and Sommer (1966) in a study of 130 American students, and Cattell and Krug (1967) in another study of American students. Further investigators to report the same association include Evans, Borgatta, and Bohrnstedt (1967) and Smith (1967, 1969).

The evidence of the relationship of cigarette consumption to anxiety is rather less clear-cut. The original study by H. J. Eysenck (1965) found no significant relationship between cigarette consumption and neuroticism, and this was subsequently confirmed by Smith (1967) and Cattell and Krug (1967). On the basis of these three large-scale studies, it would appear that cigarette consumption is largely unrelated to anxiety, although some smaller scale studies claiming a positive relationship can be found. In general, however, the studies lead to the prediction that cigarette consumption among nations will be a positive function of national levels of extroversion but unrelated to national levels of anxiety. Examination of Fig. 2 will show that this was found to be the case.

B. Crime

An association between extroversion and crime would be expected on theoretical grounds because important components of the extroverted personality are impulsiveness and poor socialization. Both the theory and the evidence relating extroversion to crime have been reviewed in detail by H. J. Eysenck (1964). Perhaps the first major investigation to report the relationship is that of Glueck and Glueck (1950). In their classical study of 500 delinquent boys, they estimated that 57% were extroverted compared with 28% of a control group. This relationship between extroversion and a propensity to commit crime was confirmed in a longitudinal study reported by Miller (1956). He took 551 children attending a child guidance clinic in Dallas, Texas, and assessed them for introversion–extroversion. Over the subsequent 28 years, 25% of the extroverts committed crimes compared with only 5% of the introverts.

There have been a number of studies of the scores of prisoners on extroversion questionnaires and the results have not been altogether clear. The first investigation of this type was published by Bartholomew (1959). He took three groups of 50 first offenders, 50 recidivists, and a second group of 54 recidivists and gave them the Maudsley Personality Inventory. The results showed that the first offenders scored slightly less extroverted than the normal population, but both recidivist groups scored substantially more extroverted. The result for the first offenders is discrepant, but it should be noted that questionnaire results may be distorted when they are obtained from prisoners. An important component of extroversion is sociability; since a prisoner has little opportunity for being sociable, his score on these questions may be spuriously shifted towards introversion.

Results showing a comparatively high level of extroversion in criminals, although not always at a statistically significant level, have been reported by H. J. Eysenck and S. B. G. Eysenck (1964), S. B. G. Eysenck and H. J. Eysenck (1970), Burgess (1972a), Iwawaki, Sujiyama, and Nanri (1964), Cattell, Eber, and Tatsuoka (1970), Pierson and Kelly (1963), Warburton (1965), and Sanocki (1969). There are a few studies failing to show the relationship, for example, Hoghughi and Forrest (1970), Little (1963), and Burgess (1972b).

In addition to its relation with extroversion, criminal behavior also appears to be related to anxiety. This relationship has been found in all the questionnaire studies listed above, generally, although not invariably, at a statistically significant level. The evidence therefore suggests that criminal behavior is a joint function of extroversion and anxiety. Accordingly, national crime rates are posited as joint functions of national levels of extroversion and anxiety in our model of national personality dimensions.

C. DIVORCE

There are some theoretical grounds for expecting a relationship between divorce and extroversion. These lie in the greater needs for stimulation, sensation, excitement, and novelty apparently felt by extroverts and their weaker inhibitions in breaching social mores for the gratification of these needs (e.g., H. J. Eysenck, 1967). One of the first findings of this type was the discovery that extroverts have a greater preference than introverts for pictures painted in bright and vivid colors, presumably because these afford stronger stimulation (H. J. Eysenck, 1947). Subsequently, it has been found that extroverts take larger risks in gambling (Lynn & Butler, 1962) and the development of sensation-seeking questionnaires has shown that extroverts have a greater liking for sensation (Farley & Farley, 1967). If the extrovert seeks to gratify his or her needs for sensation and novelty in sexual adventure, then it would seem probable that the outcome would be a greater tendency to divorce.

In addition to these general needs, there is some direct evidence that extroverts have stronger tendencies than introverts to gratify their needs for sexual novelty and variety. This appears to have been demonstrated first in Germany by Giese and Schmidt (1968). They found that extroverts began to have sexual intercourse earlier than introverts and, once started, engaged in it with more partners, apparently betraying the extrovert's need for novelty and stimulation. A later study by H. J. Eysenck (1972) of 800 young people in Great Britain obtained the same result. Thus, it seems that extroverts have a stronger drive for sexual variety and it would be surprising if this were not associated with a tendency to have a higher divorce rate.

The only direct evidence on the relationship between divorce and extroversion appears to be a study by Cattell and Nesselroade (1967). They took 102 stably married couples, defined as those where there had been no known step towards dissolution of the marriage, and compared them with 37 couples who had either separated or sought advice because of marital difficulties. The separated couples were found to be more extroverted than the stably married. There was no difference between the stably and unstably married couples on Cattell's anxiety factor. Hence, the prediction for national differences is that, among nations, divorce rates will be positively associated with extroversion but will have no association with anxiety.

D. ILLEGITIMACY

An association between extroversion and the procreation of illegitimate children is one that would be expected on the basis of the general nature of the extroverted personality. An important feature of the extrovert's personality is impulsiveness. Furthermore, the extrovert is relatively unsocialized and has not absorbed so well the moral values of society. With this personality structure it would be surprising if the extrovert were not a stronger candidate than the introvert for illegitimate parenthood.

Direct confirmation of this inference is available in a study by S. B. G. Eysenck (1961). She compared the extroversion scores of 100 unmarried mothers admitted to a maternity hospital with those of 100 matched married mothers. The unmarried mothers proved to be highly extroverted. They also scored somewhat higher than the normal population on neuroticism, so that we are led to the prediction that, among nations, the illegitimacy rate should be a positive function of both extroversion and anxiety.

E. ACCIDENT-PRONENESS

The classical work on the personality structure of the accident-prone is that carried out by Tillmann and Hobbs (1949) in Canada in the years immediately following the close of World War II. This work was specifically concerned with driving accidents, and the investigators concluded that how a person drives is determined by his general personality structure. As they put it, "a man drives as he lives."

Tillman and Hobbs compared 20 taxi drivers with exceptionally good driving records with another 20 whose records had been exceptionally poor. They found that the poor taxi drivers had long life histories of comparatively psychopathic and irresponsible behavior, including criminal records and poor employment histories. The good drivers had well-socialized hobbies like gardening and voluntary church work. Although they did not use the term extroversion, it seems fairly clear from the descriptions that the taxi drivers with the poor accident records were in fact extroverted and somewhat psychopathic, while the good taxi drivers tended to introversion.

One of the first investigators to link accident-proneness explicitly to extroversion was Fine (1963). His investigation of the accident records of nearly 1000 male students at the University of Minnesota found a significant association between the numbers of accidents and the degree of extroversion. This result was confirmed in a study of accident-proneness among South African bus drivers by Shaw and Sichel (1971). By the use of a number of measures these authors report a correlation of +.61 between accident-proneness and extroversion. A similar result has been obtained in Holland, where Buikhuisen (1968) has reported a high level of extroversion among people convicted of drunken driving. Others who have found this relationship include Biesheuvel and White (1949) in an investigation of accident-prone pilots in South Africa, Manheimer and Mellinger (1967) in a study of children in California, and Cattell and his associates in a number of investigations (Cattell *et al.*, 1970, p. 164).

Accident-proneness is also associated with anxiety. The association has been found in numerous studies and the literature has been reviewed by Shaw and Sichel (1971). The implication for national differences is, therefore, that national rates of accidents should be associated both with national levels of extroversion and with national levels of anxiety.

F. CORONARY HEART DISEASE

There is evidence that coronary heart disease is related to both low anxiety and extroversion. This may be surprising in view of the common supposition that coronary disease is associated with stress, and, hence, possibly with a high level of anxiety, but this belief has been discredited by the research on approximately one-quarter of a million Bell Telephone Company employees, which showed that coronaries are less prevalent among managers than among blue-collar workers (Hinkle, Whitney, Lehman, Dunn, Benjamin, King, Plakun, & Flehinger, 1968).

One of the problems in evaluating the personality of coronary patients is that of obtaining a control group. The coronary patient has the stress of the illness and the most satisfactory controls are probably other patients. Three studies of this kind have been published. One reported that coronary patients were "more cheerful and better socializers" (O'Leary, Schwab, John, & McGuinnies, 1968), suggesting a low level of anxiety and a high level of extroversion. Questionnaire evidence for a low level of anxiety in coronary patients has been published by Sainsbury (1980). Bendien and Groen (1963) report a tendency in the same direction and also that coronary patients are more extroverted than normal. Taking the evidence as a whole, the indications seem to be that coronary patients tend to be low on anxiety and high on extroversion, and, hence, we are led to the prediction that the prevalence of coronary heart disease in nations should be associated both with a low level of anxiety and with extroversion.

G. Suicide

There are several lines of evidence to indicate that people who commit suicide tend to be characterized by a high level of anxiety. In the first place, it has often been found that such people are frequently in a state of anxiety as a result of stresses of various kinds, such as bereavement and bankruptcy, and have turned to suicide as a way out of their stressful situation (e.g., Stengel, 1964; Roberts & Hooper, 1969). It is probably reasonable to assume that such people would score high on a test of anxiety.

The difficulty of measuring the personality of the person who commits suicide can be overcome by testing a large sample and then comparing the scores of those who subsequently commit suicide with the norms. A study along these lines has been published by Paffenbarger and Asnes (1966) using graduates of the University of Pennsylvania. All students were given an anxiety questionnaire over a 10-year period and 50 subsequently committed suicide. These were matched with a control group and it was found that the suicide group had been significantly more anxious as students. A similar study has been published by Bunney and Fawcett (1965). They first determined the urinary 17-hydroxycorticosteroid (17-OHCS) level of 36 patients in a mental hospital. Subsequently, three of these patients committed suicide, and inspection of the record showed that these three had had high urinary 17-OHCS. High urinary 17-OHCS is generally regarded as a sign of high anxiety, so that this result indicates that people who commit suicide tend to be high on anxiety.

Another approach to the suicidal personality is to measure by questionnaire the personality structure of those who attempt suicide but fail. One such study was made by Philip (1970) in Edinburgh, Scotland, and the result showed that the attempted suicides score highly on the anxiety scale of Cattell's 16 PF test. The only study of this type using the neuroticism scale of one of Eysenck's questionnaires (the Maudsley Personality Inventory) appears to be that of Colson (1972) on a sample of students at the University of Illinois who had attempted or seriously considered suicide. He found that their neuroticism scores were considerably above the mean for American students.

In addition to the relationship with anxiety, the questionnaire studies of attempted suicides showed that they were somewhat more introverted than the normal population. This leads us to the prediction that a high national suicide rate should be a function of a high national level of anxiety and also have a smaller correlation with introversion. As noted above, the results indicated a relation with extroversion rather than introversion.

H. CAFFEINE CONSUMPTION

Caffeine is a drug that has a stimulating effect on the nervous system (e.g., Gooch, 1963). This leads to the expectation that caffeine would be taken in larger quantities by people who are low on anxiety. The reason for this is that stimulants activate the sympathetic nervous system. People who score highly on anxiety tend to have a sympathetic nervous system that is easily activated and, hence, require less stimulation to obtain sympathetic activation. They should, therefore, tend to take less caffeine. Direct evidence showing that caffeine consumption is negatively associated with neuroticism has been reported (Lynn, 1973). In this study no relationship was found between caffeine consumption and extroversion. We are therefore led to the prediction that national per capita consumption of caffeine should be a negative function of national levels of anxiety, but be unrelated to national levels of extroversion.

I. ALCOHOLISM

Alcohol is a drug which has broadly the opposite properties of caffeine. Where caffeine stimulates the sympathetic nervous system, alcohol sedates it. Hence, while individuals who are low on anxiety apparently tend to take larger quantities of caffeine, those high on anxiety would be expected to take larger quantities of alcohol.

The effect of alcohol on sedating the sympathetic nervous system and reducing the emotions of anxiety and fear are well established. At the physiological level it is known that alcohol has depressant effects on the nervous system, dampening the system as a whole and the sympathetic system in particular (e.g., Block, 1962; Rosen & Gregory, 1965). At the psychological level the best known classical experiments are probably those of Masserman and his colleagues on cats (Masserman & Yum, 1946). They subjected cats to frightening stresses and found that they developed a taste for alcohol and that the alcohol reduced the cats' phobias. In the case of humans there is a good deal of evidence that people who suffer from excessive anxiety are prone to alleviate their condition by consuming alcohol. For instance, Vallance (1965) has reported a study of 65 male, alcoholic patients admitted to Glasgow General Hospital in which he found that a substantial proportion had a history of neurotic symptoms and took alcohol as a means of relief. Other studies finding a high level of anxiety in alcoholics have been reported by Rosenberg (1969) in Sydney, Australia, Hoy (1969) in Great Britain, and Golightly and Reinehr (1969) in the United States. Numerous other studies are listed by Cox (1979). In addition there is some tendency for alcoholics to be extroverted (MacAndrew, 1980). Thus, it appears that alcoholism is largely a function of anxiety with a small correlation with extroversion and this leads us to the prediction that among nations the prevalence of alcoholism will have similar correlates.

J. Calorie Intake

There are theoretical reasons for regarding calorie intake as a negative function of anxiety. These lie in the reciprocally inhibiting relationship between the parasympathetic nervous system, which is involved in the ingestion of food, and the sympathetic system, which mediates fear and anxiety. If one system is active it tends to suppress the other (Morgan, 1965). An early demonstration of this reciprocally inhibiting relationship between fear and eating was given in the studies carried out in John Watson's laboratory on the counterconditioning of infants' phobias by the use of sweets (Jones, 1924). Experimental evidence demonstrating the inverse relation between calorie intake and anxiety has been published by Schachter, Goldman, and Gordon (1968). They stressed subjects in an experimental situation and obtained a reduction in eating. Questionnaire evidence that in normal populations obesity is associated with below-average anxiety scores has been found by Silverstone (1968) and Kalucy and Crisp (1974). On the other hand, anorectics are characterized by high anxiety (Hsu & Crisp, 1980).

There is corroboratory evidence from a variety of other sources. For instance, damage to the frontal lobes has the effect both of reducing anxiety and nervous tension and of increasing the appetite (e.g., Hofling, 1963). Conversely, stimulant drugs increase anxiety and nervous tension and reduce appetite. Although it is sometimes maintained that anxiety can motivate eating, a large-scale study of normal eaters and overeaters among 1000 children carried out by Brandon (1968) in Newcastle, England, showed that the emotionally disturbed had poor appetites rather than large ones and also had lower body weights; there was no evidence of emotional disturbance among voracious overeaters.

There appears to be no evidence for a relationship between calorie intake and extroversion. We are therefore led to the prediction that there should be an inverse relation between national levels of calorie intake and of anxiety.

K. Chronic Psychosis

There are several sources of evidence to indicate that the level of anxiety tends to be low among chronic psychotics. Many chronic psychotics are cases of simple schizophrenia and Bleuler's classical description of these patients as emotionally blunted or unreactive continues to stand in psychiatric descriptions of the condition. For instance, Hofling (1963) writes of "pervasive apathy" as the commonest symptom of these patients. This lack of emotional reactivity is suggestive of a low level of anxiety. More objective studies of a low level of anxiety in chronic psychotics comes from questionnaire data. It is important here to distinguish the questionnaire results of chronic psychotics from those of other kinds of psychotic patients. Reports on chronic patients as a distinct category are rare, but at least two have been published. The first is by Al-Issa (1964) and reports the mean scores of 34 chronic psychotics with a mean stay in hospital of 14.2 years; these patients had a mean neuroticism score at approximately one-third of a standard deviation below the mean of the normal population. A similar result has been reported in the United States by Farley (1970). He tested 20 chronic psychotics who had been in hospital for an average of 14.9 years. The test used was the Maudsley Personality Inventory, and the psychotics obtained a mean neuroticism score approximately one-half of a standard deviation below the mean of the normal population. These results are corroborated by the work of Cattell (1957). In Cattell's personality system the psychoticism factor (UIT 25) is negatively correlated with the anxiety factors O (Guilt) and Q_4 (Ergic Tension).

In addition to these questionnaire results, there is an extensive physiological literature indicating that typically there is a low level of sympathetic reactivity in chronic psychotics. The best-known studies in English are probably those of Gellhorn (1957) and Nelson and Gellhorn (1957) showing that the majority of chronic psychotics show little sympathetic and central nervous reactivity to stimulation, for example, a poor generation of heat following exposure to cold, low psychogalvanic reactions, and reduced desynchronization of the EEG alpha rhythm.

The same conclusion has been reached in a considerable Russian literature. This originates from Pavlov's observations of the apathy of many chronic psychotics and his theory that protective inhibition has spread from the cerebral cortex to the subcortical centers and reduced the reactivity of the nervous system. Russian experimental studies of sympathetic reactivity have confirmed that it is low in chronic psychotic patients. The Russian work is reviewed in some detail in Lynn (1971).

Neither of the questionnaire studies of chronic psychotics (Al-Issa, 1964; Farley, 1970) shows any significant deviation from normality on extroversion. We are therefore led to the prediction that national prevalence rates of chronic psychosis should be a function of a low national level of anxiety and independent of national levels of extroversion.

L. MURDER

Singh (1980) has demonstrated high anxiety and high impulsiveness in a sample of 160 murders in India. Both Warburton (1965) and Iwawaki *et al.* (1964) had murderers in their groups of criminals showing high anxiety and extroversion levels. Although the evidence may be a little weak, it will probably seem reasonable to regard murder as a special case of crime and, hence, to predict that national rates of murder will follow those of crime and be related to national levels of both extroversion and anxiety.

In addition to these studies relating the 12 demographic phenomena to anxiety and extroversion, it would also be expected that pairs of the demographic variables would be correlated among individuals in approximately the same manner as they are correlated among nations. There are a few reports which confirm that this is the case. For example, alcoholism and suicide were found to be associated in a London sample of alcoholics, whose tendency to commit suicide was 80 times greater than the general population (Kessell & Grossman, 1961). Similarly, in our international data, national prevalence rates of alcoholism and suicide correlate $+.42$ (see Table II). Another pair of correlated variables among individuals consists of caffeine consumption and coronary heart disease. In a sample of approximately 12,000 patients it was found that those who drank six or more cups of coffee a day had a 120% greater risk of infarction (Jick, Miettinen, Neff, Shapiro, Heinonen, & Slone, 1973). In our international data, caffeine consumption and the prevalence of coronary heart disease are correlated $+.56$.

The international data show a positive association between national rates of suicide and murder ($r = +.14$; see Table II) and there are a number of studies showing a similar association among individuals. Thus, three American studies found that among samples of suicides a significant proportion had previously committed murder [5, 4, and .8%, respectively, in the studies of Cavan (1927), Dorpat (1966), and Schmid (1933). All these percentages are, of course, very much greater than the prevalence rate of suicide in the American population.]. Similarly, murderers have a relatively high propensity to commit suicide. An English study found that over the period 1900–1939 no less than 30% of murderers committed suicide, while in the United States percentages of murderers committing suicide range from 2 to 9 in four studies (Morris & Blom-Cooper, 1967; Durret & Stromquist, 1925; Dublin & Bunzel, 1933; Wolfgang, 1958; Guttmacher, 1960). Certainly in both countries the chances of a murderer dying by suicide are very much higher than his chances of dying from execution.

Finally, studies of accident-prone individuals have found that as a group they have a tendency to alcoholism and crime (Shaw & Sichel, 1971). Once more this is consistent with our international data where there are correlations between accidents and alcoholism of $+.64$ and between accidents and crime of $+.57$ (see Table II).

These few citations are not presented as a full review of the studies showing relationships at the individual level between the phenomena with which we are concerned as aggregates at the national level. The studies cited are given only as examples to indicate the consistency which can be found between the individual and national levels of analysis. No doubt a thorough survey of the literature would reveal many more studies of this kind. This concludes our attempt to justify the interpretation of the two factors found among national demographic phenomena in terms of anxiety and extroversion, and we turn now to the question of scoring the nations on these two personality dimensions.

IV. Scoring Nations for Anxiety and Extroversion

It will no doubt have been noted that the procedure adopted in the factorial analysis of demographic phenomena follows conventional psychometric techniques applied to individuals. In the analysis the nations are treated as subjects and the demographic data as scores on a battery of tests. Thereafter we analyze the data by intercorrelation and factor analysis as in orthodox psychometrics. This allows us to score the "subjects" on the "tests," that is to say, to calculate scores for the nations on anxiety and extroversion.

To make these calculations we have taken the factor scores obtained by the nations on the two factors. The factor scores were derived from the first two eigenvectors. On the basis of these factor scores the position of each nation can now be plotted on the two dimensions. These plots are shown in Fig. 3. The results indicate that the most extroverted nation is the United States, while the most introverted is Japan. The most anxious nation is Austria; the least anxious Ireland. The values of the factor scores of the nations are given in Table V.

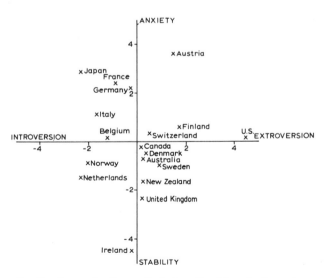

Fig. 3.   Scores of nations on the factors of anxiety and extroversion.

TABLE V
FACTOR SCORES OF THE NATIONS ON THE FIRST TWO COMPONENTS

Nation	Factor 1 (anxiety)[a]	Factor 2 (extroversion)
Australia	−.75	.36
Austria	3.73	1.62
Belgium	.15	−1.29
Canada	−.29	.15
Denmark	−.55	.41
Finland	.61	1.73
France	2.37	−.94
Germany	2.11	−.19
Ireland	−4.58	−.17
Italy	1.05	−1.61
Japan	2.95	−2.37
Netherlands	−1.52	−2.30
New Zealand	−1.61	.29
Norway	−.86	−2.03
Sweden	−.86	.99
Switzerland	.28	.47
United Kingdom	−2.41	.30
United States	.18	4.56

[a] Signs on the anxiety factor are reversed to make high positive scores represent high levels of anxiety.

V. Criticisms of the Theory

In this section we consider criticisms of the use of demographic data for the measurement of national differences in anxiety and extroversion. There are three principal kinds of objection. The first proposes that national differences in the prevalence rates of suicide, alcoholism, accidents, and the other demographic phenomena may be due simply to local cultural and social factors specific to each nation. Thus, the suicide rates in Ireland and Italy may be determined by the strength of Roman Catholicism, the tendency of coroners to return accurate verdicts, and so forth. Criticism along these lines has been advanced by Maher (1975) who concentrates particularly on rates of chronic psychosis.[1] He argues that hospitalization rates in any country may reflect substantially the availability of hospital beds—a resource likely to be influenced by variables such as national affluence and attitudes towards health care, and not only by the actual rates of illness. In countries with a high ratio of beds per unit of the population, we might

[1] The presentation of Maher's criticism beginning here and extending to the subsequent paragraph has been written by the Editor with Professor Lynn's consent.

expect a higher rate of reported hospitalization than in countries with low bed/ population ratios. In the latter the psychotic patient may never see a physician and, thus, never be diagnosed nor assigned to in-patient status and, in turn, never appear in the national statistics. Thus, before we may conclude anything about the true rates of an illness in a given country we must control statistically for the bed/population ratio. A proper datum, Maher implies, would consist of a valid count of psychotic patients regardless of their in-patient, out-patient, or nonpatient status.

A possible rebuttal to Maher's criticism is to suggest that the bed/population ratio does directly reflect the rate of illness in any country (i.e., that there are no significant differences between the countries studied by Lynn in terms of their devotion of resources to the care of the sick) and, hence, may be used as a valid measure of the true illness rate in a country. This rebuttal implies that the actual differences in bed/population observed by Maher in Lynn's sample of countries reflected substantial differences in the overall rates of sickness in these countries. A resolution of the problem clearly requires data free from the possibility of bed/population ratio confounds.[2]

Turning to Maher's more general point to the effect that the national variations in the demographic phenomena merely reflect unique social and cultural conditions of one kind or another, the answer is that this criticism does not deal with the intercorrelations between the variables and the existence of the two factors. It may be noted here that the factors account for substantial proportions of the variance, namely 33.6 and 23.7%, respectively, for the two factors, which may be compared with around 10–15% of the variance typically accounted for by the first two factors in questionnaire studies. There is, therefore, considerable common variance to be explained. If the measures were simply functions of local cultural and social conditions, there would be no intercorrelations among them and no factors. The logic here seems quite straightforward and is the same as Spearman advanced at the beginning of the century when he argued that the presence of intercorrelations among a number of cognitive tests indicates the existence of a factor of general intelligence. Of course, each individual intelligence test result also has other determinants, for example, vocabulary tests are affected by how much a child reads and mechanical aptitude tests by a child's interest in machines. Similarly, in the national demographic measures there are no doubt specific conditions which affect the prevalence rates of the various phenomena in different countries. However, these specifics are of little general interest and the significant fact lies in their intercorrelations which indicate the presence of underlying factors. This is the essential point of both the data and the theory and is the empirical discovery with which the critic has to deal.

---

[2]Such data are provided by the demonstration that Irish immigrants in Britain have rates of psychosis approximately the same as those in Ireland (Cochrane & Stopes-Row, 1979).

A second possible criticism of the theory lies in proposing an alternative explanation of the factors. This is potentially a more damaging line of attack and one to which the theory could be vulnerable. Criticism on this front recognizes that there is a curious set of data which requires explanation, namely the intercorrelations and the two factors among this set of demographic phenomena. Our theory that the factors are anxiety and extroversion can be overturned by proposing some more convincing alternatives. One of the more obvious possibilities is per capita income, since more affluent populations are likely to consume more alcohol and have more accidents (because of greater car ownership), which could explain the positive correlation between these two variables. It is possible that one of the factors might be explained along these lines and a similar alternative found for the other factor. Because of the potential damage to the theory which could come from alternative explanations of the factors, the most obvious possibilities have been examined. These include the per capita income, the age structure of the population (e.g., with more old people there would be high rates of suicide and mental illness), and urbanization (associated with higher rates of suicide and lower calorie intake). We have discussed these and other possibilities in some detail in *Personality and National Character*. Here it was shown that none of these social variables has any significant association with the anxiety factor and they cannot, therefore, explain it. On the other hand, the second factor which we have identified as extroversion has quite a strong association with national per capita income. Thus, for the year 1960, the correlation between national levels of extroversion and per capita income is $+.66$ (Lynn & Hampson, 1977). This raises the question of whether the factor could not simply be interpreted as per capita income and whether introduction of the concept of extroversion may not be superfluous.

It is considered that this alternative explanation of the second factor is not a feasible one. To interpret the factor we have to examine the variables which have high loadings on it. The highest loading variables are national rates of crime, murder, illegitimacy, divorce, and cigarette consumption. Now it can hardly be supposed that the possession of greater incomes as such motivates people to higher response rates on these five variables. If you, the reader, have more money in your pocket this surely does not directly increase your propensity to commit crimes. If this were true we should expect that the prevalence rates for them would be higher among the more affluent social classes within countries, whereas in general the contrary is the case. Thus, the explanation for the association of this factor with per capita income would seem to lie in some more indirect mechanism. The most probable line of explanation would seem to be that increasing affluence at a national level tends to shift the population towards extroversion and this, in turn, raises the prevalence rates of the phenomena of crime, divorce, illegitimacy, and so forth that we find loaded on the factor.

A third possible line of criticism is that the theory is at present rather weak and requires further substantiation if it is to be taken seriously. It would be difficult not to concede that there is some substance to a criticism along these lines. We have, therefore, attempted to strengthen the theory by an examination of two predictions from it, and it is to these that we now turn.

VI. Effects of World War II on National Levels of Anxiety and Extroversion

In this section data are presented for the two factors for a number of years over the period 1935–1970. The interest in extending the measurement of national levels of anxiety and extroversion to a number of years over a period of several decades is threefold. First, it makes it possible to examine whether the factor structure of the demographic and epidemiological variables, found for the year 1960, holds for other years. If this proves to be the case, we can proceed to a second problem, which is to analyze trends in the national levels of anxiety and extroversion over the period. And third, in making this analysis we can test a prediction concerning the effects of World War II on national levels of anxiety.

War is a stress which should raise the level of anxiety, particularly in nations suffering military defeat and occupation. These nations ought to show increases in their levels of anxiety in World War II and for some time afterward, followed by a decline to prewar levels. This rise and fall should not be found in the neutral nations. This is a stringent prediction and its verification would do much to strengthen the theory.

The object of this study was to collect data for the 12 demographic and epidemiological variables at five yearly intervals over the period 1935–1970. Unfortunately, little of the data was collected during the Second World War and for several years afterward, so that there is a gap here in the series. It has, however, proved possible to collect the data for the years 1935, 1950, 1955, 1960, 1965, and 1970. Copies of the raw data can be obtained from the author or from the SSRC data bank at the University of Essex.

The data were first considered for each year independently. Principal components analyses and varimax rotations were carried out for each year and the factors were similar in all six years to the 1960 factors already shown in Table III. It can, therefore, be concluded that the factor structure is stable over this period.

In order to measure trends over time in the nations' levels of anxiety and extroversion, the following procedure has been adopted. Each nation at each year is treated as an independent subject and the demographic and epidemiological variables are treated as the subjects' scores on tests. Thus, there are 108 subjects in this treatment, consisting of the 18 nations by the six years. This set of data has been intercorrelated and factored by principal components analysis with unities inserted in the principal diagonal of the correlation matrix. The correlation matrix is shown in Table VI and the loadings of the variables on the first two factors are

TABLE VI
The Correlation Matrix[a]

Variable	1	2	3	4	5	6	7	8	9	10	11	12
1. Chronic psychosis	—											
2. Calorie intake	65	—										
3. Caffeine consumption	55	57	—									
4. Coronary heart disease	61	61	58	—								
5. Alcoholism	-38	-23	-42	-37	—							
6. Suicide	-40	-31	-21	-13	33	—						
7. Murder	-10	-06	-07	13	07	10	—					
8. Crime	-29	-29	-30	-06	07	33	67	—				
9. Divorce	01	05	13	24	22	15	53	12	—			
10. Cigarette consumption	21	27	26	27	05	-17	31	07	40	—		
11. Illegitimacy	-11	04	03	31	13	52	04	12	29	-10	—	
12. Accidents	-19	09	-01	-03	57	35	33	31	26	28	17	—

[a] From Lynn and Hampson (1977).

TABLE VII
PRINCIPAL COMPONENTS AND VARIMAX SOLUTIONS[a]

	Principal components solution		Varimax solution	
Variables	I	II	I	II
1. Chronic psychosis	83	13	82	−18
2. Calorie intake	75	30	81	00
3. Caffeine consumption	75	27	80	−02
4. Coronary heart disease	68	49	81	21
5. Alcoholism	−61	22	−49	42
6. Suicide	−58	28	−43	48
7. Murder	−25	69	02	74
8. Crime	−50	44	−30	59
9. Divorce	−06	73	21	70
10. Cigarette consumption	24	57	43	45
11. Illegitimacy	−15	42	01	44
12. Accidents	−35	61	−10	70
Variance	3.50	2.63	—	—
Percentage variance	29.21	21.94	28.23	22.92

[a] From Lynn and Hampson (1977).

shown in Table VII. These loadings are similar to those obtained on individual years and shown already for 1960 in Table III. The first factor is interpreted as anxiety and the second as extroversion. The two factors were rotated to orthogonal simple structure by varimax and the results are shown in Table VII. The varimax solution is fairly similar to the principal components analysis. The loadings obtained from the principal components analysis are used for the next step involving the calculation of nations' factor scores.

The nations' factor scores (component scores) were calculated for both factors for each year, and converted to t scores based on a mean of 50 and SD of 10 for the entire set of data. These t scores are given in Tables VIII, IX, and X.

We can now consider the possible effect of World War II on national levels of anxiety and examine the hypothesis suggested earlier to the effect that national levels of anxiety would be expected to rise in the nations experiencing the stress of military defeat and occupation and then fall to approximately their prewar level. It so happens that nine of the 18 nations suffered military defeat and occupation, while the remaining nine escaped this experience and can be regarded as a control group. The fluctuations of the levels of anxiety in the two sets of nations are shown in Figs. 4 and 5. It will be noted that in all nine nations experiencing military defeat and occupation there was a rise in anxiety from 1935 to 1950 and a fall from 1950 to 1960. Among the other nine there was no rise from 1935 to 1950 in six and small increases in the other three. The statistical significance of the difference between the defeated and the undefeated nations in their 1950 anxiety scores, adjusted for differences in 1935 levels, was tested by

TABLE VIII
NATIONAL ANXIETY SCORES[a]

Country	1935	1950	1955	1960	1965	1970
Australia	44.10	44.21	45.05	44.79	46.46	47.55
Austria	63.04	66.49	64.31	64.56	62.48	66.27
Belgium	49.80	51.19	52.33	50.29	51.04	51.69
Canada	50.71	48.17	47.38	47.82	47.90	50.77
Denmark	43.68	51.98	48.84	45.83	43.91	44.92
Finland	59.53	52.60	58.00	50.63	48.21	46.90
France	56.20	63.41	63.17	60.22	62.21	61.52
Germany	60.60	62.93	59.34	59.33	59.45	60.85
Ireland	30.47	27.00	24.99	26.29	27.02	31.43
Italy	59.93	62.10	59.43	56.75	55.74	57.05
Japan	69.78	73.93	72.00	67.85	63.26	61.69
Netherlands	48.14	49.09	47.23	44.55	42.88	44.46
New Zealand	40.35	37.39	40.26	40.39	39.75	44.36
Norway	46.55	50.33	46.49	46.72	46.35	45.02
Sweden	41.93	45.44	45.48	42.84	41.16	42.95
Switzerland	52.79	50.74	51.48	49.08	48.51	51.50
United Kingdom	36.99	37.76	37.13	37.32	38.48	40.28
United States	55.42	47.70	47.32	47.00	49.38	51.58

[a] From Lynn and Hampson (1977).

TABLE IX
NATIONAL EXTROVERSION SCORES[a]

Country	1935	1950	1955	1960	1965	1970
Australia	45.82	47.65	49.58	51.25	54.61	57.42
Austria	53.73	55.30	56.39	61.19	58.96	67.02
Belgium	40.21	40.39	42.07	44.14	47.53	51.74
Canada	42.83	46.94	48.58	50.09	54.12	60.75
Denmark	44.28	50.24	50.16	52.19	55.60	60.23
Finland	62.16	54.76	55.62	58.32	59.48	61.42
France	43.99	47.02	45.08	48.53	50.03	53.17
Germany	48.65	47.67	48.54	51.06	56.01	58.59
Ireland	40.60	46.21	47.12	45.39	47.34	51.35
Italy	39.81	38.32	39.33	42.09	43.98	44.65
Japan	34.75	38.18	39.41	39.26	38.55	40.48
Netherlands	32.10	34.25	34.42	36.94	40.60	43.10
New Zealand	45.58	47.19	45.97	49.63	53.09	59.16
Norway	35.71	34.83	38.17	38.75	41.68	45.11
Sweden	44.62	44.14	48.20	53.40	56.64	62.35
Switzerland	54.22	51.84	51.99	53.56	55.09	56.12
United Kingdom	48.55	45.69	47.96	49.37	51.85	54.28
United States	78.38	75.16	72.20	73.72	78.20	88.20

[a] From Lynn and Hampson (1977).

TABLE X

MEAN SCORES FOR THE 18 NATIONS ON ANXIETY AND EXTROVERSION, 1935–1970[a]

Year	Anxiety		Extroversion	
	Mean	SD	Mean	SD
1935	50.56	9.81	46.44	10.52
1950	51.25	11.11	46.99	9.05
1955	50.57	10.73	47.82	8.22
1960	49.01	9.77	49.94	8.57
1965	48.57	9.23	52.41	8.78
1970	50.04	8.59	56.40	10.51
	50.00	10.00	50.00	10.00

[a] From Lynn and Hampson (1977).

analysis of covariance. The F ratio between the means of the two groups for 1950 anxiety scores was 21.89 and is statistically significant at $p < .01$.

It seems clear that the results support the theory that the first factor should be identified as anxiety. The rise and fall occurred in all nine of the defeated nations. In contrast, of the nine nations which escaped military defeat and occupation, six show a fall in anxiety. Australia and the United Kingdom show marginal increases and Sweden shows a larger increase. Thus, the only seriously

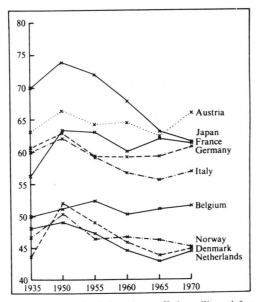

FIG. 4.   Rise and fall of anxiety levels in nations suffering military defeat in World War II.

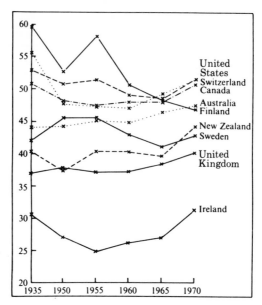

FIG. 5.   Anxiety levels in nations escaping military defeat in World War II.

discrepant case is Sweden. With this exception the magnitude of the increase in anxiety from 1935 to 1950 discriminates perfectly between the defeated and the undefeated nations, since the rises in Australia and the United Kingdom are smaller than in any of the nine defeated nations. The discrimination is probably sufficiently clear to implicate the wartime experiences or some factor associated with them as the cause of the differential rises in anxiety over the period. There is one psychological trait which is generally agreed to rise with stress, and that is anxiety. Hence, the increase in this trait in the defeated nations goes some way toward validating our original thesis that anxiety is the common factor underlying the covariation of this set of epidemiological and demographic phenomena.

It may be worth noting another point concerning the long-term trend in the level of anxiety over time in the advanced Western nations. The overall picture is that the level is fairly steady over the 35-year period. In 10 of the nations the level of anxiety was higher in 1970 than in 1935, while in the remaining eight it was lower. It appears that, apart from powerful stresses like military defeat and occupation, levels of anxiety in the advanced Western nations have been more or less constant. This result tells against the theory sometimes proposed to the effect that the populations of the advanced nations are becoming more neurotic as a result of the increasing complexity, stress and strain, and so forth of modern life.

The secular trend of the level of extroversion over the period is quite different. Here there has been a steady rise in extroversion, so that the level in 1970 is higher than in 1935 in all the nations except Finland, and even here there has been a steady increase from 1950 to 1970. The general rise in extroversion levels over the 35-year period has been associated with increasing affluence, and this suggests a closer look at the relationship between national levels of extroversion and per capita income. This relationship has been examined between nations in each of the six years and also over time. The correlations are given in Table XI. Here it can be seen that in five of the six years national per capita income is significantly correlated with extroversion; it is only in 1935 that the correlation does not reach statistical significance. The final correlation of $+.60$ is derived from treating each nation in each year as an independent subject and expresses the magnitude of the association between national levels of extroversion and per capita income over the 35-year period. These correlations indicate that a population's level of extroversion is substantially associated with its per capita income both between nations at various points in time and within nations over time. The consistency of the association between extroversion and affluence suggests that the two are causally related. The principal demographic indices of extroversion (crime, divorce, illegitimacy, and cigarette consumption) are evidently all tapping a socialization dimension. This is a component of extroversion, as H. J. Eysenck has shown in numerous publications (e.g., Eysenck, 1964, 1965, 1972). It would appear that increasing affluence in the advanced Western nations has tended to undermine the strength of socialization to the canons of traditional morality and that this is the explanation for our syndrome appearing as a factor and its correlation with per capita income. Why this would be the case is not altogether clear.

TABLE XI

PRODUCT MOMENT CORRELATIONS BETWEEN NATIONAL INCOME, ANXIETY, AND EXTROVERSION[a,b]

Year	Anxiety	Extroversion
1935	-40	36
1950	-44	65
1955	-30	66
1960	-25	66
1965	-17	73
1970	02	65
All years	-14	60

[a] Correlations above .59 are statistically significant at $p < .01$.

[b] From Lynn and Hampson (1977).

VII. Questionnaire Data on National Differences in Anxiety and Extroversion

The evidence presented so far is to the effect that there are two factors among national demographic phenomena for which an interpretation as anxiety and extroversion has been proposed. And, in addition, it has been shown that the anxiety factor rose differentially in the nations suffering defeat in World War II as compared with those which escaped defeat. The second finding adds some predictive validity to the thesis. Nevertheless, the reader may well feel that the theory has about it something of the air of a building from which the cornerstone is missing. It is clear that the crucial data for the establishment of the theory must lie in a direct demonstration that the proposed national differences in anxiety and extroversion can be confirmed by questionnaire studies from samples of the populations of the nations. What is required is the administration of anxiety and extroversion questionnaires to comparable samples of the populations of all the nations, and the demonstration that the differences in the mean anxiety and extroversion levels are similar to those derived from the demographic data. The theory would surely stand or fall on the results of an investigation of this type.

Unfortunately, there are formidable problems in obtaining questionnaire results from representative samples of the populations of a large number of nations and the task has never been completely satisfactorily accomplished. Nevertheless, work by Hofstede (1976) in Belgium has gone some way toward providing the necessary data. Hofstede has collected self-reported anxiety data from approximately 70,000 subjects employed in a multinational organization in 40 different nations. The data consist of answers to the question, "How often do you feel nervous or tense at work?" scored on a five-point scale (1 = always, 5 = never). It has to be admitted that, as a one-question questionnaire, the instrument is a bit on the short side. Nevertheless, this is to some extent compensated by its good face validity, its high reliability, and the large numbers of subjects from which the mean scores were derived. The data were collected for 32 of the nations in two separate surveys in 1967–1969 and 1971–1973 and for these it was possible to estimate the test's test–retest reliability. The rank correlation was +.94, indicating a highly reliable instrument.

Before considering what conclusions can be drawn from these data, it is worth considering their methodological strengths and weaknesses where several points deserve some discussion. To take the weaknesses first, the most obvious is no doubt the shortness of the questionnaire. This gives rise to two particular difficulties which may have involved a reduction in the validity of the data. In the first place, a single question concerned with nervousness and tension at work only taps one manifestation of anxiety. A person of a generally anxious disposition may be nervous and tense in his relations with his family, anxious about money, and so forth, and yet be relatively unanxious at work because of fortunate circumstances in his employment. Normally, where a construct like anxiety is measured by a questionnaire consisting of some 12–20 questions, any particular question would correlate somewhere between .2 and .6 with the anxiety factor. Thus, any single question is only a coarse measure of the construct. It should, however, be noted that this would be a more serious weakness in the assessment of anxiety in an individual than in the measurement of a mean for a population, as Hofstede is using it. The reason for this is that the various chance circumstances which tend to generate anxiety in different areas of life in different individuals would tend to cancel each other out in a population. Hence, unless there is any consistent tendency in certain countries for work to be more anxiety provoking than in others, a single question concerned with anxiety at work should give reasonably good validity for national anxiety levels. It is suggested, therefore, that criticism on these grounds is less damaging than might appear at first sight.

A second criticism, which may be more serious, concerns the distortion which could arise in the translation of a single question. Just how the subject answers the question will depend to some extent on the nuance of the words used to convey "nervous" and "tense" in the various languages into which the question was translated. Where there is a full questionnaire with further questions tapping different facets of anxiety these translation problems are less serious, since any slight over emphasis or underemphasis in any particular question is likely to be either compensated for or swamped by other questions.

The study involved the translation of the questionnaire into 17 languages and it seems likely that with this number of translations at least one or two distortions would have arisen. It is considered that such translation errors have probably occurred in the case of the mean for Belgium, which appears as an exceptionally high anxiety nation in Hofstede's data. It is difficult to believe that anxiety levels in Belgium can be so much higher than in neighboring France and The Netherlands. In the assessment of national anxiety levels from demographic phenomena, Belgium scores very similarly to her Western European neighbors and certainly not in a class by herself. It is, therefore, proposed that the mean for Belgium is erroneous and that the true reading is that indicated by the demographic data to the effect that the anxiety level in Belgium is about halfway between that in France and The Netherlands, as might be expected.

In spite of these reservations about Hofstede's data, there are compensating strengths which make them worth taking seriously. First, there is the sheer size of the study. With results for over 70,000 subjects from 40 nations, these are by far the largest questionnaire data available. In this respect the study certainly compares favorably with, for example, Spielberger and Diaz-Guerrero's (1976) results on anxiety in Greece which is based on 17 subjects, which may be considered somewhat on the small size as a sample of the Greek nation. Second, the collection of results on two separate occasions (1967–1969 and 1971–1973) for 32 nations and the high correlation between the two testings (.94) clearly indi-

cate high reliability. However, this does not overcome the possibility of translation distortions, since any distortion in meaning would be reproduced on the
second testing. A third strength of the study lies in the comparability of the
samples across the countries. As mentioned above, the samples were all employees of a multinational corporation and were all white-collar managerial or
technical staff. This provides a valuable control for socioeconomic and occupational status in making national comparisons. On the other hand, the mix of the
sexes was not controlled. This could be a point of weakness since females
generally score more anxious than males and, thus, a high proportion of females
in some countries would probably give a spurious bias towards high anxiety in
the mean. This is another possible source of error in the anomalous scores for
Belgium to which reference has been made previously.

Having attempted to discuss the strengths and weaknesses of Hofstede's data,
we now turn to the relation between his questionnaire measures of anxiety and
our own demographic measures.

To obtain a single reading for national anxiety scores from Hofstede's data, the
two scores (for 1967–1969 and 1971–1973) have been averaged. The resulting
figures are shown in Table XII. Also shown are our own anxiety scores for the
nations for the year 1970 calculated independently from demographic data and
reported in Lynn and Hampson (1977). The product moment correlation between
the two sets of results is $-.57$, statistically significant at the 5% level (the
correlation is negative because in the Hofstede data low scores represent high
anxiety levels, whereas in our own data high scores represent high anxiety
levels).

Considering the imperfections in the data, and in particular the difficulty of
capturing exactly equivalent meanings in the translation of a questionnaire into a
number of different languages, the magnitude of the correlation would appear to
give satisfactory corroboration for the thesis that our demographic factor has
been correctly identified as the level of anxiety present in the populations of
different nations.

In addition to Hofstede's results, there is one other source of cross-cultural
questionnaire data which can be used to test the validity of the demographic
theory. This source is derived from the data on Eysenck's questionnaires of
neuroticism and extroversion which have been administered to samples in many
countries in different parts of the world. In some cases the sampling is less
representative than would have been desired, but even when these have been
discarded there remain a considerable number of usable studies.

The Eysenck questionnaires have appeared in several different editions and
have been standardized in different countries on samples of the general population and also on students. This necessitates conversion to a single scale on which
the means of different countries can be placed. A methodology for this has been
devised and the literature as a whole reviewed in Lynn (1981). There are results

TABLE XII
ANXIETY SCORES

Nations	Hofstede anxiety scores[a]	Lynn anxiety scores[b]
Australia	3.31	47.55
Austria	3.22	66.27
Belgium	2.74	51.69
Canada	3.21	50.77
Denmark	3.68	44.92
Finland	3.22	46.90
France	3.02	61.52
Germany	3.14	60.85
Ireland	3.32	31.43
Italy	2.99	57.05
Japan	2.55	61.69
Netherlands	3.23	44.46
New Zealand	3.34	44.36
Norway	3.48	45.02
Sweden	3.50	42.95
Switzerland	3.08	51.50
United Kingdom	3.33	40.28
United States	3.31	51.58

[a] From data of Hofstede (1976). Low scores indicate high anxiety.

[b] From data of Lynn and Hampson (1977). High scores indicate high anxiety.

for 9 of the 18 advanced Western nations and these are given in Table XIII. The national scores for neuroticism derived from the Eysenck questionnaire correlate $+.70$ ($p < .01$) with the demographic scores for anxiety for the year 1970. In the case of extroversion, the questionnaire and the demographic measures are correlated $+.84$ ($p < .01$). Both results clearly give reasonably good validation for our interpretation of the two demographic factors as anxiety and extroversion.

VIII. Some Possible Causes of National Differences in Personality

In this section we consider some of the possible causes of national differences in anxiety and extroversion. This problem has been touched on in passing in previous sections, particularly in Section VI where it was shown that military defeat and occupation in World War II apparently acted as a stress and raised anxiety levels in the affected populations. It seems a plausible hypothesis that

TABLE XIII

MEAN SCORE FOR NINE ADVANCED WESTERN NATIONS ON EYSENCK'S CONSTRUCT OF NEUROTICISM
AND EXTROVERSION BASED ON QUESTIONNAIRE DATA[a]

Country	Neuroticism	Extroversion	National income per capita (1970)
Australia	50.56	51.53	2644
Canada	50.73	53.81	3214
France	54.11	48.08	2550
Germany	51.84	49.10	2711
Italy	50.46	50.48	1591
Japan	53.85	46.56	1664
Sweden	41.71	50.81	3736
United Kingdom	50.00	50.00	1991
United States	50.13	56.16	4274

[a] From Lynn (1981).

other stresses might also be present and responsible for some of the national differences in anxiety. In *Personality and National Character* the possible role of climatic stresses was discussed. It was noted that anxiety levels were higher in nations exposed to greater heat in the summer, for example, Japan and Italy as compared with Great Britain and Ireland, and suggested that heat might be acting as a stress such as would elevate anxiety levels in a number of the more anxious populations. Other more subtle climatic variables which had significant associations with national anxiety levels and which might act as stresses include solar radiation, storm frequency, and exposure to electromagnetic long waves. For all these climatic variables there is some evidence at the individual level for a stimulating effect on anxiety. The subject has been reviewed in detail and will not be covered again here (see Lynn, 1971).

Hitherto we have been concerned only with national differences in anxiety and extroversion among the 18 advanced Western nations. These, of course, are fairly homogeneous populations and in trying to identify possible causes of national differences in the two personality traits it would seem useful to attempt to get data for a larger and more heterogeneous group of nations. Such more extensive data as are available are presented in this section.

We consider first a hypothesis proposed by Cattell and Scheier (1961) to account for some national differences in anxiety measured on samples of students by the 16PF. The samples came from the following countries, which obtained anxiety means in descending order from high to low: Poland, India, France, Italy, Great Britain, and the United States. This early finding that national anxiety levels are higher in France and Italy than in Great Britain and the United States is consistent with a number of other results reviewed earlier in this article.

As an explanation for these national differences, the authors suggested that a low standard of living and lack of political freedom might be the relevant factors tending to generate relatively high anxiety levels in countries like Poland, India, France, and Italy as contrasted with Great Britain and the United States. Both a low standard of living and politically authoritarian systems can be regarded as imposing stresses on the populations and the explanation offered can consequently be regarded as an extension of the stress theory of anxiety. The thesis seems plausible and apparently fits the data. Subsequent results, however, have complicated the picture and shown that the relationship of national anxiety levels to the stresses of poverty and totalitarian political systems is not so straightforward as this initial study suggested.

The possibility that national differences in income might be a factor determining national anxiety levels was considered in our initial study (Lynn, 1971, p. 13). It was found that national anxiety levels were correlated $-.37$ with per capita incomes. The correlation is negative, as expected from the Cattell hypothesis. It is not statistically significant, but as this set of nations may be considered the universe of advanced Western nations and not a sample, considerations of statistical significance may be judged irrelevant. Thus far the evidence does appear to give some limited support to Cattell's hypothesis.

For a more extensive test of the thesis, we turn to the full set of data provided by Hofstede (1976) for 40 nations. The data have already been described in Section VII and are shown in Table XIV. The correlation between these anxiety means and national per capita income is $-.08$, indicating the total absence of any straightforward linear association between the two phenomena among this wide range of nations. However, Hofstede divides the sample into two groups of the less and more affluent. Among the less affluent the correlation between national per capita income and anxiety is $+.45$ (statistically significant at $p < .05$), that is, there are higher anxiety levels in more affluent nations in this group. On the other hand, among the 19 more affluent nations the correlation turns negative. Thus, considering the nations as a whole, there is a curvilinear relationship between affluence and anxiety such that anxiety is low in very poor nations such as India and Pakistan, increases to a peak among nations of intermediate national wealth (e.g., Greece, Portugal, Yugoslavia, and the South American republics), and then declines among the most affluent nations (e.g., the United States, Norway, Sweden, and Denmark).

It is evident that these results fail to give any support to the original hypothesis of Cattell and Scheier to the effect that poverty is a stress generating high anxiety. If anything, the data run in the opposite direction, since it is particularly among the poorer group of nations where poverty is experienced most acutely that the relationship would be expected to hold. Once countries reach moderate levels of affluence, such as those of Latin America, it might be expected that any stresses arising from poverty would cease or at any rate diminish, especially for

RICHARD LYNN

TABLE XIV
MEAN SCORES ON THE "STRESS" QUESTION, "HOW OFTEN DO YOU FEEL NERVOUS OR TENSE AT WORK?"[a]

Country	1967–1969[b]		1971–1973[c]		Mean of 1967–1969 and 1971–1973		
	Country mean score	Rank of 32 countries	Country mean score	Rank of 32 countries	Country score (a)	Rank of 40 countries	Reversed stress score[d]
Japan	2.64	1	2.45	1	2.55	1	145
Greece	2.74	3	2.52	2	2.63	2	137
Belgium	2.77	4	2.71	3	2.74	3	126
Argentina	2.69	2	2.81	6	2.75	4	125
Peru	2.85	5	2.78	5	2.82	5	118
Chile	2.88	—	n.s.	—	(2.84)	6	116
Colombia	2.86	6	2.84	7	2.85	7	115
Portugal	3.01	9	2.74	4	2.88	8	112
Yugoslavia	n.s.	—	2.92	—	2.92	9	108
Mexico	2.96	8	2.94	9	2.95	10	105
Venezuela	2.94	7	2.98	10	2.96	11.5	104
Taiwan	n.s.	—	2.92	—	(2.96)	11.5	104
Italy	3.03	—	n.s.	—	(2.99)	13	101
Spain	3.10	11	2.90	8	3.00	14	100
France	3.05	10	2.99	11	3.02	15	98
Switzerland	3.11	12.5	3.05	13.5	3.08	16	92
Brazil	3.11	12.5	3.06	15	3.09	17.5	91
Turkey	3.15	15	3.03	12	3.09	17.5	91
Israel	3.18	16	3.08	16.5	3.13	19	87
Germany	3.14	14	3.14	18.5	3.14	20	86
South Africa	3.29	20	3.05	13.5	3.17	21	83
Canada	3.26	19	3.16	20	3.21	22	79
Austria	3.30	21	3.14	18.5	3.22	24	78
Finland	3.36	24	3.08	16.5	3.22	24	78
Thailand	n.s.	—	3.18	—	(3.22)	24	78

(continued)

the middle class from which the Hofstede data were derived. Thus, on the basis of the poverty→stress→anxiety hypothesis, we might expect that the relation of poverty to national anxiety levels would be strongly positive among poor countries and then peter out among the affluent, advanced Western democracies. The Hofstede results are clearly contrary to this model. Even allowing for the various weaknesses in the data to which attention has been drawn, they must cast serious doubts on the hypothesis.

Particularly damaging to the poverty–stress model is the low level of anxiety in India, which comes thirty-sixth out of the 40 nations. Anxiety is also low in neighboring Pakistan. This result is clearly a difficult one for the poverty→

TABLE XIV—*Continued*

Country	1967-1969[b]		1971-1973[c]		Mean of 1967-1969 and 1971-1973		
	Country mean score	Rank of 32 countries	Country mean score	Rank of 32 countries	Country score (a)	Rank of 40 countries	Reversed stress score[d]
Netherlands	3.22	17	3.23	22	3.23	26	77
Philippines	3.25	18	3.26	24	3.26	27	74
Australia	3.37	25	3.24	23	3.31	28.5	69
United States	3.35	—	n.s.	—	(3.31)	28.5	69
Ireland	3.32	22.5	3.31	26	3.32	30	68
Great Britain	3.38	26	3.27	25	3.33	31	67
New Zealand	3.46	27	3.22	21	3.34	32.5	66
Hong Kong	3.32	22.5	3.36	27	3.34	32.5	66
Norway	3.57	29	3.39	28	3.48	34	52
Sweden	3.52	28	3.47	29	3.50	35	50
India	3.57	—	n.s.	—	(3.53)	36	47
Iran	3.63	30	3.59	30	3.61	37	39
Singapore	n.s.	—	3.59	—	(3.63)	38	37
Denmark	3.69	31	3.66	31	3.68	39	32
Pakistan	3.79	32	3.80	32	3.80	40	20
Mean of 32 countries surveyed twice	3.19		3.10				
Mean of 40 countries						3.15	85

[a] Scores were computed from seven occupations in each of 40 countries at two points in time. Total number of responses was 70,895.

[b] Total number of responses was 30,310.

[c] Total number of responses was 40,585.

[d] Scores were computed from the formula, $100 \times (4 - a)$.

stress→anxiety theory of national differences in anxiety and also for our earlier theory of climatic stress as a possible factor.

If we look inductively at the set of data provided by Hofstede, probably the most striking result is the high level of anxiety in the Latin American republics. All seven nations for which there are data (Argentina, Peru, Chile, Colombia, Mexico, Venezuela, and Brazil) obtain means in the top half of the distribution. The mean for the group is clearly higher than the relatively low means obtained by the 15 advanced Western democracies since there is virtually no overlap between the two distributions. If we omit the mean for Belgium as being unreliable for reasons discussed above, the difference between the two sets of nations is highly statistically significant ($t = 4.91$, $p < .001$). This result is perhaps not too surprising, since the Latin American republics are characterized by considerable political instability, high inflation, and general lawlessness of a kind which seems likely to generate high anxiety in the populations. It is also possible that high anxiety levels would play a causal role in generating political, social, and economic instability, giving rise to a positive feedback effect where high anxiety levels generate a variety of social tensions, which in turn serve to maintain or augment the anxiety level.

In addition to the Hofstede data, we can examine the results collated from the Eysenck questionnaires for a variety of countries beyond the advanced Western nations. The details of the compilation are given elsewhere (Lynn, 1981) and the results shown in Table XV. Also shown in this table are the per capita incomes for 1970, a median year for the collection of the questionnaire results. The correlation between the national means for neuroticism and per capita income is $-.31$, indicating a tendency for more affluent nations to have lower levels of neuroticism of the same order as that found among the advanced Western nations. The correlation is not statistically significant but may be read as offering some limited support for the thesis. On the other hand, the Eysenck questionnaires confirm the low level of anxiety found in India by Hofstede. In this connection it may be noted that subsequent work with Cattell's 16PF, as reported in Cattell and Child (1975), also indicates a low anxiety mean for India, contrary to the initial results of Cattell and Scheier (1961). The consistency of the results on India is impressive and undoubtedly poses difficulty for the poverty→stress thesis of national differences in anxiety.

Looking more inductively at the data from the Eysenck questionnaires, it is evident that the mean levels of neuroticism are generally low in the advanced Western democracies as compared with those elsewhere. Perhaps the most reasonable explanation is that life in the advanced Western democracies is relatively unstressful. They are politically stable with a high degree of consensus among the populations on political and economic fundamentals, and there are no violent revolutions or military coups. The economies are stable and free from the worst ravages of hyperinflation. There are means for nine of the advanced Western democracies and these cluster together within one-third of a standard deviation of the British mean. There is a clear contrast between this group of nations and the Islamic nations of the Near and Middle East. It will be seen that means of the Islamic nations all lie between one- and two-thirds of a standard deviation above the British mean, and, indeed, there is no overlap between the two groups of nations. The difference between the means of the two groups is clearly statistically significance ($t = 2.37$, $p < .05$).

It seems reasonable to explain the difference between the two sets of nations in terms of differences in stress. In contrast to the economic and political stability of the advanced Western nations, the Islamic nations have been embarking on a

TABLE XV

MEAN SCORE FOR 24 NATIONS ON EYSENCK'S CONSTRUCT OF NEUROTICISM AND EXTROVERSION
BASED ON QUESTIONNAIRE DATA[a]

Country	Neuroticism	Extroversion	National income per capita (1970)
Australia	50.56	51.53	2644
Canada	50.73	53.81	3214
Egypt	62.96	48.46	202
France	54.11	48.08	2550
Germany	51.84	49.10	2711
Ghana	53.07	42.29	238
Greece	54.47	52.50	1051
India	48.56	50.82	94
Iran	55.22	48.01	316
Italy	50.46	50.48	1591
Japan	53.85	46.56	1664
Jordan	56.27	57.11	260
Kuwait	60.81	54.25	3148
Lebanon	54.58	53.01	521
Nigeria	50.82	50.17	135
Poland	55.14	51.93	—
South Africa			
Black	55.05	51.63	728
White	52.22	51.66	—
Sweden	41.71	50.81	3736
Syria	57.74	49.50	258
Turkey	44.60	49.44	344
Uganda	57.19	44.72	127
United Kingdom	50.00	50.00	1991
United States	50.13	56.16	4274
Yugoslavia	49.21	47.63	—

[a] From Lynn (1981).

program of rapid economic development with inevitable disruption of the traditional way of life of the people. In addition, they were engaged in the 1960s and 1970s in a struggle with Israel over the Palestinian problem and the populations imbued with a form of militant Islamic fervor which may foster high levels of anxiety.

The stress theory of national differences in anxiety levels receives further support from a consideration of some of the other nations whose mean levels of neuroticism are given in Table XV. First, the high level of neuroticism in Uganda (57.19) is clearly in line with the theory, as are the elevated neuroticism means in Greece (54.47) and Ghana (53.07). A little surprising, perhaps, is the relatively low level of neuroticism in Nigeria (50.82) which saw some political instability in the civil war of the 1960s. Also consistent with the stress theory are the differences in levels of neuroticism between Negro and Caucasian populations in the United States and South Africa. It seems reasonable to infer that in both countries the Negroes are subject to a certain degree of stress by virtue of their underprivileged position, and in both countries they have higher neuroticism means than Caucasians.

The data from the Eysenck questionnaires also provide means on extroversion for a number of countries. Comparing these with the national scores on the extroversion factor derived from the demographic data, there are nine countries for which there are scores on both measures, namely Australia, Canada, France, Germany, Italy, Japan, Sweden, the United Kingdom, and the United States, and it will be noted that on both measures the United States scores the most extroverted and Japan the most introverted. The product moment correlation between the two scores is .84 ($p < .01$), indicating a high degree of consistency.

It is an interesting question why extroversion scores should be so high in the United States. This phenomenon was noted a number of years ago and the suggestion made that the explanation might lie in selective emigration of more extroverted individuals to the United States (Lynn & Gordon, 1962). It is known that extroverts are, in general, more susceptible to boredom than introverts and have greater enjoyment of novelty, excitement, and risk such as would seem to be involved in emigration to a new country. Thus, emigrants might be expected to come from the more extroverted members of a population. This would give rise to high extroverted means among the new populations of countries established by emigration and these high means would remain a characteristic of these populations, passed on down the generations by hereditary and environmental transmission. It is possible to test this hypothesis by examining extroversion means in several new nations whose populations are almost entirely made up of relatively recent emigrants (viz. Australia, Canada, and South African Whites, as well as the United States) and comparing these with the means of the nation states of northwest Europe, from which the emigrants largely came. Examination of these means given in Table XV shows that the two groups are differentiated with no overlap and the differences are clearly statistically significant although quite small ($t = 2.95$, $p < .05$). Thus, the emigration hypothesis receives some support as a factor determining national means for extroversion.

In our derivation of national extroversion scores for the 18 advanced Western nations based on demographic indices, we again found an exceptionally high mean for the United States. Since the United States is economically the most affluent of the countries, this suggested that perhaps high levels of affluence might shift populations toward extroversion. Further examination of the data seemed to support this hypothesis since there were significant positive associations between extroversion and affluence among the whole set of 18 nations. Thus, the correlation between extroversion and per capita income for 1970 was

+.65 (statistically significant at $p < .01$). Furthermore, over the period 1935–1970, all the 18 national populations were growing more extroverted, as measured by the demographic indices, and at the same time were also growing more affluent. The results of this analysis are shown in Fig. 6. This again seemed to suggest that as the advanced Western nations increased in economic prosperity so the extroversion levels of their populations rose.

It is now possible to examine this thesis further in light of the additional data on national levels of extroversion derived from the Eysenck questionnaires given in Table XV. The product moment correlation between these questionnaire means and per capita income in 1970 (also given in Table XV) is +.38. This correlation is not statistically significant for the 22 nations although it is in the expected direction, suggesting higher levels of extroversion in more affluent nations among the wider set of countries represented in the Eysenck questionnaire data. We do not have any suggestions to offer for the causes of this apparent association between affluence and extroversion.

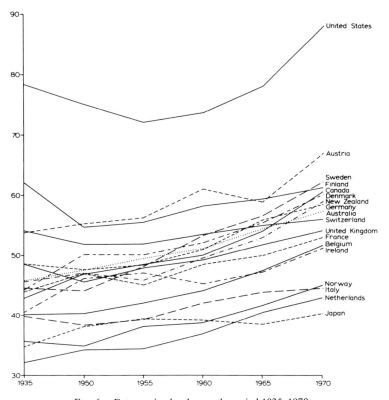

FIG. 6.   Extroversion levels over the period 1935–1970.

The possibility of genetic differences in introversion–extroversion between nations of different races has been suggested by H. J. Eysenck (1977). The starting point of the hypothesis lies in the finding that among Europeans introversion is associated with the AB blood group (Angst & Maurer-Groeli, 1974). Eysenck also notes that the introverted Japanese have a somewhat higher proportion of AB among their population than the British (approximately 9% of Japanese are AB compared with approximately 3% of British). The data are certainly suggestive and deserve further research on this association, both within countries such as Japan and between larger sets of nations.

Considering more generally the possibility of racial differences in extroversion, we can note relatively low means for extroversion in the Negro nations of Ghana (42.29), Uganda (44.72), and Nigeria (50.17). This tendency is confirmed by the lower level of extroversion among United States Negroes (52.56) compared with Caucasians (56.56), although in South Africa there is virtually no difference between Blacks and Whites. As far as Mongoloids are concerned, the only representative is Japan (46.56) where the low level of extroversion is consistent with the results of our earlier analyses on demographic data. Further results on other Mongoloid populations should make it possible to determine whether low extroversion is a general characteristic of Mongoloid peoples or whether it is a more limited feature of contemporary Japan.

IX. Summary

This article summarizes and discusses the author's theory that there are national differences in anxiety and extroversion among the populations of the advanced Western nations, and that these personality differences account for substantial proportions of the variance in a number of demographic phenomena, for example, prevalence rates of alcoholism, suicide, accidents, crime, murder, divorce, illegitimacy, cigarette consumption, chronic psychosis, coronary heart disease, calorie intake, and caffeine consumption.

The theory rests on three lines of evidence. First, factor analysis shows the existence of two strong factors among this set of phenomena, accounting for approximately 50% of the variance; and there is considerable evidence at the level of individuals to substantiate the interpretation of the two factors as anxiety and extroversion. Second, it is shown that the anxiety factor increased in nations suffering military defeat and occupation in World War II, thereby providing predictive validity for the interpretation of the factor. Third, the interpretation of the two factors is validated directly against questionnaire data derived from samples of national populations.

The article concludes with some speculations and discussion of the possible causes of national differences in anxiety and extroversion. It is suggested that stresses of various kinds are to some degree responsible for national differences in anxiety and that affluence is a factor determining national differences in extroversion.

References

Al-Issa, I. The Eysenck Personality Inventory in chronic schizophrenia. *British Journal of Psychiatry,* 1964, **110**, 397-400.

Angst, J., & Maurer-Groeli, Y. A. Blutgruppen und Personlichkeit. *Archiv Für Psychiatrie und Nervenkrankheiten,* 1974, **218**, 291-300.

Bartholomew, A. A. Extraversion-introversion and neuroticism in first offenders and recidivists. *British Journal of Delinquency,* 1959, **10**, 120-129.

Bendien, J., & Groen, J. A psychological-statistical study of neuroticism and extraversion in patients with myocardial infarction. *Journal of Psychosomatic Research,* 1963, **7**, 11-14.

Biesheuvel, S., & White, M. E. The human factor in flying accidents. *South African Air Force Journal,* 1949, **1**, 25-31.

Block, M. A. *Alcoholism.* London: Day, 1962.

Brandon, S. Eating disorders in a child population. *Acta Paedopsychiatria,* 1968, **35**, 317-323.

Buikhuisen, W. *A research programme on drunken driving.* Groningen: Criminologisch Institut, 1968.

Bunney, W. E., & Fawcett, J. A. Possibility of a biochemical test for suicidal potential: An analysis of endocrine findings prior to three suicides. *Archives of General Psychiatry,* 1965, **13**, 232-239.

Burgess, P. K. Eysenck's theory of criminality: A new approach. *British Journal of Criminology,* 1972, **12**, 74-82. (a)

Burgess, P. K. Eysenck's theory of criminality: A test of some objections to disconfirmatory evidence. *British Journal of Social and Clinical Psychology,* 1972, **11**, 248-256. (b)

Cattell, R. B. *Personality and motivation structure and measurement.* New York: World Book, 1957.

Cattell, R. B., & Child, D. *Motivation and dynamic structure.* New York: Holt, 1975.

Cattell, R. B., Eber, H. W., & Tatsuoka, M. M. Handbook for the 16 PF Questionnaire. Champaign, Ill.: Institute for Personality and Ability Testing, 1970.

Cattell, R. B., & Krug, S. Personality factor profile peculiar to the student smoker. *Journal of Counseling Psychology,* 1967, **14**, 116-121.

Cattell, R. B., & Nesselroade, J. R. Likeness and completeness theories examined by 16 PF measures on stably and unstably married couples. *Journal of Personality and Social Psychology,* 1967, **7**, 351-361.

Cattell, R. B., & Scheier, I. H. *Measurement of neuroticism and anxiety.* New York: Ronald Press, 1961.

Cavan, R. *Suicide.* Chicago, Ill.: Univ. of Chicago Press, 1927.

Cochrane, R., & Stopes-Row, M. Psychological disturbance in Ireland, in England, and in Irish emigrants to England: A comparative study. *Economic & Social Review,* 1979, **10**, 301-320.

Colson, C. E. Neuroticism, extraversion and repression-sensitization in suicidal college students. *British Journal of Social and Clinical Psychology,* 1972, **11**, 88-89.

Cox, W. M. The alcohol personality. In B. A. Maher (Ed.), *Progress in experimental personality research* (Vol. 9). New York: Academic Press, 1979.

Dorpat, T. Suicide in murderers. *Psychiatry Digest,* 1966, 51-55.

Dublin, L., & Bunzel, R. *To be or not to be.* New York: Harrison Smith and Haas, 1933.

Durkheim, E. *Suicide: A study in sociology*. London: Routledge & Kegan Paul, 1897.

Durret, M., & Stromquist, M. Preventing violent death. *Survey*, 1925, **59**, 437.

Estabrook, M., & Sommer, R. Study habits and introversion-extraversion. *Psychological Reports*, 1966, **19**, 750.

Evans, R. R., Borgatta, E. F., & Bohrnstedt, G. W. Smoking and MMPI scores among entering freshmen. *Journal of Social Psychology*, 1967, **73**, 137–140.

Eysenck, H. J. *Dimensions of personality*. London: Routledge & Kegan Paul, 1947.

Eysenck, H. J. *Crime and personality*. London: Paladin, 1964.

Eysenck, H. J. *Smoking, health and personality*. London: Weidenfeld & Nicolson, 1965.

Eysenck, H. J. *The biological basis of personality*. Springfield, Ill.: Thomas, 1967.

Eysenck, H. J. *Psychology is about people*. London: Allen Lane, 1972.

Eysenck, H. J. National differences in personality as related to ABO polymorphism. *Psychological Reports*, 1977, **41**, 1257–1258.

Eysenck, H. J., & Eysenck, S. B. G. Manual of the Maudsley Personality Inventory. London: Univ. of London Press, 1964.

Eysenck, S. B. G. Personality and pain assessment in childbirth of married and unmarried mothers. *Journal of Mental Science*, 1961, **107**, 417–430.

Eysenck, S. B. G., & Eysenck, H. J. Crime and personality: An empirical study of the three-factor theory. *British Journal of Criminology*, 1970, **10**, 225–239.

Farley, F. H. Moderating effects of psychopathology on the independence of extraversion and neuroticism. *Journal of Clinical Psychology*, 1970, **26**, 298–299.

Farley, F. H., & Farley, S. V. Extraversion and stimulus-seeking motivation. *Journal of Consulting Psychology*, 1967, **31**, 215–216.

Fine, B. J. Introversion-extraversion and motor vehicle driver behaviour. *Perception and Motor Skills*, 1963, **16**, 95–100.

Gellhorn, E. *Autonomic imbalance and the hypothalamus*. Minneapolis: Univ. of Minnesota Press, 1957.

Giese, H., & Schmidt, A. *Studenten Sexualitat*. Hamburg: Rowohlt, 1968.

Glueck, S., & Glueck, E. *Unravelling juvenile delinquency*. Cambridge, Massachusetts: Harvard Univ. Press, 1950.

Golightly, C., & Reinehr, R. C. The 16 PF profiles of hospitalized alcoholic patients: Replications and extension. *Psychological Reports*, 1969, **24**, 543–545.

Gooch, R. N. The influence of stimulant and depressant drugs on the central nervous system. In H. J. Eysenck (Ed.), *Experiments with drugs*. Oxford: Pergamon, 1963.

Guttmacher, M. *The mind of the murderer*. New York: Farrar, Strauss and Cudahy, 1960.

Hinkle, L. E., Whitney, L. H., Lehman, E. W., Dunn, J., Benjamin, B., King, R., Plakun, A., & Flehinger, B. Occupation, education and coronary heart disease. *Science*, 1968, **161**, 238–246.

Hofling, C. K. *Textbook of psychiatry for medical practice*. Philadelphia, Pennsylvania: Lippincott, 1963.

Hofstede, G. *Nationality & organisational stress*. Mimeographed report. Brussels: European Institute for Advanced Studies in Management, 1976.

Hoghughi, M. S., & Forrest, A. R. Eysenck's theory of criminality. *British Journal of Criminology*, 1970, **10**, 240–254.

Hoy, R. The personality of in-patient alcoholics in relation to group psychotherapy as measured by the 16 PF. *Quarterly Journal of Studies on Alcohol*, 1969, **30**, 401–407.

Hsu, L. K. G., & Crisp, A. H. The Crown-Crisp experimental index profile in anorexia nervosa. *British Journal of Psychiatry*, 1980, **136**, 567–573.

Iwawaki, S., Sujiyama, Y., & Nanri, R. *Japanese manual of the Maudsley Personality Inventory*, 1964.

Jick, H., Miettinen, O. S., Neff, R. K., Shapiro, S., Heinonen, O. P., & Slone, D. Coffee and myocardial infarction. *New England Journal of Medicine*, 1973, **289**, 63–67.

Jones, M. C. The elimination of children's fears. *Journal of Experimental Psychology*, 1924, **7**, 383–390.

Kalucy, R. S., & Crisp, A. H. Some psychological and social implications of massive obesity. *Journal of Psychosomatic Research*, 1974, **18**, 465–473.

Kessell, W. I. N., & Grossman, G. Suicide and the alcoholic. *British Medical Journal*, 1961, **2**, 1671–4.

Little, A. Professor Eysenck's theory of crime: An empirical test on adolescent offenders. *British Journal of Criminology*, 1963, **4**, 152–163.

Lynn, R. *Personality and national character*. Oxford: Pergamon, 1971.

Lynn, R. National differences in anxiety and the consumption of caffeine. *British Journal of Social and Clinical Psychology*, 1973, **12**, 92–93.

Lynn, R. (Ed.) *Dimensions of personality*. Oxford, Pergamon, 1981.

Lynn, R., & Butler, J. Introversion and the arousal jag. *British Journal of Social and Clinical Psychology*, 1962, **1**, 150–151.

Lynn, R., & Gordon, I. E. Maternal attitudes to child socialisation. *British Journal of Social and Clinical Psychology*, 1962, **1**, 52–55.

Lynn, R., & Hampson, S. L. National differences in extraversion and neuroticism. *British Journal of Social and Clinical Psychology*, 1975, **14**, 223–240.

Lynn, R., & Hampson, S. L. Fluctuations in national levels of neuroticism and extraversion, 1935–1970. *British Journal of Social and Clinical Psychology*, 1977, **16**, 131–138.

MacAndrew, C. Male alcoholics, secondary psychopathy and Eysenck's theory of personality. *Personality and Individual Differences*, 1980, **1**, 151–160.

Maher, B. Neurosis is small potatoes. *Contemporary Psychology*, 1975, **20**, 360–361.

Manheimer, D. I., & Mellinger, G. D. Personality characteristics of the child accident repeater. *Child Development*, 1967, **38**, 491–513.

Masserman, J. H., & Yum, K. S. An analysis of the influence of alcohol on experimental neurosis in cats. *Psychosomatic Medicine*, 1946, **8**, 36–52.

Miller, C. M. Follow-up studies of introverted children. III. Relative incidence of criminal behaviour. *Journal of Criminal Law and Criminology*, 1956, **47**, 414–422.

Morgan, C. T. *Physiological psychology*. New York: McGraw-Hill, 1965.

Morris, T., & Blom-Cooper, L. Homicide in England. In M. Wolfgang (Ed.) *Studies in homicide*. New York: Harper, 1967.

Nelson, R., & Gellhorn, E. The action of autonomic drugs on normal persons and neuropsychiatric patients. *Psychosomatic Medicine*, 1957, **19**, 486–494.

O'Leary, J. P., Schwab, R. L., John, L., & McGuinnies, N. H. Anxiety in cardiac patients. *Diseases of the Nervous System*, 1968, **29**, 443–448.

Paffenbarger, R. S., & Asnes, D. P. Chronic disease in former college students. III. Precursors of suicide in early and middle college life. *American Journal of Public Health*, 1966, **56**, 1026–1036.

Philip, A. E. Traits, attitudes and symptoms in a group of attempted suicides. *British Journal of Psychiatry*, 1970, **116**, 475–482.

Pierson, G. R., & Kelly, R. F. Anxiety, extraversion and personality idiosyncrasy in delinquency. *Journal of Psychology*, 1963, **56**, 441–445.

Roberts, J., & Hooper, D. The natural history of attempted suicide in Bristol. *British Journal of Medical Psychology*, 1969, **42**, 303–312.

Rosen, E., & Gregory, J. *Abnormal psychology*. Philadelphia, Pennsylvania: Saunders, 1965.

Rosenberg, C. M. Young alcoholics. *British Journal of Psychiatry*, 1969, **115**, 181–188.

Sainsbury, P. Psychosomatic disorders and neurosis in out-patients attending a general hospital. *Journal of Psychosomatic Research*, 1960, **4**, 261-273.

Sanocki, W. The use of Eysenck's personality inventory for testing young prisoners. *Przeglad Penitencjarny*, 1969, **7**, 53-68.

Schachter, S., Goldman, R., & Gordon, A. Effects of fear, food deprivation and obesity on eating. *Journal of Personality and Social Psychology*, 1968, **10**, 91-97.

Schmid, C. Suicide in Minneapolis, Minnesota, 1928-32. *American Journal of Sociology*, 1933, **49**, 47.

Schubert, D. S. Arousal seeking as a central factor in tobacco smoking among college students. *International Journal of Social Psychiatry*, 1965, **11**, 221-225.

Shaw, L., & Sichel, H. *Accident proneness*. Oxford: Pergamon, 1971.

Silverstone, J. T. Psychosocial aspects of obesity. *Proceedings of the Royal Society of Medicine*, 1968, **61**, 371-378.

Singh, A. A study of extraversion, neuroticism, psychoticism and adjustment of murders. Doctoral dissertation, Panjab University, 1980.

Smith, G. M. Personality correlates of cigarette smoking in students of college age. *Annals of the New York Academy of Sciences*, 1967, **142**, 308-321.

Smith, G. M. Relations between personality and smoking behaviour in preadult subjects. *Journal of Consulting and Clinical Psychology*, 1969, **33**, 710-715.

Spielberger, C. D., & Diaz-Guerrero, R. *Cross-cultural anxiety*. New York: Wiley, 1976.

Stengel, E. *Suicide and attempted suicide*. Harmondsworth: Penguin, 1964.

Tillmann, W. A., & Hobbs, G. E. The accident-prone automobile driver. *American Journal of Psychiatry*, 1949, **106**, 321-331.

Vallance, M. Alcoholism: a two-year follow-up study of patients admitted to the psychiatric department of a general hospital. *British Journal of Psychiatry*, 1965, **111**, 348-356.

Warburton, F. W. Observations on a sample of psychopathic American criminals. *Behavior Research and Therapy*, 1965, **3**, 129-135.

Wolfgang, M. An analysis of homicide-suicide. *Journal of Clinical Experimental Psychopathology*, 1958, **19**, 208-18.

INDEX